THE
VICTORY
PROJECT

ADVANCE PRAISE FOR *THE VICTORY PROJECT*

'Today we live in a world which is knowledge- and data-rich, but time-starved. At the same time, we need to keep our skills current, to keep pace with rapid changes and disruption. This book provides an elegant framework for structuring continuous learning and for amplifying our creativity and potential while dealing with the intense pressure of our work'—Nandan Nilekani, chairman and co-founder, Infosys, and founding chairman, UIDAI (Aadhaar)

'At a time when the formal education system in India is struggling to cope with the rapidly evolving skilling needs of the economy, this book provides a framework that industrious professionals can use for sustained personal development'—T.V. Mohandas Pai, chairman, Manipal Global Education, and former CFO, Infosys

'In a complex and fast-changing world, common sense, simplicity and focus bring tremendous competitive advantage. I think the book highlights the best attributes of all these important virtues'—Motilal Oswal, managing director and CEO, Motilal Oswal Financial Services

'I wish I'd had the benefit of the perceptive analysis and practical advice in this book when I was starting out'—Avinash K. Dixit, John J.F. Sherrerd '52 University Professor of Economics, Emeritus, Princeton University

'Books which fuse the best practices from India with the teachings of leading Western gurus are rare. This one is an addition to that short list. The case studies and interviews contained in the book are particularly useful'—Arundhati Bhattacharya, former chairman, State Bank of India

'In a networked and VUCA (volatility, uncertainty, complexity, ambiguity) world, where collaboration, grit and emotional maturity are often more important than functional knowledge, this book offers a powerful template for development as a holistic leader'—Saugata Gupta, MD and CEO, Marico Limited

PRAISE FOR SAURABH MUKHERJEA'S PREVIOUS BESTSELLERS

Coffee Can Investing: The Low-Risk Road to Stupendous Wealth
(co-authored with Rakshit Ranjan and Pranab Uniyal)

'*Coffee Can Investing: The Low-Risk Road to Stupendous Wealth* . . . is a must-read for all . . . For those who worship moolah, this book could be a Bible'—*Outlook Money*

'Besides discussing the coffee can portfolio, the book packs in a number of lessons that investors will find relevant to these times'—*Business Standard*

'The shift in savings away from physical towards financial assets is one of the defining changes of this decade. *Coffee Can Investing* captures the underlying reasons for this change and then lays out a route map to wealth creation that almost everyone can follow'—Manish Chokhani, Enam Holdings

'Anyone who wants to invest sensibly and retire happily should read this book'—Sanjay Bakshi, adjunct professor, Management Development Institute, Gurgaon

'. . . [W]ell-researched, informative and thoughtfully structured'—*The Hindu BusinessLine*

The Unusual Billionaires

'Saurabh Mukherjea describes incisively how some great Indian companies have achieved corporate success and made a great deal of money for investors along the way'—John Kay, author of *Other People's Money*, and former professor of economics, London School of Economics

'An insightful—and reassuring—exposition of how steady good sense can consistently beat the unsteady Sensex'—Rama Bijapurkar, author and management consultant

'Mukherjea's book is insightful and makes for easy reading'—*The Financial Express*

'Mukherjea is one of our most erudite writers in the field of investment banking'—*Mint*

'Books that are able to describe successful businesses through a common theme of analytical framework are rare in India. This one is an addition to that small collection'—*Moneylife*

'This book does not just list the winning pack, but also traces the history of these companies'—*The Hindu BusinessLine*

THE VICTORY PROJECT

Six Steps to Peak Potential

SAURABH MUKHERJEA
and ANUPAM GUPTA

PORTFOLIO
PENGUIN

An imprint of Penguin Random House

PORTFOLIO

USA | Canada | UK | Ireland | Australia
New Zealand | India | South Africa | China

Portfolio is part of the Penguin Random House group of companies
whose addresses can be found at global.penguinrandomhouse.com

Published by Penguin Random House India Pvt. Ltd
7th Floor, Infinity Tower C, DLF Cyber City,
Gurgaon 122 002, Haryana, India

Penguin
Random House
India

First published in Portfolio by Penguin Random House India 2020

Copyright © Saurabh Mukherjea and Anupam Gupta 2020

All rights reserved

10 9 8 7 6 5 4 3 2 1

ISBN 9780670093250

Portraits by Antra K.
Typeset in Adobe Caslon Pro by Manipal Technologies Limited, Manipal
Printed at Thomson Press India Ltd, New Delhi

www.penguin.co.in

To my maternal grandparents, Archana and Pranab Kumar Chatterjee, for planting the reading bug in my head

Saurabh Mukherjea

To my mother, Shubhra Saran, for the encouragement to read and write from as far back as I remember

Anupam Gupta

Contents

Section 4: Applications

Foreword

The subject of Saurabh Mukherjea and Anupam Gupta's book is high performance. They prescribe a number of steps to achieve it and narrate sparkling stories to illustrate it. This is altogether fitting, for Indians have always learnt how to live their lives from stories, and this is why India has one of the richest storytelling traditions in the world. In this spirit, I would like to narrate a couple of my favourite tales that will illustrate the fundamental principles in this book.

The first one, called 'The Mouse Merchant', is from an eleventh-century Shaivite Kashmiri anthology, *Kathasaritsagara*. It is a story about entrepreneurship, in tune with our age of start-ups, and demonstrates some of this book's principles in action: simplicity, collaboration, innovation and determination. The hero of the story is a young man whose father, a merchant, had died when his mother was pregnant, and his wicked uncles had stolen his inheritance. His mother had since supported him by cleaning houses and doing other menial work. Though poor, she persuaded a teacher to instruct her son in writing and mathematics. When the boy grows up, his mother says to him, 'Remember, you are the son of a great merchant. Go and make a fortune. Meet Vishakhila, the richest merchant in our city, and he will give you advice.'

The next day, the young man goes dutifully to the rich man's mansion. While waiting outside, he sees a dead mouse in his courtyard. When the rich merchant appears, he asks him if he can have the dead mouse. Vishakhila laughs.

'People come to me for money and favours; don't you want anything?'

'No, sir,' says the young man, and he thanks him for the dead mouse.

He sells the mouse to a widow with a cat, who lives near his house. With a few paisa that she gives him for the mouse, he buys two handfuls of channa, which he grinds and makes into little packets of snack food. With a pot of water and his snack food, he goes and stands under a shady tree at the crossroads outside the city. In the afternoon, loggers arrive from the forest, put down their bundles of timber and sit down to rest. The young man offers each of them a snack packet and water. They are grateful but since they have no money to repay his kindness, each one gives him a log of wood. On the way home, he sells one log to buy channa and stores the other logs at home. The next day he repeats the same thing, and then every day for the next three months, until the logging season stops with the arrival of the monsoon rains.

Because of its scarcity in the market, the price of timber begins to climb. His house is by now full of wood and he slowly begins to unload it in the timber market. By the end of the season, he has made a killing. He buys a shop in the timber market from his profits, and by the next season he has become a timber merchant. He also finds that he has a competitive advantage over other merchants because the loggers know him as the young man who was once kind to them at the crossroads. Since they prefer to deal with him, his market share begins to climb. Before long, he becomes the richest merchant in the timber market.

A few years later, he discovers that the profit margin from building ships from wood is much higher than from trading the same wood in the timber market. He looks for a master carpenter who knows the art of building ships and persuades him to take him on as his partner. Soon he has become a major player in the ship-building business. Before long, he discovers that his shipping customers are making even higher margins than shipbuilders like him. He seeks and finds a shipper in distress, provides him with capital and common sense, and before long he is running a successful shipping company. By now, still in his early twenties, he has become the richest merchant in town. He visits a jeweller and asks him to make a mouse of gold. When it arrives, he takes the mouse to Vishakhila, the wealthy merchant who had given him the dead mouse. He narrates his story and thanks him for getting him started with the sole capital of a dead mouse. The old man is delighted to hear this tale of entrepreneurial success and gives him his daughter in marriage.

'The Mouse Merchant' contains most of the six steps to reach peak potential that Saurabh and Anupam describe in this book, and it may well inspire a generation of young entrepreneurs in our age of start-ups. Some of you will protest, arguing that this story is fiction and not a real-life case study, such as the kind you read and learn from in an MBA class. I shall say in my defence that I have learnt that the line between fiction and nonfiction is very thin. The difference is that fiction has to make sense but nature and life do not. If you are not persuaded by my tenuous logic, I offer you this story from real life.

When I was a practising manager, I learnt more about high performance from our new assistant security guard than from the two summers I spent at the Advanced Management Program at Harvard Business School. We called him Kawade—no one was quite sure if it was his first or last name. He appeared one evening at our office at 5.30 p.m. to man the night shift. He was from a small town in western Maharashtra, where he had completed tenth grade. He didn't know much English, and we laughed at the way he mispronounced our company's name.

Kawade had a childlike curiosity and learnt quickly how the office functioned. In the first few days he picked up how to make tea and coffee, and between his rounds he was happy to make it for anyone who wanted it. Even though he didn't know much English, he learnt to operate the telex machine—we used telexes in those days!—and soon he began to send simple telex messages. The same went for the switchboard. Between his security duties, he could be found answering the company phone after hours. Before long, with his inquiring mind, he trained himself to operate the film projector. As a result, young marketing executives of a consumer products company began to enjoy the unbelievable luxury of reviewing the advertising of their brands after office hours.

I got a taste of Kawade's magic late one evening when I needed to speak urgently to our finance director. I knew he was travelling but wasn't sure how to reach him. Kawade made a few calls, discovered that he was staying at the Ashok Hotel in Delhi and connected me to him within minutes. If you needed anything after hours, the mantra became, 'Ask Kawade!' As a result, I noticed that people began to stay later and later at work because our office seemed to function more efficiently after hours than during the day.

Nine months after Kawade arrived, our telephone operator had to go on maternity leave. I learnt through the grapevine that Kawade had requested to fill in for her temporarily—he said he was tired of working at night. The personnel manager refused flatly, saying that ours was a multinational company that received phone calls from around the world. How could he, with his poor English, answer incoming calls when he couldn't even pronounce the company's name correctly? I gently suggested that we try out Kawade for a few days, and if it didn't work out, we could always get another person. The personnel head agreed reluctantly. 'He may surprise us!' I said as I left his room.

So Kawade had a new job. A few days later, our company lawyer asked me in passing if we had acquired a new EPABX system (which expands to Electronic Private Automatic Branch Exchange, a business telephone system). I looked at him quizzically.

'Your phone is now answered promptly on the second ring; earlier I had to hold on till the fifth or sixth ring.'

I smiled and told him that Kawade was our new EPABX system.

As I was going for lunch, I stopped by at Kawade's booth and asked him, 'Why do you answer the phone so promptly?'

He gave a reply that took my breath away. 'There may be a customer at the other end,' he said, 'and we might lose an order.'

Kawade brought the same curiosity, a bias for smart improvisation, a positive energy and an attitude of service to the daytime office. He quietly went on to become a role model and gradually transformed the atmosphere around him. Eventually, this modest, self-effacing, non-English-speaking non-graduate rose to great heights in our company. The lesson I learnt from Kawade's success is that attitude often matters more than skill or intelligence in creating a high-performance organization. Unfortunately, companies consistently make the mistake of recruiting on the basis of credentials, skills and intelligence. If you want to create more Kawades, hire for attitude and train people in skills. You can teach skills but not attitudes, which are formed early in life.

Both 'The Mouse Merchant' and Kawade teach us some of the same principles laid out in Saurabh and Anupam's book: 1) simplicity is an unblemished virtue; 2) innovation in business is often more important than capital; 3) collaborative skills will always take you far; 4) it is determination and persistence that move the world, often more than intelligence and credentials; 5) the mundane attention to detail and the ability to implement are as important as ambition and strategy.

Kawade's most endearing quality, however, was something rare, and I would like to dwell on it before ending this foreword. He had a childlike quality to turn every activity into play, no matter how menial or routine. And so he seemed to love the work he did when others got quickly bored. In fact, he tended to get so absorbed in it that he would forget himself. As a result, he didn't seem to care who got the credit. He was happy to act for the sake of the activity rather than for a personal reward associated with it. In other words, he came close to being a karma yogi that the Bhagavad Gita talks about. I was always a little sceptical about Krishna's advice to Arjuna to act selflessly until I met Kawade. I didn't believe that human beings could shrink their egos that far. It seemed like a nice ideal to strive for but it seemed hopelessly idealistic, somewhat like Marx's ideal of absolute equality. Kawade taught me the rare art of self-forgetting, which is not only the path to human happiness but also to high performance.

Every CEO would obviously like to fill his company with Kawades but the question is: can one institutionalize the attitudes and practices associated with Kawade? Can our companies create a culture of self-learning, self-development, simplicity and collaboration? If we learn to recruit people on the basis of attitude rather than credentials, if we can foster and reward the spirit of curiosity and service, then we might get ordinary people to do extraordinary things.

New Delhi   Gurcharan Das
January 2020

Section 1

Introduction

Prologue

'Ae dil hai mushkil jeena yahan,

Zara hat ke, zara bach ke

Ye hai Bombay meri jaan . . .'

—*C.I.D.*[1]

It was 9 p.m. on a Friday night at PrimeOne Towers in Lower Parel, Mumbai. The twenty-fifth floor housed the offices of CerysIn, one of India's largest fast-moving consumer goods (FMCG) companies. The office was nearly empty, and the security guard at the desk was catching his daily dose of news and outrage. One of the cabins was occupied. 'Why does she work so late? It's a Friday night; does she have no social life?' Arpita, an intern, asked her colleague, Aman. Arpita, new to CerysIn, did not know who was in the sole lit cabin on the twenty-fifth floor. 'Dude, that's Akanksha Sharma, senior vice-president of personal care products. If she's not here on a Friday night, our sales would be hit!' Aman was only half-joking. Akanksha was a legend. Twenty years into her job—her first and only job so far—she had been instrumental in the company beating the stock market's expectations every quarter.

In her cabin, Akanksha was staring at the latest monthly volumes, and they made for grim reading. 'Madam, *kya karega* (what to do)? That new foreign company, Deknext, has doubled the commission for me and is even offering me incentives! I couldn't say no, I have a family to support,' a CerysIn dealer had confided just last week. Deknext had made inroads into CerysIn's market. Akanksha had done nothing about this until now because CerysIn's products were far superior and she knew most of the company's large dealers on a first-name basis. But now CerysIn's market share was under threat. 'You need to crack this one, Akanksha, and I know you will. This is small beer for you,' Mukul Gupta, CerysIn's executive director, personal products, and Akanksha's boss, had told her. What Mukul didn't know was that Akanksha was under real pressure this time and not because of Deknext; the stress from other areas of her life refused to go.

With bleary eyes, Akanksha glanced into her inbox and read the invite. 'Manish and Smriti invite you to Arya's eighth birthday!' Manish and Smriti were a young couple who stayed as tenants in the apartment complex where Akanksha owned a four-bedroom apartment. Arya and Ria—Akanksha's daughter—were best friends. 'How are you? Long time, let's catch up soon?' was the most common thing Akanksha heard from her friends, including Manish and Smriti. And her standard reply was 'Sure, will try; travelling this week, but come over next Sunday?' Next Sunday never came, and Akanksha's friends knew that only too well.

Even as she stared at her sleek, top-of-the-line laptop, Akanksha's iPhone chirped with a notification. Zoya had posted a new photo on her Instagram. Zoya was her best friend from school and a freelance consultant. 'YOLO Akanksha, YOLO' was what Zoya kept telling Akanksha—You Only Live Once. Zoya was at Ko Samui enjoying the sunset while smoking a cigarette and sipping a cosmopolitan. 'I don't have a huge flat and a big bank balance, but hey, I am the master of my time!' Zoya had told her when they last met six months ago at a school reunion.

Zoya had recently got a divorce after fifteen years of marriage. 'I couldn't take it any more yaar, seriously, I gave it my best,' Zoya had told her then, and Akanksha recalled how guilty she had felt for not being there for her friend. India had among the lowest divorce rates in the world but Akanksha was a numbers person. She knew that the low rate was an optical illusion, a meaningless statistic. She recalled a BBC article which said, 'The number of people separated is almost thrice the number of people divorced . . . More women are divorced and separated than men.'[2] And then there was the stark reality of living in a metro city such as Mumbai, where, she recalled from a newspaper article, divorce rates are heading towards 40 per cent.[3] So she knew that the low rate of divorce at an all-India level was meaningless. Society didn't take a woman divorcing her husband well. Her mother once told her, '*Duniya main sabse bada rog, kya kahenge log?*'[4]

Akanksha's own marriage wasn't exactly a prized possession. '*Beta*, why don't you spend more time at home?' her mother-in-law kept telling her. 'Ma, why can't you make kheer like Dadi?' Ria had once told her. 'Why can't you take more days off? Work is going bonkers; you know how it is,' Akash, her husband, told her. Akash had recently been promoted to the position of CEO of one of India's largest mobile operators, and the pressure on him had only increased. The previous CEO was booted out after he failed to respond adequately to a massive price war triggered by a rival. It was now Akash's job to recover the lost market share in a ruthlessly competitive market.

Compared to Akash, Akanksha had been more successful in her career. 'Just keep doing your job, Akanksha; I can assure you that you will succeed me as the head of the personal care products division one day,' Mukul had told her just last week. But Akanksha's success wasn't celebrated at home; it was envied. Zoya had once told her, 'Akash has an inferiority complex; just face it. When we women outperform Indian men in the working environment, they feel increasingly insecure. Indian men have never been trained to accept women as bosses at their workplace, and even at home, husbands and their mothers still expect housewives.'

Akanksha's head and heart were heavy as she finally left the office at 10 p.m. 'It's showing now; you've got bags under your eyes and you've got dark circles. Your designer clothes can't hide your emptiness inside forever, Akanksha; you need help,' Zoya had told her many months ago. After all the hard work, all the success at her job, her stellar reputation among her clients and her friends, Akanksha still felt an emptiness. She looked through her purse and found the number of a counsellor and psychologist that Zoya had given her. It was time to get professional help.

Twenty kilometres north of Akanksha's housing complex, young Suraj Trivedi extricated himself out of a jam-packed 'Virar fast' Mumbai local at Kandivali station. 'Super dense crush load' is the technical term describing the high concentration of railway passengers that Suraj recalled reading. Suraj, who was twenty-seven years old and an IIT-IIM graduate, was a product of the best that Indian education has to offer. 'Why are you choosing this small investment bank, bro? The best offers from Singapore to San Francisco are out there for you!' his friends at IIM had told him. But Suraj wanted to work from the ground up with Vedanga Capital, a boutique investment bank located at the Bandra Kurla Complex in Mumbai, and wanted to stay back in India and close to his mother. As his batchmates left for plum, overseas jobs, Suraj stayed back convinced that the risk was worth it. The first week in Vedanga Capital smashed his hopes.

'So listen, Suraj, you need to clean up client records for the compliance department. Cross-check client names, addresses from filings and tally them with what was entered by data entry operators into Excel files,' Gaurav Lakhani, Suraj's boss, told him in the first week of his job. 'Dude, seriously? You're an IIT-IIM grad; that's not your job,' Amit, his batchmate, had pinged him on WhatsApp. Amit was at Google's headquarters in Mountain View, California and was very clear on the privileges of an IIT-IIM education.

Back to the reality of Mumbai, sitting in the autorickshaw from Kandivali station to his house and stuck at the signal, Suraj asked the driver, 'Boss, *kitna* time (how much longer)?' The driver replied, '*Aadha ghanta, maalik; bridge bandh hai* (Half an hour, chief; the bridge is closed).'

'Find a house in Kandivali where the rent is low, and you can use the savings to build up a corpus,' he had been advised by his friends. The rent was indeed lower compared to Bandra West, but the commute was tortuously longer—the classic trade-off of staying in Mumbai. And the commute had only increased—first because of the Metro construction work and now due to the closure of an unsafe bridge on S.V. Road. He gave a mirthless laugh remembering an old joke: 'Mumbai *meri jaan . . . lekar rahegi*' ('Mumbai will eventually take my life'; the phrase 'Mumbai *meri jaan*' literally means, 'Mumbai is my life'). The city's pulverized infrastructure was getting to Suraj now.

'You've put on so much weight, Suraj; signs of prosperity? Hehehe,' Karan, his Wall Street friend, pinged him in the night, after seeing Suraj's latest Facebook check-in. 'You need to reduce weight. Your backache is a combination of bad posture, a sedentary lifestyle and increased weight,' his orthopaedic doctor had told him. Suraj hadn't visited the gym since he joined Vedanga Capital. Twelve hours at work and a two-hour commute left him with hardly any time to focus on working out. And his diet consisted of junk food ordered at odd hours. 'The prosperity is only for Vedanga and my bosses; I'm only getting the extra weight. Things not good bro,' Suraj replied to Karan.

'Did you see this? Please do yoga, *beta*; take care of yourself,' Suraj's mom had forwarded him an article on India being the sixth most depressed country in the world.[5] 'Thanks, Mom, that's all I wanted,' he told her. The stress was real. Just a few weeks ago, his IIM batch's WhatsApp group was abuzz with the news of the suicide of a young associate at a multinational investment bank who had jumped off the Bandra-Worli Sea Link. Everyone was shocked by the incident for a few days but everything settled down soon. This was India; the race to a better life was brutal.

News was easy to come by since Suraj was completely obsessed with social media. 'Cheap data, Suraj, cheap data— that's the paradigm shift! India is among the top markets in the world for Internet—streaming, gaming and any damn thing online,' Gaurav told him. On his other WhatsApp groups, Suraj's close friends were sharing photos of their latest conquests—from late-night parties to holidays at Machu Picchu and corporate team-building trips in Las Vegas and Macau. 'Bro, *tu aaja, yaar,* come over during your next holidays, and we'll do a road trip on the West Coast. Karan is also coming over,' Amit pinged him late at night. 'Can't do, bro; no holidays for at least six to nine months, have a packed deal-book and travel plan,' Suraj replied to him. It was already 1 a.m., and Suraj had spent close to two hours on his phone on WhatsApp, Facebook and Instagram, and it was running out of battery. He lit a cigarette and took a deep drag. He began smoking when he was at IIT, but it had never become a habit, until now.

'Suraj, you've got serious analytical skills, and we like your sales pitch' was how his boss, Gaurav, and Vedanga Capital had roped him in during the placements. 'This job will open doors for you; you're going to meet a lot of important people. The network is yours to build,' he had promised him. On the first day at his job, Gaurav told him, 'Suraj, the world is yours; save aggressively, build your corpus and your network. If you want to become a start-up founder, every top venture capital firm will fund your start-up. In five years, you won't recognize yourself.' But at just five months into the job, Suraj could already not recognize himself. The grind had got to him; the peer pressure had got to him. His life was not going anywhere. He opened his smartphone and entered 'Counsellor psychologist in Mumbai' in the search box. It was time to seek help.

* * *

Akanksha and Suraj are fictional characters loosely based on people that we, the authors, have met. At various points in our own careers, we have also gone down similar paths. Things were not like this, our parents told us. But our parents lived in simpler times in a world of closed economies, government jobs, cocooned from the rest of the world, happy with 10 per cent increments and one-month bonuses. Their biggest dreams were to send their kids abroad and enjoy a retired life on government pensions in government colonies. T.V. Mohandas Pai, the former chief financial officer (CFO) of Infosys and current chairman of Manipal Global Education, tells us: 'When I was growing up, we had a very simple life. We were happy with whatever we had—from a radio to a cycle to a company-owned car. We'd go to the library, read a book or read a comic. There was not much growth for us and no impetus to change. We had lower incomes and we didn't know what more we could do as opportunities were scarce. The economy grew slowly! There wasn't even a television to show us the world outside.'[6]

Nearly thirty years after India opened up its economy to the world, our lifestyles—and those of youngsters after us—have seen a sea change that makes our lives almost unrecognizable to our parents. The plus side is the immense wealth created and enjoyed as new sectors and new careers propelled us forwards. The minus side is the price we have paid in physical and mental health. India's weak infrastructure, unable to cope with decades of rapid economic growth, has only added to the pressures. Our aspirations might be on a par with developed countries, but we are trying to fulfil those aspirations with gridlocked traffic, overflowing local trains and decrepit bridges. Pai says, 'China invested in human capital to export to the world. They took the surpluses from that and put the money into improving infrastructure, improving the school and college networks. They incentivized heavy industry and so they went to a commanding position. We never put enough money into infrastructure. Now in India, human capital hasn't grown much. The economy can grow at 8 per cent compound annual growth rate (CAGR) for a long time but employees simply can't grow at that pace in their jobs and be more productive, and the infrastructure simply can't keep up with the economy. As a result, the stress on their managers, on the C-Suite has gone up . . . All these things have resulted in the increased stress of urban living in India.'[7]

When our ambitions get shackled by the limitations of the world around us, we seek help to cope. And the Internet is at our service. In all probability, while you are reading this book, you have notifications for twelve unread emails, fifteen WhatsApp pings and sundry other alerts on your mobile clamouring for your attention. And then there is infotainment—everything from TED Talks to National Geographic documentaries, from books on pop psychology and behavioural finance to podcasts on history, science and politics.

Thanks to the Internet, we have easy access to enormous amounts of wisdom and—remarkably enough—most of it can be accessed for free or at a nominal charge. And yet this cornucopia of knowledge flatters to deceive. As we show in the next chapter, psychologists and cognitive and behavioural scientists are now moving towards a view that our brains are experts at fooling us.

How does this cluttered mind affect us? For one, we lose focus and our attention span suffers. There is also the small matter that this diversity of material does not seem to be making us wiser or happier or less stressed. In fact, stress levels in India are: (a) higher compared to other countries; and (b) rising ever higher for the employed workforce.

What is the way out? In this book, we build a structure called the Simplicity Paradigm, whose foundation consists of three types of practices—specialize, simplify, and spiritualize (more on these in Chapters 2, 3 and 4 respectively). On top of this foundation, we propose three specific behaviours—clutter reduction, creativity and collaboration (refer to Chapters 5, 6 and 7 respectively). Each practice stands alone as a desired behaviour but in this book, we will also show how the foundation is connected to these practices and how without the foundation, the benefits of the practices would be temporary at best. Finally, we show you their applications and what is possible when you apply the foundation and practices in real life—simplicity in business and simplicity in investing (in Chapters 8 and 9 respectively). Finally, Chapter 10 pulls everything together to give you a Simplicity Checklist.

Each chapter ends with an interview with an expert who we believe exemplifies the core values from the chapter. We have drawn these experts from a wide array of fields because for all of us our lives aren't just our jobs. The stories of these remarkable experts contain lessons for all of us.

The Simplicity Paradigm

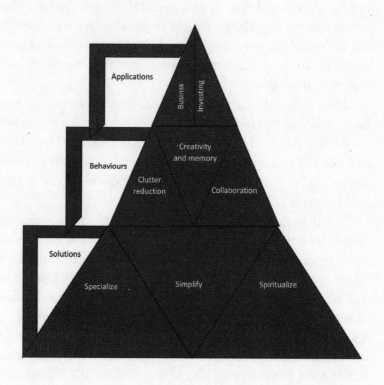

CHAPTER 1

A Peek into the Human Mind[1]

'The world is a looking-glass, and gives back to every man the reflection of his own face. Frown at it, and it will in turn look sourly upon you; laugh at it and with it, and it is a jolly kind companion; and so let all young persons take their choice.'

—William Makepeace Thackeray[2]

The mind supreme

If you were a teenager in the 1990s, you may remember En Vogue's chart-topping song which went: 'Free your mind and the rest will follow.' Western philosophy has celebrated the past three centuries or so—the modern era, if you will—as an era dedicated to the freeing of the human mind. (The eighteenth century, for instance, is known as the Age of Enlightenment or the Age of Reason.) Indeed, this time period has been dominated not only by the rise of Western democracies but also, in parallel, by the rise of scientific thought and technological progress—most spectacularly embodied in the Industrial Revolution.

Even with the benefit of hundreds of years of hindsight, the mind boggles at the sheer number of inventions produced by this revolution—the steam engine, the internal combustion engine, the telegraph, the light bulb, the sewing machine and much more.

The human mind created all this, and therefore it stands to reason that the human mind must be a supercharged supercomputer powering the progress of civilization. Baruch Spinoza, the Dutch philosopher, said in proposition twenty-three of *Ethics*, 'The human mind cannot be absolutely destroyed with the body, but there remains of it something which is eternal.'[3] His exaggerated faith in the human mind was symptomatic of the era he lived in (1632–77).

And what of our brain—that physical human organ which is closely related to our intangible mind? The mind might truly be without limits, but psychologists have shown us over the past ten years that there is a gulf between our perception of how powerful our brains are and their true abilities. One manifestation of this gulf is our vision. As a reader, you will confidently claim that you can see this page in its entirety. You are utterly convinced that all of the 300-odd words on this page are clearly visible to you. And yet your confidence is misplaced; eye-tracking software has conclusively shown that when we read a book, our eyes can see only twelve to fourteen letters at a time. The perception that we can see the whole page is actually a visual illusion—we can only see specific points on this page. In fact, while our eyes are focused on this specific word, if the rest of this page were to be altered, we would not be able to notice it. Although in the context of reading a book this visual illusion can be harmless, in other spheres of life—say, professional sport or aviation or warfare or surgery—not coming to terms with the limited abilities of the human eye can have devastating consequences.[4]

The irrational mind

The first people to openly question the idea of a rational mind were two brilliant Israeli psychologists, Nobel laureate Daniel Kahneman and his friend and collaborator, the late Amos Tversky. In what is the most popular paper written on behavioural economics, titled 'Judgment under Uncertainty: Heuristics and Biases'[5], the two psychologists showed how three biases have a bearing on how our brains assess probabilities and predict values:

- **Representativeness:** We tend to judge or evaluate things based on stereotypes. For example, when introduced to chartered accountants, people assume that accountants can't think beyond debit and credit, whereas in reality accountants are able to surprise us with occasional bouts of humour as well. In fact, we know a few doctors and accountants in Mumbai who moonlight as performing artists.
- **Availability:** We take decisions based on instances or occurrences that are first and most easily brought to our mind. For example, we might steer clear of trees on the road after reading in the news that a man walking on the road died when a tree fell on him.
- **Anchoring:** We get fixated or anchored on the first (or initial) thing we see and use that as a reference point for decisions. For example, when the Nifty hits 10,000 Anupam sells his stocks because 10,000 is optically a very large number that the Nifty has hit for the first time.

Therefore, Anupam expects the Nifty to fall after hitting this threshold, and hence sells his investments.

What psychologists like Kahneman and Tversky did was focus on the top-right box of the Johari window (see Exhibit 1), the one that represents blind spots, or that part of our mind which we cannot see but others can. For example, Saurabh does not realize it but everyone else can see that he suffers from 'anchoring' when it comes to his travel habits—in the month following a plane crash anywhere in the world, he avoids all air travel (because his mind is now anchored on the crash).

While Kahneman was felicitated with the Nobel Prize in Economics in 2002, the validity of his work came into question. In response to a February 2017 post titled 'Reconstruction of a Train Wreck: How Priming Research Went off the Rails' by Ulrich Schimmack, Moritz Heene, and Kamini Kesavan, Kahneman admitted[6] that some studies that he relied on were 'significantly weaker' than he believed them to be when he co-wrote his 1974 paper. However, Kahneman said that he still believed that 'actions can be primed, sometimes even by stimuli of which the person is unaware.'

While we view the debate around Kahneman's work to be a healthy one, we believe that most of us can benefit from the core of his teachings on the limits of the human mind. In fact, as we explain further on in this chapter, the more we understand the human mind, the more keenly we appreciate the pioneering work of Kahneman and Tversky.

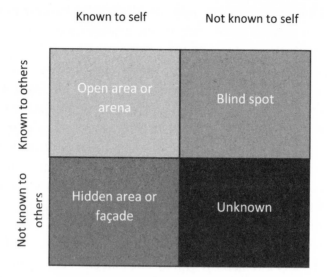

Exhibit 1: The Johari window[7]

The knowledge illusion

Donald Rumsfeld, the former US defence secretary, was famous for saying, 'There are known knowns. There are things we know we know. We also know there are known unknowns. That is to say, we know there are some things we do not know. But there are also unknown unknowns, the ones we don't know we don't know.'[8]

That is quite a mouthful. There is a simpler and older way to depict this. Created by psychologists Joseph (Jo) Luft and Harrington (Hari) Ingham in 1955, the Johari window is an approach that helps us understand how we see ourselves and how others see us.

This two-by-two grid looks decidedly plain, but delving into these four boxes is the start to better understanding ourselves and harnessing our capabilities.

It plots what we know of ourselves against what others know about us. Each box reveals something different about us. The first box, on the top left, contains the things we know about our own minds that others also know—straightforward enough. The second box, on the top right, contains things about ourselves we don't know, but others do. The third, on the bottom left, has those things that we know but are hidden from others.

But the most interesting box of them all is the last one, on the bottom right—what we don't know about our minds and which no one else knows either. The unknown unknown.

Thanks to new technology, the current generation of psychologists are using techniques such as MRI imaging, eye tracking and novel experiments to focus on this box. For example, eye-tracking software revealed that we do not always read text in a linear manner but instead tend to focus only on certain areas.

Not only are they showing the world that the box is far bigger than what anyone else had imagined, they are also identifying some of the reasons which underpin our inability to understand our own abilities (or lack thereof).

In particular, psychologists and cognitive scientists such as Nick Chater, Steven Sloman and Philip Fernbach are telling us that we suffer from the following two 'illusions'.[9]

The knowledge illusion: We think we know far more about the world than we actually do. In fact, most of us don't even understand how basic things like bicycles, toilet flushes and zippers work, let alone understand complex things like global warming, genetically-modified foods, what is inside an iPhone and how Reliance Industries Limited makes money. Anupam once talked to his son's paediatrician completely convinced that he had become an expert of children's healthcare. Expectedly, the paediatrician shut Anupam down. Twitter is full of ordinary people ignorantly taking on established subject experts. For example, astrophysicist Dr Katie Mack has become famous for her calm handling of climate change deniers, who are usually people with no qualifications whatsoever in science but with strong opinions on climate change (or the lack thereof).[10]

The grand illusion: We perceive our senses to have a richer picture of the world than they actually do. We cannot multitask because our brain can only do one thing at a time and our memory is extremely fallible. In fact, we actually remember the past only in bare-bones outlines but because our mind fills in the gaps with colours and sounds (which often have no bearing with the real world). We often mistakenly believe that we can recall the past in vivid detail.

Let us delve further into these illusions to understand why our minds struggle to understand the world around us even as we struggle to comprehend the scale of the illusion that is deceiving us.

The hubris of the free mind

Everyone agrees that traffic sucks. But here is the problem: over the past fifty years, urban planners across the world have struggled to predict traffic flows. In spite of sustained efforts to address the problems of traffic jams, we still lack a proper understanding of the dynamic behaviours of urban traffic. The difficulty stems from two distinct factors: the lack of systematic and accurate data on traffic flows across entire cities and the diversity of drivers' self-adaptive decisions with regard to the routes they take.

To complicate matters further, the advent of GPS has made these decisions even more self-adaptive. In December 2018, we took the Western Express Highway to go to IIT Bombay for the Mood Indigo festival because Google Maps had told us so. But Google Maps had also told the same thing to another 150 people. The result? By the time we reached the college, our friends, who had taken the Eastern Express Highway, reached earlier than us.

Complex traffic flows are like the complex neural networks in our mind. Vanilla or chocolate ice cream, mid-cap or small-cap stocks, route one or route two—there is a battle royale raging in the different factions of your brains over simple decisions. Understanding this chaotic complexity of the brain—and abandoning the computer-related analogies of the brain—is central to coming to terms with its strengths and weaknesses. Neuroscientist David Eagleman describes these neural wars vividly in his 2015 book *The Brain: The Story of You*[11]:

Imagine you're making a simple choice, standing in the frozen-yogurt store, trying to decide between two flavours you like equally. Say these are mint and lemon. From the outside, it doesn't look like you are doing much . . . But inside your brain, a simple choice like this unleashes a hurricane of activity.

By itself, a single neuron has no meaningful influence. But each neuron is connected to thousands of others, and they in turn connect to thousands of others, and so on, in a massive, loopy, intertwining network . . .

Within this web, a particular constellation of neurons represents mint. This pattern is formed from neurons that mutually excite each other. They're not necessarily next to one another; rather, they might span distant brain regions involved in smell, taste, and your unique history of memories involving mint . . .

At the same time, the competing possibility—lemon—is represented by its own neural party. Each coalition—mint and lemon—tries to gain the upper hand . . . They fight it out until one triumphs in the winner-takes-all competition. The winning network defines what you do next.

If choosing an ice-cream flavour stresses so many neurons, do you actually think you can understand this text while responding to pings on WhatsApp? In fact, research has now conclusively shown that the brain cannot multitask—we can only think one thought at a time.

In his path-breaking book *The Mind is Flat*, Chater shows that while doing something routine and well-practised, humans can do two things at once, like driving and talking. But when anything non-routine is introduced (such as driving and thinking through the budget for your next holiday), then multitasking becomes really difficult. Chater was quoted in a newspaper article as follows:

Most of the things that we find reasonably challenging we can only do one at a time. We think we are multi-tasking but in fact we are jumping from one task to the next quite rapidly, something we don't have to do if we practice. If we practice we get very fluent at something and it requires almost no mental effort, like driving while listening to the radio . . . We can't keep mental processes entirely separate from each other. If we are doing routine things that is fine, but if we do something non-routine suddenly other parts of the brain start to engage and interfere with routine things like walking.[12]

So the next time you try to respond to an email on your smartphone while listening to your colleague talk about his latest achievement, you should stop and ask yourself which of the two mental processes you really want to engage in. Your brain is better equipped at handling one complex process instead of two. So isn't it more practical to respond to that email with your undivided attention? Remember the destructive potential of 'reply all'? When you accidentally used it to declare your undying love for Arijit Singh to the entire sales team instead of just one colleague?

On top of the limitations of the brain, our memories are also fallible. Anupam was absolutely sure that his child's first movie was *Kung Fu Panda* (2008), until his wife showed him the photo she had clicked next to an *Iron Man* (2008) cut-out at the multiplex.

These mental limitations would not have restricted us so much had our memories been powerful. A highly retentive brain would allow us to remember, for example, all our previous choices with regard to ice-cream flavours in, say, the month of September at 9 p.m. in Bandra. It would then retrieve those memories and reduce the amount of neural perturbation involved in choosing a flavour here and now. Unfortunately, our memory is weaker—much weaker—than we perceive it to be. Professor Chater illustrates this using a brilliant thought experiment involving a Royal Bengal tiger, in Chapter 4 of *The Mind is Flat*.

Visualize a tiger. Surely, you have seen tigers in the zoo, on TV and in books dozens of times. Hence you would have no trouble visualizing this majestic animal. Now ask yourself whether the stripes on the tiger's body flow vertically or horizontally? Write down your answer on a sheet of paper. How about the stripes on the tiger's tail—how do they flow? Finally, ask yourself whether the stripes on his leg flow vertically or horizontally? Once you have written down all three answers, Google the image of a tiger and compare your answers with the image. If you have written 'vertical, horizontal, horizontal', you either work in a zoo or have superior memory. Hardly anybody gets these basic questions about a tiger right (we didn't either). By the way, the tiger's front legs don't have stripes at all—something which we had never spotted until we went through this thought experiment.

Like the flawed and incomplete image of the tiger we have in our head, most of our memories are manufactured by us—they have a lot less to do with what really happened than what we would like to believe. We imagine our past to a significant extent and in so doing, we invent memories and invent feelings such as nostalgia. Forget the number of stripes on a tiger, sometimes we can't even remember the combination of the number lock on our bicycles. And we won't even get into how we have faulty memories of what our spouses wore on special occasions.

The practical implications of the mind's limitations

There are two clear implications of the limitations of our minds and the fallibility of our memories: first, we are bad decision-makers; and second, our minds can be manipulated easily.

Let us consider the first one. We are prone to making some bad, even random, decisions without fully thinking things through. Faced with the same choices in the same circumstances on two consecutive days, we might take two totally different decisions. On one day, we took Tulsi Pipe Road from Bandra to Lower Parel, and on the next day, we took the Bandra–Worli Sea Link. Both decisions make perfect sense to us and we have the same goal—reaching work on time. And yet, we didn't have any reason for taking the different routes.

The Indian government's ever-changing rationalization for the demonetization of Indian currency in 2016 (black money, terrorism, corruption, counterfeiting, etc.), extensively documented in the Indian press, is a public demonstration of post-facto rationalization of a policy decision which must have arisen from a neural storm in our policymakers' heads.[13]

Legendary trader and philanthropist George Soros's son, Robert, claimed that his illustrious father's trades weren't based on grand theories of reflexivity but rather on his back pain. George Soros admitted as much in the book *Soros on Soros: Staying Ahead of the Curve*[14], in a section on how he found out when things were going wrong: 'I feel the pain. I rely a great deal on animal instincts. When I was actively running the Fund, I suffered from backache. I used the onset of acute pain as a signal that there was something wrong in my portfolio. The backache didn't tell me what was wrong—you know, lower back for short positions, left shoulder for currencies—but it did prompt me to look for something amiss when I might not have done so otherwise. That is not the most scientific way to run a portfolio.'

Which brings us to the second issue: our vulnerability to manipulation. As our brain reaches almost every meaningful decision through neural war, it is highly prone to suggestion and manipulation (without realizing that it is being manipulated).

In his book *The Brain: The Story of You*, Eagleman describes an interesting experiment to illustrate this vulnerability. Alvaro Pascual-Leone, a professor of neurology at Harvard Medical School, used transcranial magnetic stimulation (TMS), i.e. a magnetic pulse which excites a part of the brain, to initiate movement in either the left or right hand. Participants sat in front of a computer screen and were told to raise their right or left hand as the screen cued the colours red, yellow and green. At red, participants made their choice of right or left hand and activated this decision when the lights turned green.

Then, a twist was introduced. A TMS pulse was used when the colour changed to yellow. The pulse was specifically designed to make participants more likely to lift their right hand. Interestingly enough, the participants thought that they changed their decision on their own free will, even though the TMS was influencing their decision. As Eagleman says, 'The conscious mind excels at telling itself the narrative of being in control.' In fact, psychologists have shown that the illusion of being in control is even stronger than the visual and knowledge illusions which we have discussed earlier in this chapter.

The susceptibility of the human mind to external suggestion obviously creates the risk of brainwashing not just at the level of the individual but also at the collective level. Followers of cults who commit mass suicide (for example, the more than 900 followers of the Reverend Jim Jones who committed suicide together in 1978 by drinking poisoned fruit punch[15]) and ordinary people who become a murderous mob (for example, the people who lynch members of a minority community, or ordinary Germans who ganged up to send six million Jews to their death in Nazi concentration camps) are extreme manifestations of this. Less extreme manifestations are faddish games such as Tamagotchi[16] (all the rage in Japan in 1996), social media like Instagram, and the latest, hottest, must-buy apparel designs.

The same stimulus can provoke different responses in different people

So absorbed are we in our internal world that we often don't see and hear what's right in front of us. Why? Because all vision and hearing involves inference and perception, implying that each of us can perceive the same thing differently depending on what our brain has been exposed to before. For example, the language that you are exposed to as an infant refines your ability to hear the particular sounds of your language and, in parallel, reduces your capacity to hear the sounds of other languages. At birth, a baby born in a Bengali family and a baby born in a Punjabi family can hear and respond to all the sounds in both languages. As she ages, the baby raised in the Bengali family will lose the ability to distinguish between the 's' and 'sh' sounds—two sounds that aren't separated in Bengali. (So in Bengali there is no 'Saurabh'; there is only 'Shourobh'.)

How we are primed in life also has a bearing on not just what we can hear but also what we can see. Many of you would have seen the picture[17] given below. What do you see when you see this picture?

Saurabh usually sees an old woman with a beak-like nose. Saurabh's wife, Sarbani, sees the profile of a young woman staring into the distance. This phenomenon—where the same image evokes two different responses—is called perceptual bistability. Saurabh and Sarbani see the same image completely differently because their brains have been primed differently during the course of their lives. However, in a further illustration of priming, now that Sarbani has shown Saurabh how the picture also represents a young woman's profile, Saurabh too can see the young woman!

This phenomenon of the same thing being perceived differently by different people was immortalized by legendary Japanese film director Akira Kurosawa in his 1950 movie *Rashomon*. In this movie, a murder is described in four mutually contradictory ways by its four witnesses. Since then the term 'Rashomon effect' is used to refer to contested interpretations of the same event, subjectivity versus objectivity in human perception, in memory and in reporting. The Rashomon effect arises from, both, differences in our perception of the same event (perceptual bistability) and the weakness of our memory in remembering exactly what happened (especially what happened in complex and/or ambiguous situations). A famous example of such a situation is US President John F. Kennedy's assassination on 22 November 1963 in Dallas, Texas. While it is clear that former US Marine Lee Harvey Oswald shot and killed the American President, what observers present on the scene still cannot agree upon is whether there was another gunman who also fired a bullet at the president. As a result, half a century on from the tragic event, there are still numerous unresolved questions around this infamous assassination.

Taking shortcuts

So far, we have shown that our brains have limited power and our memories are fallible. The fallout of this is that we are lousy decision-makers and prone to manipulation. If you're wondering how we survive despite these limitations, the answer is by using heuristics, shortcuts that our brains use to simplify the world for us.

There is nothing inherently wrong with this. These shortcuts or mental rules of thumb help us make decisions and solve simple problems quickly. The problem is that heuristics can also manifest as biases or even delusions.

As toddlers, we loved hearing stories; as grown-ups, we love believing them. Our brain indulges us in our desire to see the world in black and white, just as our body indulges us in our desire to have junk food and skip gym sessions. Unfortunately, many of our stories are based on heuristics as mental illusions and biases.

Cultural stereotypes, for example, reduce our understanding of different people to superficial traits. For a country as diverse and as culturally rich as India, we do a disservice to our own countrymen when we limit our understanding of them to generalities. For example, the stereotype of Marwaris and Gujaratis as being great at business totally ignores the huge amounts of wealth created by entrepreneurs elsewhere, such as in the south. And in Mumbai's stock market, the 'Delhi discount' was denigratingly used to ascribe lower valuations for stocks of companies belonging to promoters from north India.

So what remedies can this book provide?

What can we do to deal with the fact that the human mind is not a computer, the fact that faced with an identical decision in identical circumstances on two consecutive days the brain can make different choices? What can we do to mitigate the fact that even when faced with simple decisions our brain goes into a tizzy? How do we live with the fact that even the same image can be interpreted differently by different people? What can we do to cope with the fact that our brain creates heuristics or shortcuts which are often faulty?

Repetitive practice allows us to reduce the amount of neural processing activity and generate more consistent outcomes. Science has shown that we are able to, quite literally, mould our brains through practice and intense application. Our brains are plastic—not just in childhood but right through adulthood, our brains change physically. Prolonged practice and persistent skill improvement has a marked impact on our brains.

Let us go back to our example of driving. We talked about how we often make suboptimal decisions with regard to routes or brainlessly rely on GPS. The men and women who drive the famous black cabs of London are specifically trained to avoid both of these behaviours. They spend years memorizing every street and back alley in the city. Then they have to sit for and pass a torturous exam called The Knowledge[18], as part of which they are repeatedly given two obscure points in the city and have to immediately come up with the best route.

As we discuss in more detail in the next chapter, neural imaging (or imaging of the brain and its functioning) has allowed psychologists to see how the brains of these taxi drivers change as they go through the long process of memorizing thousands of routes, then passing The Knowledge and then—even more interestingly—becoming experts in the decade after they have passed the test.

The next couple of chapters are centred on techniques similar to these which can be applied to a broader range of professions, techniques which help one build focused specialisation. Then from Chapter 4 onwards we focus on a different set of techniques to increase our efficiency and our effectiveness. Chapters 4 and 5 focus on how to declutter our minds while reducing stress and anxiety. Chapters 6 and 7 delve into juicing up our ability to come up with original ideas at a rapid clip in the context of the highly competitive industries in which most of us have to work. Chapters 8 and 9 then provide case studies of how these techniques have been applied in the real world.

* * *

Key takeaways from this chapter

- Psychologists have shown us over the past ten years that there is a gulf between our perception of how powerful our brains are and their true abilities. We suffer from the knowledge illusion (i.e. we think we know everything) and the grand illusion (i.e. we think our faculties are stronger than they actually are).
- Research has conclusively shown that the brain cannot multitask—we can only think one thought at a time. And most of our memories are manufactured by us; they have a lot less to do with what really happened than what we would like to believe happened.
- Given the above, we are bad decision-makers and our minds can be manipulated easily. How do we survive despite these shortcomings? By using heuristics—shortcuts that our brains use to simplify the world for us.
- What remedies does this book provide? We start with the concepts of simplicity, specialization and spiritualization. We then move on to specific behaviours, namely clutter reduction, creativity and memory, and collaboration. Finally, we provide applications where the solutions and behaviours provide actual results.

Navigating Modern India's Mental Health Issues with Dr Sharmila Banwat

Dr Sharmila Banwat is an occupational therapist and clinical psychologist practising for more than nineteen years in the bustling suburbs of Mumbai. She believes in and propagates preventative interventions for all age groups of individuals. We met Dr Banwat on 25 May 2019 at her clinic in Andheri, a western suburb in Mumbai, and spoke with her about a wide range of topics, starting with her education and training and how she began her practice. Hailing from a typical middle-class Indian family, Dr Banwat graduated in occupational therapy from Topiwala National Medical College in Mumbai.

During the course, she became interested in psychiatry and psychology and decided to pursue the subjects. After completing her post-graduation in clinical psychology, Dr Banwat worked under Mumbai's eminent psychiatrists for a year, before opening her own clinic at the turn of the century. Since then she has been testing and counselling a cross section of people who typically live in and around the western suburbs of Mumbai. In 2012, Dr Banwat completed her PhD (in psychology and management) from SNDT Women's University.

Until about a decade ago, psychiatrists and paediatricians would refer patients to psychologists for psychometric evaluation, therapy or counselling. There were hardly any walk-in patients into clinics then. But everything has changed over time. As mental health awareness has risen, the idea of treating mental health issues, challenges and disorders under the guidance of specialist mental health professionals such as clinical psychologists has also increased manifold. Now, Dr Banwat tells us, there are more walk-ins into her clinic. People check online for psychologists and as word spreads, recommendations from old patients, friends and family have also become a source of patient referrals.

Dr Banwat has an extensive experience of working with children and adults. In the first ten years of her practice, she worked as a child psychologist. Through this period, she gained insights into the family dynamics of children and incorporated family psychology into her practice. As her interest in the subject grew, she underwent training in counselling techniques to equip herself as a psychotherapist and counsellor to treat adult cases as well.

Dr Banwat now sees patients across all age groups: infants for developmental screening; children for cognitive and temperamental issues; adolescents for addressing teenage angst, life-skill training, personality evaluation etc.; adults for mental health check-ups, marital counselling; senior citizens for neuro-psychological assessment and screening for cognitive impairment, dementia or will-making.

The western suburbs of Mumbai have upmarket schools and colleges and from these come children with multifold issues. Of late, she has been seeing many adolescents who are undergoing a range of emotional, behavioural, academic and drug-abuse problems. We are talking serious drugs here—not just marijuana—which are becoming extremely common substances now. Next on the list of problems are relationship breakdowns, because kids even at a young age are in and out of many relationships, leaving them very vulnerable. In some cases, children experience angst because of their family going through distress, their parents' marital discord or their extravagant social life. Dr Banwat's experience suggests that addressing unhealthy family dynamics yields good and enduring results. As she says, 'We need to nip it in the bud.'

Among adults, Dr Banwat sees many people who cannot figure out how to strike a work-life balance. They understand it conceptually but can't implement it practically—for example, everyone knows they want to leave office at 7 p.m. but find it impossible to do so. Some take sabbaticals to think it through, others switch from one job to another. Everybody has their own trajectory. Some can't even articulate their problem and reach the psychologist in a state of confusion and distress. Some don't know what's happening and where their life is taking them; they see no purpose or meaning, while some have figured out that something is not right but are not able to place a finger on it. Especially in the corporate sector, very few adults accept that they're going through a mental crisis and understand the need to address it.

And then there are certain stressors or triggers, either at the workplace or at home, such as not being able to do justice to your role as a father, as a spouse, as an employer, or as a boss to one's juniors. Increasingly, midlife crisis has become a well-recognized issue in India. But how we respond to it is still evolving. In many cases, people just let it pass, expecting that time will heal it. Some people feel that their job is not their calling and that they ended up doing things that were different from what they wanted to do. Some people want to figure out midway through their careers what exactly life has to offer, and this becomes a quest for self-discovery.

These mental issues have ballooned in the past decade. It is tough to pinpoint a single reason. Anecdotally, India is a rapidly developing country. As a society we seem to be moving from a joint family to a nuclear-family system. As a result, not only is the family constitution changing but the support systems available to families and their children have also changed. Add to that the overexposure of children to media and the uncensored availability of a plethora of information at a much younger (and, arguably, inappropriate) age.

Not all of this is bad news though. For the children, there is a lot of hope. Greater exposure to the broader world at a younger age means that children today are more emotionally aware than their parents were at a comparable age. So if we work on the emotional intelligence part and make them stable, then these children can thrive. We can work at a preventative level by teaching teenagers about mental well-being in schools (especially in the age band of twelve to eighteen), in colleges and in awareness talks and group therapies.

For adults, Dr Banwat believes that things need to change at the corporate level. Since companies are now more aware than ever about the impact of stress on work performance, they should be willing to invest in solutions. Such solutions do not just entail making counsellors available for stressed employees but also involve providing ongoing emotional coaching to: (a) help employees become aware of the stressors which characterize contemporary urban life, (b) improve stress management skills, and (c) build resilience.

Dr Banwat repeatedly stresses the importance of emotional coaching because in an upwardly-mobile society, the 'fear of missing out' on the best schools, tuition teachers, tutorial classes, activity classes, colleges, jobs, etc. is a big factor. Education has become commercialized and this generation of kids is paying the price for that.

Physical health has a big role to play in mental health too. Dr Banwat believes that three changes in lifestyle can contribute significantly to mental wellness: adequate (seven to eight hours) sleep, healthy food eaten as per a schedule (instead of erratic meals) and regular physical exercise. There is a fourth tip as well: at the end of each day, give yourself ten minutes to self-reflect and evaluate your day—what were the highlights, what were the positive and negative events. This helps break what she calls the 'compare and despair' cycle. Instead of comparing our lives to others and despairing over our deficits, we could take time to see how we grow in our own individual lives.

Finally, while explaining how therapy works, Dr Banwat told us about how the rational emotive behaviour therapy (REBT) approach separates rational and irrational belief systems and works at disputing irrational beliefs (which tend to further creep in when stress preoccupies the human mind) to achieve realistic solutions. When her patients walk in, they don't have insights into what and how these irrational beliefs are affecting their lives. REBT therapy is aimed at increasing their awareness, their coping skills, and at building resources to strengthen the rational belief systems. Since she believes in preventive measures, she propagates individual- and group-therapy programmes for children starting in grade-I until adolescence, so that they become happy, self-accepting and well-functioning and ready to face the world. Today's children face not only normal developmental problems but also a myriad of potentially overwhelming stressors unimaginable in previous generations. As mental health professionals, parents and educators, we need all the resources we can muster to help safeguard our children from self-doubt, irrational thinking, debilitating emotions and self-defeating behaviours.

While emotional intelligence must be instilled in children, the good news is that it can also be developed among adults through psychotherapy. Yet another psychotherapy modality used by Dr Banwat is eye movement desensitization and reprocessing (EMDR) for trauma cases. She has found that EMDR delivers faster and more durable results in challenging cases.

At the end of our interview, she told us that work on mental health is not optional but necessary to improve the quality of life by psychologically engineering your mind through objective and empirically-tested methods.

Section 2

Solutions (The Three S's)

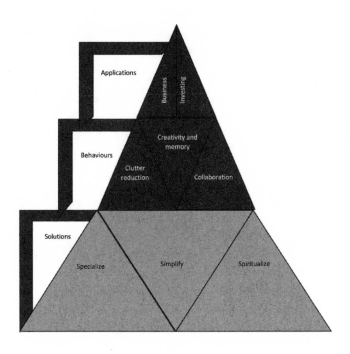

CHAPTER 2

Discovering the World of Specialization[1]

'Everyone holds his fortune in his own hands, like a sculptor the raw material he will fashion into a figure. But it's the same with that type of artistic activity as with all others: We are merely born with the capability to do it. The skill to mould the material into what we want must be learned and attentively cultivated.'

—Johann Wolfgang von Goethe[2]

'Use only that which works, and take it from any place you can find it.'

—Bruce Lee [3]

Introduction

On most Sunday evenings, Saurabh's family plays out what must be a ritual of modern urban life in millions of households across the world—they argue about what genre of movie they will watch over dinner. While Saurabh's teenage son usually votes for action adventures and his daughter loves detective serials, his wife prefers comedies. As Saurabh oscillates between these three opinionated individuals, he reminisces about a very different time and place—1980s Delhi—in which he grew up.

At that time, Indians used to have only two channels at their disposal, and every Sunday evening, Doordarshan, India's state-owned broadcaster, would air the only Bollywood movie of the week. So not just Saurabh's family, the whole country would watch the same movie together. Thanks to technological progress and greater affluence, we now have a plethora of choices. However, it is not obvious that these choices have actually made us unequivocally better off. The painful dilemmas posed by plentiful choices are most apparent when it comes to the crunch point in the careers of most industrious young professionals—deciding what to specialize in.

Why specialize?

The first thinker to clearly articulate the merits of specialization was the Scottish economist Adam Smith. In 1776, he published a book that would lay the foundations of free market economics— *The Wealth of Nations*[4]. The book explained the merits of the division of labour, i.e. the division of a large job into smaller jobs and then the assignment of these small jobs to specific workers such that each worker becomes a specialist in executing a narrowly defined task. So, in one of the most famous case studies ever narrated by an economist, the Scotsman explained how the task of making a pin (from a wire) could be broken down into the following sequential tasks: cut wire, sharpen one end, stamp the head and, finally, solder the head to produce the finished product. Each task would be given to one worker who by dint of doing the same thing all day long would become extremely proficient in that specialized task.

Smith's idea provided the basis for how factories would be organized during the Industrial Revolution and for a long time thereafter. In the first decade of the twentieth century when Henry Ford built the assembly line for the first mass-produced car, the Model T, he drew upon Smith's theory of the division of labour; each worker would work at one station all day long and do just one thing. This not only enhanced the worker's efficiency but training the workers also became easier as they only had to be trained in a narrow, specific task. Almost a century later, cars are still made in much the same way in a silent salute to the Scottish economist who explained why specialization by workers radically improves efficiency for the manufacturer and productivity for the worker (who can thus command a better wage).

In the context of the post-industrial world, the man who has taken Smith's thinking and turned it into practical principles is Malcolm Gladwell. In his provocative book *Outliers: The Story of Success*[5], Gladwell laid out a template for specialization or expertise development which we will revisit repeatedly in this book. This template hinges on relentless application, ideally from an early age, to develop a skill under the tutelage of a master or in the confines of a progressive organization.

More specifically, Gladwell challenged the conventional view of success that it is mostly about innate talent possessed by almost superhuman individuals. Using examples as diverse as Bill Gates, the Beatles, Canadian ice-hockey players and Jewish lawyers in New York, Gladwell illustrates that success arises from a mixture of immense application (usually thousands of hours of practice) and social circumstances (for example, being born to the 'right' parents, in the 'right' place and at the 'right' time).

Matthew Syed, a former British number-one table tennis player, turned Gladwell's template into an inspirational self-help book. In *Bounce: The Myth of Talent and the Power of Practice*[6], using examples ranging from chess players and violinists to firefighters, Syed debunks many of our cherished myths about talented super-achievers.

Syed explains that success has three distinct drivers:

- **Relentless practice**: 10,000 hours of practice, as codified by Gladwell, to develop a specific skill is a necessary but not sufficient driver of success. To quote Syed, '. . . from art to science and from board games to tennis, it has been found that a minimum of ten years is required to reach world-class status in any complex task . . . In *Outliers*, Malcolm Gladwell points out that most top performers practise around one thousand hours per year . . . so he redescribes the ten-year rule as the ten-thousand hour rule. This is the minimum necessary for the acquisition of expertise in any complex task.'
- **Coaching**: 'Purposeful practice' under the guidance of coaches and/or high-quality institutions helps optimize the skill development derived from 10,000 hours of practice. In other words, the whole process of learning becomes more efficient if done under the tutelage of experts who can spot the budding star's mistakes and provide remedies while harnessing her strengths.
- An **enabling environment** makes all of the above possible. Without this environment—without the support of parents, coaches and without the right infrastructure—and the opportunities that it creates, we would not have the Virat Kohlis, the Sachin Tendulkars, the Warren Buffetts or the Steve Jobses. Given access to such an environment, more youngsters will blossom to become successful professionals.

In fact, in Saurabh's first book, *Gurus of Chaos: Modern India's Money Masters*[7], he showed that the template laid out above goes a long way towards explaining the success of several of India's leading fund managers. Looking at the careers of Indian investment legends such as Sanjoy Bhattacharyya, Akash Prakash, K.N. Sivasubramanian and B.N. Manjunath, Saurabh found that success in managing large sums of money over long time periods comes from:

- 'A decade or so of intense training in analysing companies, quizzing management teams, cultivating primary data sources and understanding the business cycle;
- An almost obsessive focus on intellectual integrity (an avoidance of shortcuts in researching, understanding and diligencing a company) even after the initial period of apprenticeship is over to ensure that clients' wealth is preserved and harnessed in an optimal fashion; and
- The ability—created through training, self-awareness and humility—to successfully deal with greed and fear on a daily basis and thereby peel away from other investors who succumb to these primal emotions.'

For example, the chief investment officer (CIO) of one of India's largest fund management houses, ICICI Prudential Asset Management Company, Sankaran Naren, started investing his father's money in Indian stocks when he was fourteen years old. He continued investing through his years in IIT Madras and IIM Calcutta. This hobby was sustained through his early years in the world of work— as a stockbroker in Chennai through the 1990s. In 2000, Naren joined a prominent brokerage in Mumbai first as vice president (Operations) and then as head of research. In 2004, he became a fund manager at ICICI Prudential at the age of thirty-eight. Six years later, he became the CIO of ICICI Prudential.

From his entry into investing in his early teens, Naren's journey to the peak of his profession had taken nearly thirty years. Those years were spent reading thousands of annual reports, understanding market cycles, understanding the investing styles of other investment legends, investing money, losing money, discussing those mistakes with other investors, learning from the mistakes, improving the investment process and gradually, through sustained effort, learning how to deliver healthy returns without taking high levels of risk. That is the level of time and effort it takes to achieve mastery in difficult, demanding jobs.

In fact, in the decade since the publication of *Outliers*, the benefits of 10,000 hours-style specialization in terms of superior expertise and the attendant mental development required for the demonstration of superior expertise have now been scientifically proven in numerous fields. Take, for example, the London taxi drivers we encountered in the previous chapter. The men and women who drive the famous black cabs are specifically trained to: (a) have a very detailed mental map of the city in their heads; and (b) be able to use this map to identify the shortest route between two locations. Their accelerated mental development has been studied in detail by psychologists.

In his book *Peak: Secrets from the New Science of Expertise*[8], Swedish psychologist Anders Ericsson writes:

To master the Knowledge, prospective cabbies . . . spend years driving from place to place in London, making notes of what is where and how to get from here to there. The first step is to master a list of 320 runs in the guidebook provided to taxi-driver candidates. For a given run, a candidate will generally first figure out the shortest route by physically travelling the various possible routes, usually by motorbike, and then will explore the areas around the beginning and end of the run . . . After repeating this process 320 times, the prospective cabbie has accumulated a foundational set of 320 best routes around London . . . even after passing all the tests and getting licensed, London taxi drivers continue to increase and hone their knowledge of London's streets . . .

Neural imaging has allowed psychologists to see how the brains of these taxi drivers change as they go through the long process of memorizing thousands of routes, then passing The Knowledge and then—even more interestingly—becoming experts in the decade after they have passed the test.

Thus, many years of deliberate practice gives London cabbies extraordinary and valuable knowledge of London's roads; it also gives Olympic male gymnasts massively developed arms and shoulders; it gave Steve Jobs the extraordinary ability to perceive, to understand and to create simple, intelligent and yet highly functional designs which have changed the way we use and perceive our phones.

Is it better to be a 'generalist' than a 'specialist'?

Before we delve deeper into how to specialize, it is worth questioning the whole notion of specialization. As highlighted earlier in this chapter, Gladwell's bestseller *Outliers* popularized the concept that with 10,000 hours of 'deliberate' practice under the guidance of an expert/coach, anyone could become a world-beater at anything. That in turn led to ambitious parents enrolling their kids into coaching classes as early as they could to ensure that their children started clocking those 10,000 hours as soon as possible.

However, in an equally well-written book entitled *Range: Why Generalists Triumph in a Specialized World*[9], David Epstein says that the '10,000 hours of practice' theory is not only misguided, it could also be damaging. Epstein argues that specialists flourish in 'kind' learning environments (such as golf, classical music, technology innovation, chess), where patterns recur and feedback is quick and accurate. By contrast, generalists flourish in 'wicked' learning environments (business, politics, fund management, medicine, day-to-day life), where patterns are harder to discern and feedback is delayed and/or inaccurate. Why so?

Epstein cites two reasons why generalists outperform specialists in 'wicked' learning environments. Firstly, generalists tend to have a more rounded set of skills and hence are able to adapt to difficult/fluid learning environments better than specialists (who tend to be more unidimensional in their talents and training). Secondly, generalists have better 'match' quality—since they have done a broader range of things in life, the odds are relatively high that generalists have settled upon/specialized in an activity which fits (or matches) their talents better. As it happens, another book—*Bruce Lee: A Life*[10] by Matthew Polly—provides an almost ideal exemplification of Epstein's theory in a context many of us can identify with, namely, the rise of Asia after World War II.

Bruce Lee: The ultimate 'generalist'

Polly begins the book by giving us the outline of Bruce Lee's life. He was born in San Francisco in 1940 to Chinese parents who were in the USA on a working visa. He then grew up in Hong Kong and became a child movie star before he was banished by his father to the USA when he was eighteen. He finished his schooling in Seattle and set up his first martial arts (kung fu) school there even before he went to the University of Washington. Another kung fu school in Oakland followed three years later, before Hollywood discovered Bruce Lee at the Long Beach Karate Championships in 1964.

Small roles in US TV serials followed, but Hollywood couldn't get over its mental block about an Asian man helming a movie. Instead, Bruce Lee's big break came from Hong Kong; his lead role in *The Big Boss* (1971) made him a superstar in Asia. Over the next two years, four more hit movies—the final one being *Enter the Dragon* (1973), widely considered the finest martial arts movie of all time—established Bruce Lee as a global superstar before his tragic death in Hong Kong in 1973 in mysterious circumstances. While some say that Bruce Lee died due to an allergic reaction to a prescription painkiller, Polly says that Bruce's death was caused due to his body overheating as he had had the sweat glands in his armpits removed so as to help him film for longer without having to change shirts. Without sweat glands, Polly claims, Bruce's body could not cool down swiftly enough in the peak of the Hong Kong summer.

More than his death in mysterious circumstances, what makes Bruce Lee interesting is his fusion of many different styles of fighting to create not just a unique style of combat (which would go on to be called mixed martial arts) but also a new genre of cinema—the martial arts movie.

As a schoolboy, Bruce Lee began by learning wing chun, an obscure style of kung fu, in Hong Kong from his first and only formal guru, Ip Man. He then studied other styles of kung fu while learning judo from his pupil in Seattle, Jesse Glover, and taekwondo from his friend in Oakland, Jhoon Rhee, also known as the 'father of American taekwondo'. In fact, Bruce Lee learnt martial arts from so many that when he became a star, several people—from film star Chuck Norris to Jhoon Rhee—claimed to have taught him his famous side kick.

While still in his early teens, Bruce was taught the basics of Western-style boxing by Father Gordon, a schoolteacher in Hong Kong. After he moved to the USA, Bruce studied boxing films closely, especially those of Muhammad Ali, to understand how the entire body can be used to pack an enormously powerful punch. Bruce also took from boxing its training techniques— skipping, weight training, punching heavy bags 500 times in a day and a five-mile run at the crack of dawn to build stamina.

In his early teens, Bruce also learned the basics of fencing from his brother. He would go on to read and build a library of many dozens of books on fencing. Not only did he become an expert fencer, he combined kung fu and fencing to create the pose which he holds in his iconic photographs wherein he 'leads' with his right hand and 'finishes' or signs-off with his feet. Bruce called his style of kung fu 'fencing without a sword'.[11]

In his twenties, after reading American bodybuilding magazines, Bruce Lee adopted the dietary practices recommended by them, viz. a protein-rich diet accompanied by weight training with lots of repetitions to improve muscle definition. Addicted to non-stop training, while watching TV or waiting for his shot on the sets of a movie, Bruce would do hundreds of repetitions.

Battling Hollywood's relentless racism, Bruce Lee learnt from acting coaches how to slow down his English to make it easier for Western audiences to follow him, and how to slow down his fighting so that the camera could actually see him. By slowing down his fight scenes—most of which he choreographed himself—Bruce Lee transformed the Asian martial arts movie from a sideshow to mainstream entertainment in the US market.

Alongside all this training and movie work, Bruce Lee was reading and writing at a frenetic pace. He extensively read Western, Taoist and Confucian philosophies and was particularly influenced by Jiddu Krishnamurti's[12] religion-less philosophy. Martial arts coach to the biggest Hollywood stars of his time, Bruce Lee went on to write two martial arts guides to his style of kung fu—*Chinese Gung Fu: The Philosophical Art of Self-Defense*[13] and *Tao of Jeet Kune Do*[14]. The latter book, published after his death, has become the largest selling martial-arts book of all time, as stated in Polly's book *Bruce Lee: A Life*.

In the 1971 American TV series *Longstreet*, Bruce Lee narrated lines which have almost become his epitaph: 'Empty your mind, be formless, shapeless—like water. Now you put water into a cup, it becomes the cup; put it in a teapot, it becomes the teapot. Now water can flow or creep or drip or crash. Be water, my friend.'[15]

Settling the 'generalist versus specialist' debate

While *Range* makes a compelling case that all of us should strive for broadness throughout our careers, there is no conflict between Epstein's exhortation to generalization in *Range* and Gladwell's 10,000 hours. In fact, the two notions appear to be complementary, for it seems self-evident to us that in any competitive profession, the people who will rise to the top are those who have (1) generalised skills to deal with a wide variety of challenges, and (2) deep expertise in the core skill or competency offered by the profession to its customers. For example, for the captain of a cricket team to be successful, she not only has to be a good cricketer—which is her core skill—but she also has to have more general skills, such as the emotional intelligence required to get the best out of her players.

So, regardless of whether you are a cricketer, a politician, a fund manager, a dancer or a film star, it is hard to believe that a unidimensional expert or an incompetent expert will reach the summit in the rapidly evolving flux of a complex and competitive society. The mental-model for achieving success in complex 'wicked' societies such as ours therefore resembles the letter 'T', i.e. broad-based knowledge alongside deep, focused expertise.

Building deep, focused expertise

'The two most important days in your life are the day you are born and the day you find out why.'

—From a 1970 pamphlet distributed by a church in the USA[16]

In spite of the popularity of the 10,000 hours principle, we are still left asking, 'What should I specialize in?' And even more fundamentally, 'What are the guiding principles to use to figure out what I should specialize in?'

The tussle between 'should' and 'must'

In 2018, on a flight from Delhi to Mumbai, Saurabh saw a young lady in the seat next to his settle down and spend the next hour doing some high-quality sketching on her tablet (with what looked like a high-tech stylus). Then after the in-flight meal was out of the way, she opened her laptop and started working on a conventional PowerPoint presentation for a large Indian corporate firm.

Saurabh immediately identified with the pattern in her behaviour. A decade ago, when he was her age, Saurabh used to write columns for magazines using the time allocation she was following—the first part of the flight was spent doing what Saurabh loved to do, what his creative instincts said 'I must do'. Then, once the meal was out of the way, Saurabh would switch to doing what he 'should do' to earn a living and/or to meet societal expectations, e.g. prepare research reports for institutional investors with deep pockets. (Saurabh discovered later that the lady sitting next to him on the flight from Delhi was a consultant with a prominent management consultancy.)

For millions of professionals like Saurabh's neighbour on the flight, the tussle between 'should' and 'must', between what they feel they should do (because of financial or societal reasons) and what they must do (in order to fulfil deeply felt urges) is the defining tussle of their lives. The American artist Elle Luna immortalized this internal battle in a celebrated blog published in 2014.[17]

However, it doesn't have to be like that. It has taken Saurabh the best part of twenty years to understand that there is no trade-off between what we should do and what we must do.

It is harder to excel if you are not doing what you 'must' do

What is original thinking? One way of understanding this is to ask yourself how you gain knowledge these days. Generating new thoughts on your own isn't easy. Our knowledge today is based on the expertise of others. Thanks to technology, new ideas are now disseminated rapidly and a large part of our waking hours is spent absorbing the latest ideas produced by others either for professional use (say, by attending professional courses or by subscribing to a trade website) or for personal use (say, by staying glued to Facebook or WhatsApp).

Original thinking is at the heart of professional success in the highly competitive economies which we find ourselves in. And, regardless of your profession, if you want to be an original thinker you have to do what you 'must do', not what your parents or your social circles think you 'should do'.

There is no trade-off between 'should' and 'must'

> 'Work is often seen as a means for making money so we
> can enjoy that second life we lead. Even if we derive some
> satisfaction from our careers, we still tend to compartmentalize
> our lives in this way. This is a depressing attitude . . . If we
> experience this time as something to get through on the way
> to real pleasure, then our hours at work represent a tragic
> waste of the short time we have to live. Instead you want to
> see your work as something more inspiring, as part of your
> vocation . . . Your work then is something deeply connected
> to who you are, not a separate compartment in your life.'
>
> —Robert Greene, *Mastery*[18]

Ironically, it is not so much a question of following your heart
over your head. Once you realize that the trade-off people
talk about (eg. 'you have to choose between a steady job and
the financial security that comes with it versus the fluctuating
fortunes of an entrepreneur') is a false notion—you have
neither financial nor emotional security if you are in a job you
don't enjoy—you will be on your way to a happier and more
successful career. Looking at it another way, there is no career
advancement available for unhappy executives who churn out
unimaginative slides/reports just because of the pay cheque
available at the end of the month.

However, the problem with this sort of emotional response
to a practical question is that our emotions can be fickle. If
today I want to be (or must be) the next legendary batsman to
play cricket for India and tomorrow I must be a footballer and
the day after I decide that journalism is my abiding passion, it
is hard for me to use my 'passion' as a compass for determining
what I should specialize in.

So is there a more practical and more sustainable way to determine specialization? Yes, says Greene in his deeply researched book *Mastery*. He writes:

> You possess a kind of inner force that seeks to guide you toward your Life's Task—what you are meant to accomplish in the time that you have to live. In childhood this force was clear to you. It directed you towards activities and subjects that fit your natural inclinations, that sparked a curiosity . . . In the intervening years, the force tends to fade in and out as you listen more to your parents and peers, to the daily anxieties that wear away at you. This can be the source of unhappiness—your lack of connection to who you are and what makes you unique. The first move toward mastery is always inward—learning who you really are and reconnecting with that innate force. Knowing it with clarity, you will find your way to the proper career path and everything else will fall into place.

Greene goes on to provide a three-step method to help you find your calling:

Step 1: You must connect (or reconnect) with your inclinations, with your sense of uniqueness. In that regard, Step 1 focuses on looking inward—you search your past for signs of that inner voice. You try to clear away other voices—parents, friends, teachers—that might confuse you. Greene says, 'You look for an underlying pattern, a core to your character that you must understand as deeply as possible.'

Step 2: Having nailed Step 1, you look at the career path which you are already on (or the one that you are about to begin). The choice of this path is critical. More specifically, when you are choosing this career path, you need to avoid making needless distinctions between your professional and personal lives. Greene says, '. . . you will need to enlarge your concept of work itself. Too often we make a separation in our lives—there is work and there is life outside work, where we find real pleasure and fulfilment.'

Step 3: Once you have figured out your career path, you need to give yourself a mental model of how your career will broadly pan out. Greene says,

> . . . you must see your career or vocational path more as a journey with twists and turns rather than a straight line. You begin by choosing a field or position that roughly corresponds to your inclinations . . . You don't want to start with something too lofty, too ambitious—you need to make a living and establish some confidence. Once on this path you discover certain side routes that attract you, while other aspects of this field leave you cold. You adjust and perhaps move to a related field, continuing to learn more about yourself, but always expanding off your skill base.

How to specialize?

Greene's book, published four years after Gladwell's *Outliers* became a global bestseller, also gives a detailed road map to specialization, to expertise and ultimately to *mastery*. In fact, we reckon Greene's road map to mastery is best seen as the fleshing out, the detailing of Gladwell's 10,000 hours principle with the main difference between these two American authors being their view of the role that fortune and circumstance play in attaining success.

As explained earlier in this chapter, Gladwell believes that the time, the place and the family circumstances in which you are born play a major role in the attainment of expertise. So, the fact that Bill Gates was born in an affluent American family, went to a high quality school and had access to computers from an early age played a central role in his success in creating Microsoft. In the Gladwellian world, an equally talented child born in an impoverished village in eastern or northern India is highly unlikely to become as successful as Gates.

Greene takes a different, more radical and a more exciting view, more relevant for people like us who do not hail from privileged First World families. He believes that the attainment of mastery—in their chosen vocation—is open to anyone regardless of their financial position, social standing or biological attributes. In Greene's world all you need to attain mastery is a deep commitment to your craft, your vocation allied to a ferocious willingness to learn and push yourself day after day, year after year.

In the passages which follow we have summarized the key steps outlined by Greene but anybody who is serious about gaining expertise in her craft should read Greene's book from cover to cover. Greene articulates a three-step path to mastery: apprenticeship, creative-active and mastery. To summarize each of these steps:

- **Apprenticeship**: We need mentors because life is short— we have limited time and energy to expend, especially since our most creative years tend to be our late twenties into our mid-forties. We can learn through books, courses, videos, our own practice and the occasional piece of advice from others. However, that process is a hit-and-miss because the information in books or courses is neither customized to your specific circumstances nor takes into account the quirks in your personality and mental makeup. Further, the books and courses are likely to be abstract and when you have little knowledge of the world, the utility of such knowledge is limited. Leaving books and courses aside, you can learn from your personal experiences but that is likely to be a drawn-out process. It is in this context that a mentor or a guru can be of help. Such a person can streamline your learning to suit your specific requirements.

The mentor's personal experiences allow her to not only share with you battlefield stories which you can learn from, it also allows her to tailor all the resources that are available to you—courses, books, work experience, etc.— to suit your personality and needs. The mentor's guidance reduces the chances that you will walk down blind alleys and fall prey to diversions. Her ability to give you real-time feedback will allow you to make the best use of your time. In short, the mentor can potentially help you learn in, say, five years what could have taken ten years to learn without appropriate guidance.

- **Creative-active**: As you accumulate knowledge and experience in your chosen discipline, ideally under the guidance of a mentor, you will increasingly have to choose between: (a) keeping your mind active, hungering for more knowledge, asking increasingly difficult questions and seeking out new experiences; or (b) turning conservative with your knowledge acquisition, preferring to fit into groups of people and sticking to procedures which—for you—are tried and tested. If you want to attain mastery in your craft, you will have to choose path (a) rather than path (b). In other words, as you move towards the end of your apprenticeship, you have to be bold enough to expand your knowledge of related fields. You have to experiment and look at old problems from new angles. As you do this,

Greene says that 'you will turn against the very rules you have internalized . . . Such originality will bring you the heights of power.'

- **Mastery, or the development of high-level intuition**: As you push the frontiers of your knowledge and your skill set repeatedly, you will develop an understanding of all the parts involved in the discipline that you are studying (or the craft that you are learning). The knowledge will now be internalized in you in ways that even you will not fully understand. Albert Einstein, famously, was able to see a whole new way of seeing the whole universe—the time-space continuum as he called it—in one single visual image.[19] Similarly, Thomas Edison was able to visualize how an entire city could be electrified in a single image. Greene says that this level of intuition can only be reached after 20,000—not 10,000—hours of learning and practice. Through sheer practice and experience, you transform the neural networks in your brain such that it is able to make connections no one else can. In short, you become a 'master'.

Specialization case study: Charlie Munger

A uniquely original and astonishingly capable mind, Charlie Munger has trained himself across multiple disciplines without taking a single course at university on business or finance. His life provides rich lessons for those who seek wisdom. At the core of Munger's wisdom is the realization that thinking does not come naturally to the vast majority of people in the stock market, i.e. most of us do not think most of the time; we parrot/imitate and respond reflexively to what we read, see and hear. Therefore, if we can set up systems and processes and learn tricks, which teach us to think and in fact make us think, we will gradually become better than most people around us. This central insight from Munger is extremely relevant for investors in a market such as India where the herd instinct is even stronger than it is in the developed markets and where accounting/governance inadequacies characterize even prominent companies.

Based on our reading of three superb books—*Seeking Wisdom: From Darwin to Munger* by Peter Bevelin, *Charlie Munger: The Complete Investor* by Trenholme J. Griffin and *Poor Charlie's Almanack*[20]—we provide our summary of what we are trying to learn from this titan:

1. Continuously learning, thinking, building mental models and deep knowledge: In order to benefit from this model of focused learning, we need to be patient and we need to realize that there will always be people who will be going faster than us. However, if we persist, we will benefit from what is called the second half of the chessboard—or the area where our knowledge bears fruit in a much more meaningful way.[21] In Munger's words, 'Spend each day trying to be a little wiser than you were when you woke up. Discharge your duties faithfully and well. Slug it out one inch at a time, day by day. At the end of the day—if you live long enough—most people get what they deserve.'[22]

There is another way to think about what Munger is saying. If we build a repository of knowledge and accumulated experience of real-world situations, we will gradually become more able to correlate problems we come across with the knowledge we have already accumulated. In the words of the psychologist-cum-economist Herbert A. Simon[23], 'The situation has provided a cue; this cue has given the expert access to information stored in memory, and the information provides the answer. Intuition is nothing more and nothing less than recognition.'

2. Understanding our circle of competence and staying within it: A decade ago, Munger said in a BBC interview, 'We have to deal with things that we're capable of understanding.'[24] At Marcellus Investment Managers, Saurabh and his colleagues are repeatedly asked why they don't invest in stocks which don't have high returns on capital and strong cashflows. After all, the thinking goes, great investors are all about finding decent companies at bargain prices. However, since they can't second-guess how an ugly frog will become a handsome prince, the team at Marcellus has focused on its core competence of investing in great franchises with strong moats and a clean management. To quote Munger, 'It's obvious that if a company generates high returns on capital and reinvests at high returns, it will do well. But this wouldn't sell books, so there's a lot of twaddle and fuzzy concepts that have been introduced that don't add much.'[25]

Munger also makes the broader point that '[k]nowing what you don't know is more useful than being brilliant', and '[a]cknowledging what you don't know is the dawning of wisdom'.[26] Munger's friend Li Lu has restated this nicely: 'The true insights a person can get in life are still very limited, so correct decision making must necessarily be confined to your "circle of competence". A "competence" that has no defined borders cannot be called a true competence.'[27]

3. Focus on one or two variables: Both in the businesses he invested in and in the way he gradually built a vast body of knowledge, Munger learned to focus on the one or two variables which drive success. In his words: 'In business we often find that the winning system goes almost ridiculously far in maximizing and or minimizing one or a few variables—like the discount warehouses of Costco.'

Warren Buffett has articulated this point of view from the perspective of an investor: 'You only have to be right on a very, very few things in your lifetime as long as you never make any big mistakes . . . An investor needs to do very few things right as long as he or she avoids big mistakes.'[28]

4. Focus on outstanding businesses, *not* on cheap stocks: Until he started collaborating with Munger, Buffett was focused on using Benjamin Graham's cigar-butt style of 'value investing'. Munger's influence played a major role in Buffett gradually abandoning this style through the 1970s and 1980s and moving towards investing in outstanding franchises such as Capital Cities/ABC and Coca-Cola. Munger deserves enormous credit for first saying[29]: 'Ben Graham had blind spots. He had too low an appreciation of the fact some businesses were worth paying big premiums for.'

And then saying[30]:

Ben Graham had a lot to learn as an investor. His ideas on how to value companies were all shaped by how the Great Crash and Depression almost destroyed him, and he was always a little afraid of what the market can do. It left him with an aftermath of fear for the rest of his life . . . I think Ben Graham wasn't nearly as good an investor as Warren Buffett is or even as good as I am. Buying those cheap, cigar-butt stocks [companies with limited potential growth selling at a fraction of what they would be worth in a takeover or liquidation] was a snare and a delusion . . .'

Interestingly, this resulted in an investment style for Munger (heavily influenced by the great Philip A. Fisher) which works nicely for Saurabh's colleagues at Marcellus Investment Managers in India and has given them a portfolio of moated, relatively clean, well-run companies such as Asian Paints, Pidilite, HDFC Bank and Dr Lal PathLabs. In Munger's words[31], 'Once we'd gotten over the hurdle of recognizing that a thing could be a bargain based on quantitative measures that would have horrified Graham, we started thinking about better businesses.'

5. Carefully choose the people you work with: Munger says one has to be selective about the people one works with because people who do unwise things in one setting usually proceed to do unwise things in other settings as well. In Munger's words[32], '. . . it's just so useful dealing with people you can trust and getting all the others the hell out of your life. It ought to be taught as a catechism [W]ise people want to avoid other people who are just total rat poison, and there are a lot of them.'

Learning from Charlie Munger

Saurabh and his colleagues at Marcellus Investment Managers have benefited immensely from Charlie Munger's teachings. The Marcellus team in Mumbai focuses on analysing in-depth no more than thirty stocks. This is significantly lower than the number of stocks covered by an average portfolio management house in India. Marcellus's Consistent Compounders Portfolio has only thirteen stocks in it. The firm has seven analysts in its team, and each is required to dissect only four to five stocks. Why? Because Marcellus does not think it can realistically ask its analysts to build deep knowledge on more than this number of companies.

By 'deep knowledge' Saurabh means (a) familiarity with the last fifteen years of annual reports of each of these companies; (b) a deep understanding of every single major capital-allocation decision made by these companies over the last fifteen years;

(c) a deeper understanding of the competitive advantages—or the lack thereof—of these companies than anyone else in the Indian stock market has; and (d) a full understanding of the accounting/governance tricks being used to flatter the firm's profits and its net worth.

The past decade has taught Saurabh and his colleagues that building deep knowledge of high-quality Indian firms is unusually rewarding because most analysts/investors operating in India are seldom able to focus long enough on a company to truly understand its sustainable competitive advantages. As a result, if the team at Marcellus can understand the same better than others, it should generate superior results over long periods of time. That being said, it is tough, grindingly hard work—not just because of the many hours spent reading but also because of the time and effort involved in tracking down experts who can provide deep, original insights into the workings of these companies. The fact that a legend like Charlie Munger traversed a similar path gives Marcellus the proof of concept that it needs to focus as deeply as the legendary American investor.

* * *

Key takeaways from this chapter

- The first thinker to clearly articulate the merits of specialization was the Scottish economist Adam Smith, who explained the merits of the idea 250 years ago in his famous book *The Wealth of Nations*. Smith's idea regarding the division of labour on the lines of specialization provided the basis for how factories would be organized during the Industrial Revolution and for a long time thereafter.
- Authors such as Malcom Gladwell and Matthew Syed have debunked the notion of talent as the key driver for

success. Instead, they have written about the role of social circumstances, immense application, relentless and purposeful practice, and an enabling environment as keys to success.

- In the debate on generalists versus specialists, we believe that one must be both a generalist and a specialist. The people who rise to the top are those who have: (1) generalised skills to deal with a wide variety of challenges; and (2) deep expertise in the core skill or competency offered by the profession to its customers. For example, for the captain of a cricket team to be successful, he not only has to be a good cricketer—which is his core skill—but he also has to have more general skills, such as the emotional intelligence required to get the best out of his players.

- What should you specialize in? Robert Greene provides three steps: Connect with your inclinations, choose your career in line with your inclinations, and prepare a mental model of how your career will broadly pan out. How to specialize? Follow Robert Greene's path to mastery. Find a great mentor, ignite the 'creative-active mind' and finally develop high-level intuition.

How Raamdeo Agrawal Built the Motilal Oswal Empire

Raamdeo Agrawal and his friend Motilal Oswal are legends of Dalal Street. They are a testimony to the power of specialization, given their focus on a single area: equities. Their tag line reads, 'Equity Sahi Hai' (equities are right). We met Agrawal or RA (as he is known within the company) on 23 July 2019 at the Motilal Oswal Financial Services (MOFS) Ltd headquarters in Prabhadevi, Mumbai.

MOFS is named after Oswal since, as Agrawal says, 'he went into the ring' (the trading ring at the Bombay Stock Exchange) while Agrawal 'took the trade orders'. MOFS was set up as a stockbroking house in 1987 and since then has diversified into fields such as wealth management, mutual funds and housing finance. Between the two, RA is the more visible face, seen often on business TV channels, in newspaper interviews, holding forth confidently regarding India's future and about the Indian stock market being the best avenue for an average Indian to grow his wealth.

RA gives his own example as the son of a farmer from a village in Chhattisgarh who went to Raipur, now the capital of the state of Chhattisgarh, for his schooling, Nagpur for his college, and then came to Mumbai as a broke but hugely ambitious Marwari graduate who vowed to build his own business and get rich. From those early days of setting up MOFS to the present-day Motilal Oswal HQ in a 300,000-square-foot glass tower in the central suburb of Prabhadevi, RA has traversed a long distance.

Like almost all the experts we interviewed for this book, RA is a voracious reader and this habit goes back to his school and college days. While RA was strong at sciences in school and at accounts in college, he was poor in English. Determined to address this deficiency, RA began reading newspapers and books in college—a habit that helped him easily read huge annual reports later in his career.

RA's struggle in building his career has now become a competitive advantage for him because it allows him to spot great entrepreneurs early—RA looks for driven men and women who put in immense efforts in clearing competitive exams (like the entrance exams held each year to get admission into IIT, IIM and medical colleges, the professional exams held for chartered accountants or the evaluation exam for the Indian Administrative Service). RA believes that determination to clear the exams is an indicator of an inner desire to fight and win against the odds. RA recalls his own desire to clear the hugely competitive chartered accountancy (CA) exams. RA was determined to pass the exams even if it took multiple attempts.

RA was also clear that he would never work for a salary. He stayed on track to be an entrepreneur even as all his friends settled into comfortable jobs after earning their CA qualification. RA attributes this bent of mind to the many financial fiction books that he read in his youth—books by authors such as Paul Emil Erdman (*The Billion Dollar Sure Thing*, *Zero Coupon* and *The*

Silver Bears), Irving Wallace (*The R Document*) and Arthur Hailey (*The Moneychangers*). Most of these books were easily available to read at cheap rentals in local libraries. Books from these local libraries shaped RA's mind and led him towards a career in the stock markets, preventing him from going down the traditional CA routes of accounts, audit and taxation.

As RA started understanding the stock market, he would analyse businesses everywhere he went. If he went to a restaurant, he would work out the number of customers, table turnarounds, average billings, etc. and construct a profit and loss (P & L) account within minutes. This laid an early framework to understanding businesses. It also helped RA set up a low-cost, self-funded brokerage that benefited from the long settlement periods of buying and selling shares in the physical settlement era of India's stock markets. The Harshad Mehta-led bull run (and subsequent crash) of 1991 and 1992 helped MOFS's fortunes. A hunger to learn and an ambition to succeed drove RA to focus on what he knew best—fundamental research of companies and their promoters. 'We were young and mad. The stock market is all we knew. We liked to say that if you like mad people, come work with us, else don't. And it is difficult to compete with mad people,' RA told us.

Everything changed when veteran Indian investor, Sanjoy 'Bhatta' Bhattacharyya pointed RA towards the Berkshire Hathaway (BH) founder and legendary investor Warren Buffett. In the 1990s, Buffett was an unknown name in Indian stock markets. But RA dove deep into the work and investment philosophies of Buffett, procuring all of BH's annual letters. Before reading Buffett, RA focused only on simplistic and 'primitive' price-to-earnings based investing with basic knowledge of the company from annual reports.

RA was so deeply influenced by Buffett that he even travelled to Omaha in 1994—for the first time—to meet Buffett and got a photograph clicked with him. While the trip to meet the Oracle of Omaha was an achievement for RA in those days, it has become a ritual for many Indian investors over the past few years. RA credits a lot of his investment frameworks and even management styles to Buffett. 'Investing is much more than just reading the balance sheet. So that [Buffett and his investment style] really changed everything for us in investing,' RA told us. To date, RA credits his friend Bhatta for pointing him towards Buffett, towards other global investors and towards investment philosophies—all of which have made RA a better investor. 'Buffett is my guru, but Bhatta is my Sadhguru,' RA told us.

While RA often comes across as animated in our discussions with him, he is detached and calm about how the stock market moves. Unlike many people who can't get their eyes off the stock price ticker on the TV screen or mobile phones, RA gave us his full attention for this interview. RA credits this detachment to his steadfast refusal to lever (use debt to increase his bets). He is unfazed with any stock-market boom or crash, other than propounding his beliefs in the power of equity when TV channels call him during those booms or crashes.

RA credits his chartered accountancy degree to staying focused on sensible capital allocation. 'I will never manage anything based on my market cap. I do things based on what I have in my pocket,' he told us. RA believes that an owner of a company is the chief risk officer because if the company fails, his employees may leave him, but his company is all that he has. Hence, he must manage risks more than anything else. 'Because I started from zero, I never want to go back to zero. Even if I commit mistakes, I will cut my losses in such a way that we stay safe overall,' he told us.

Finally, when we ask him for his advice to a twenty-five-year-old, RA tells us to do two simple things. First—find your passion. Unlike his time when opportunities were limited, he believes that opportunities for today's youth are global. They can even take a few years off to find their passion and then pursue it with everything they have, to literally put their lives behind finding success with an unshakeable belief in themselves. Second—have a strong value system that you hold through good and bad times. RA quotes Charlie Munger, vice-chairman of Berkshire Hathaway, 'The safest way to try and get what you want is to try and deserve what you want.'

CHAPTER 3

How to Simplify Your Life[1]

'The definition of genius is taking the complex and making it simple.'

—Attributed to Albert Einstein[2]

The iPhone: Simplicity made iconic

In his biography of Steve Jobs, Walter Isaacson[3] recalled that when the iPod was launched, a Harvard Business School professor said that it 'will likely become a niche product'. When Apple Stores were opened in 2001 to retail the company's products, *Bloomberg Businessweek* published a headline saying, 'Sorry, Steve: Here's Why Apple Stores Won't Work'.[4] In fact, and as Isaacson's book goes on to state, fourteen years prior, Apple's then CEO, John Sculley—who was instrumental in bringing Steve Jobs's first stint at Apple to a premature end—had pooh-poohed the entire effort made by the firm to create beautiful yet useful tech products for the mass market by saying, 'High tech could not be designed and sold as a consumer product.'

And yet, as Isaacson explains in his magisterial biography of this visionary entrepreneur, Jobs was so obsessed with functional yet beautiful things that he simply would not let mainstream opinion get in the way. His love for 'clean design' and 'awesome little features' can be linked partly to the house in Mountain View, California, where he grew up. It was built by the developer Joseph Eichler, who built more than 11,000 homes in California's subdivisions—these were mass-market homes which were affordable yet beautiful to see and to live in. Jobs's fondness for intelligent design was inculcated by his father, Paul Jobs, a great mechanic who taught his son how to make well-crafted objects in the backyard of their house. During the writing of his biography, he took the author, Isaacson, to see a fifty-year-old fence built by his father. Jobs said of his late father, 'He loved doing things right. He even cared about the look of the parts you couldn't see.'

Jobs's obsession with simple, intelligent designs became so well-developed that he could perceive ordinary things, like well-made knives and kitchen appliances, in a way that most of us cannot. That he admired the Cuisinart food processor he saw at a supermarket may sound unimportant, but from that food processor stemmed his idea that a moulded plastic covering might work for a computer as well. Isaacson said of Jobs in a TV interview[5], 'His genius was the ability to connect poetry to technology. That art and technology thing . . . How do you connect artistry to technology? And that comes, whether it was the cancer or his personal life or his professional life, from sort of having that new-age, alternative, beautiful side to him, the poetic side, and the technology side.'

Jobs's genius is still visible in the iPhone—in its design and functioning. For instance, the major components in an iPhone Xs Max include the screen, earpiece speaker assembly, cameras, logic boards, battery, nano SIM card reader, taptic engine, speaker assembly—all of which have their own sets of components and subcomponents. In fact, the iPhone Xs Max has more than 300 parts. These parts, in total, cost around $450 and yet the iPhone retails for more than $1,100.[6] The delta between those two numbers is the 'simplicity premium' that Apple commands.

The quote from Albert Einstein, which is cited at the beginning of this chapter, is often used in the context of Steve Jobs's remarkable life. Ironically, while numerous websites attribute this quote to the legendary physicist, it is possible that the great man never actually uttered these words. In fact, in the context of seeking to understand simplicity, it is another Einstein quote—which can be confidently attributed to the Nobel laureate—that is more appropriate: 'It can scarcely be denied that the supreme goal of all theory is to make the irreducible basic elements as simple and as few as possible without having to surrender the adequate representation of a single datum of experience . . . everything should be as simple as possible, but not simpler.'[7]

Einstein's statement on simplicity is elegant in itself. Certainly, Einstein's ideas or theories could get quite complex, as was his theory of relativity (at least initially, Einstein was the only one able to understand its math). But if one is to understand its essence, then that understanding must be conveyed as simply as possible, so that the message can be understood by a mainstream audience with no specialist subject-matter knowledge. For example, in learning how to write, there are a core number of elements, ten in all, that must be communicated simply in order for the student to gain meaning. If you try to give too many rules without any order or structure, which enables the student to see the connections, then understanding breaks down. You've got to see the forest before you can see the trees: the simple before the complexity of the details.

What is so special about simplicity?

'Simplicity is the ultimate sophistication.' That was the tagline for the Apple II personal computer in 1977. It is an admirable sentiment. But how do you define simplicity? According to the Oxford dictionary, simplicity is: (1) the quality or condition of being easy to understand or do; and (2) the quality or condition of being plain or uncomplicated in form or design.[8]

Both in the context of business and in the world of investing, simple strategies are easy to understand, easy to implement, easy to sell to others, and easy to course-correct from. In fact, a portfolio of the world's top ten largest brands ranked on simplicity has outperformed global equity benchmarks by a country mile.[9] In Chapter 8, we will discuss in more detail as to how 'simple' businesses make more money and do so on a more sustainable basis than complicated businesses.

In the world of investing, John Bogle has shown that simplicity trumps over all manners of sophisticated investment strategies. Through Vanguard—the firm that John Bogle founded in 1975—he has shown that the most sensible way to make money in the stock market is through an index tracker fund, i.e. a low-cost fund which simply mimics the main stockmarket index (and therefore does not need to pay a fund manager crores of rupees for his non-existent skill). So useful are Vanguard's offerings that the firm not only manages \$5.1 trillion worth of assets, but investors as revered as Buffett have said that the portion of their inheritance which they will leave for their families (i.e. the quantum which will not go to charitable causes) will be invested in Vanguard's tracker funds. We discuss John Bogle in greater detail in Chapter 9.

Another example of the power of simplicity in the world of investing is the systematic investment plan, or SIP in common parlance. For the uninitiated, an SIP is a way to automatically invest a certain amount every month into a mutual fund. Its simplicity lies in the fact that it takes the burden of 'timing the market' off an investor. SIPs are the best way for retail investors to save due to a phenomenon called 'dollar cost averaging'. Here is how it works: an investor invests a fixed amount at regular intervals in an investment, irrespective of the price of the asset or security. Anupam, for example, has an SIP in a mutual fund where he invests Rs 10,000 every month and he has been doing this since 2014, without missing a single month. He has set this up as an auto debit into his bank account so at most times he is not even aware that the SIP is in motion.

The SIP has exploded in popularity in India, which is a testament to its effectiveness from the average investor's point of view. The mutual fund industry's trade body, Association of Mutual Funds in India (AMFI), estimates that there are 29 million SIP accounts and the total amount invested by investors in SIPs (from April 2016 until January 2020) is Rs 2.9 trillion ($40 billion).[10] To put this number into perspective, the total investment of Indian high-net-worth investors in alternative investment funds (AIFs) and portfolio management services (PMS) amounts to $35 billion.[11]

But as easy as simplicity sounds, it is anything but easy. Most simple systems are in fact derived from complex processes. Delivering simplicity is the result of a combination of top-notch strategy and leadership, and of innovation and taking risks. Think of the modern smartphone—it is simple; it helps us get a lot of things done; and we don't have to work hard to figure it out. As far as we—the customers—are concerned, it just works. But a whole lot has gone into making that happen.

Earlier in the chapter we discussed how the iPhone Xs Max is the successful orchestration of more than 300 parts. Beyond just the physical parts is Apple's massive machinery of marketing, design, patents, employees and much more. Apple employs more than 1,20,000 people, 9,000 alone in the design department. At Apple Park, the company's headquarters in Cupertino, designers from diverse areas of creative expertise work alongside each other; industrial designers sit next to font designers, prototypers, haptic experts. 'The best haptic experts in the world are sat next to a bunch of guys who have PhDs in material science,' says Sir Jony Ive, Apple's former chief design officer.[12]

Take Amazon, which has made an art of offering literally an Amazonian range of products and then delivering it perfectly on time. Behind that massive catalogue and near-perfect delivery is a vast network of employees and processes that we can never fathom.

Amazon's famously customer-obsessive founder and CEO, Jeff Bezos, summarized Amazon's philosophy in these simple words, 'We've had three big ideas at Amazon that we've stuck with for 18 years, and they're the reason we're successful: Put the customer first. Invent. And be patient.'[13]

Achieving simplicity in thought and action, then, is not easy. So how can we do it?

Two degrees of simplification

If you think about it, the examples of simplification we have discussed so far in this chapter fall into two distinct categories. Whereas the iPhone is an example of a product where the underlying principle is that the user should be presented with an uncluttered and what—at least superficially—looks like a simple user interface, the SIP is an example of a simplification turned into a habit, namely that every month without fail I will invest a pre-specified amount of money. While simplification through habit is easier to achieve, simplification through principles yields more powerful results.

As Richard Koch says in the preface to the book he co-authored with Greg Lockwood, *Simplify: How the Best Businesses in the World Succeed*[14]:

> Principles are wonderful things, because if they are really powerful they can save us enormous effort and stop us going down dead ends. In science and business there are just a few such principles; but whereas most scientists are aware of the beautiful principles in their field, few business people are guided by principles in their daily work, preferring to rely on methods – the next level down. Yet, as the nineteenth-century philosopher Ralph Waldo Emerson said, 'As to methods there may be a million and then some, but principles are few. The man who grasps principles can successfully select his own methods. The man who tries methods, ignoring principles, is sure to have trouble.'
>
> To qualify, a principle must be so overwhelmingly powerful that ordinary mortals – such as you or me – can reliably create extraordinary results, not through personal brilliance but just by following the principle carefully and with a modicum of common sense.

We agree with Koch and Lockwood—simplification through principles is the ultimate sophistication. However, because it is harder, let us begin with the easier type of simplification—through habit, process and method.

Simplification Type 1: Simplify through habit/process/ method

> 'I must have liked the long hours, for in later life, I never
> took the attitude of "I've worked hard all my childhood and
> youth and now I'm going to take it easy and sleep till noon."
> Quite the contrary . . . I wake up at five in the morning. I
> get to work as early as I can. I work as long as I can. I do
> this every day in the week, including holidays. I don't take
> vacations voluntarily and I try to do my work even when I'm
> on vacation.'
>
> —Isaac Asimov[15]

In the five hundred years prior to the British arriving in India, the Vijayanagara empire centred in Hampi and encompassing much of present-day Karnataka, Telangana and Andhra was the mightiest kingdom south of the Vindhyas. The might of this empire reached its peak during the rule of Krishna Deva Raya when Vijayanagara's armies would routinely defeat the surrounding kingdoms in the Deccan and thus capture more territory and usurp more wealth.

In his richly entertaining book, *Rebel Sultans: The Deccan from Khilji to Shivaji*[16], historian Manu S. Pillai has this to say of the great Krishna Deva Raya: 'Every morning, reportedly, he drank a three-quarter pint of sesame oil, after which he "anoints himself all over with the same oil; he covers his loins with a small cloth, and takes in his arms great weights made of earthenware, and then, taking a sword he exercises himself till he has sweated out all the oil, and then he wrestles with one of his wrestlers". After gymming so (and making a royal display of it), "he mounts a horse and gallops about the plain in one direction and another till dawn, for he does all this before daybreak". When it was time to appear in court, he would throw on a tunic embroidered with "many roses in gold", a brocade cap crowning his head "like a Galician helmet" . . . seated on the Diamond Throne, surrounded by his ministers, Brahmins and robed eunuchs, Krishna Deva was without doubt an impressive figure . . .'

While none of us modern-day office workers can match the routine of a legendary king, path-breaking work has at its core very hard work, often done in the midst of a well-defined schedule and usually done in solitude. Research shows that the greatest minds of the past 300 years have used a surprisingly similar set of habits to grind their way to success.

Habits drive 40 per cent of our decision-making

Even though habits account for 40 per cent of the decisions that we make, the 'thinking' part of the brain does not control our habits. To quote bestselling author Charles Duhigg[17]:

> Most of the choices we make each day may feel like the products of well-considered decision making but they're not. They are habits. And though each habit means relatively little on its own, over time the meals we order, what we say to our kids each night . . . have enormous impacts on our health . . . and happiness. One paper published by a Duke University researcher in 2006 found that more than 40% of the actions people performed each day weren't actual decisions, but habits . . .
>
> When you dream up a new invention . . . it's the outside parts of your brain at work. That's where the most complex thinking occurs. Deeper inside the brain and closer to . . . where the brain meets the spinal column, are older, more primitive structures. They control our automatic behaviours,

such as breathing and swallowing . . . Towards the centre
of the skull is a golf ball-sized lump of tissue that is similar
to what you might find inside the head of a fish, reptile or
mammal. This is the basal ganglia . . . [Scientists have found
that] basal ganglia was central to recalling patterns and
acting on them. The basal ganglia, in other words, stored
habits even while the rest of the brain went to sleep.

Understanding the reflex element of habit-driven decision-
making is central to nailing down why some people consistently
achieve better results than others even though, on the face of it,
they appear to be no more able or talented than others around
them. As Gretchen Rubin says in her book on habits[18], 'Habits
are the invisible architecture of our lives . . . Habit allows us to
go from "before" to "after", to make life easier and better. Habit
is notorious – and rightly so – for its ability to direct our actions,
even against our will . . .'

Advances in science have now helped us understand how
habits (or the 'habit loop') work in a three-step framework.
Sequentially, these are:

1. **A cue**: This is a trigger (something you see, smell or hear)
   that transfers the brain into an automatic mode which
   determines which habit to use.
2. **A routine**: This is the heart of the habit and is typically a
   mental, emotional or physical routine.
3. **A reward**: This helps the brain ascertain if this specific loop
   is worth remembering for the future.

Duhigg says that the cue and reward 'become neurologically
intertwined until a sense of craving emerges'. For example,
when Saurabh wakes up on weekdays, he keeps his running
shoes close to the bed. That is his cue that he needs to get

some exercise. That cue triggers a routine for him—of putting on his gym clothes, going down to the gym and working out. Throughout this process, he needs a reward which keeps him going in the dark Mumbai mornings (which are accompanied by heavy rain from June to September). His reward is a peanut-butter sandwich with jam layered on top for breakfast. Saurabh's wife ensures that he doesn't get the sandwich if he doesn't go to the gym. That's how Saurabh's exercise habit loop works.

The nature of our habits influences our decision-making

Clearly, our habits will influence our financial decisions. While this phenomenon is multilayered, it is possible to understand the simplest layer in 200 words.

Saurabh and his colleagues at Marcellus Investment Managers are fund managers. When they meet companies, the meeting often takes place in the promoter's office itself (rather than in a meeting room). Most such offices have a TV and hence the promoter is exposed to cues emanating from the TV. Associated with these cues are likely to be the routines/habits of the promoter. For example, he might be accustomed to calling up his broker after seeing the share price of a stock he holds surge, or he might have got into the habit of calling his CEO when he hears news about a competitor.

At the end of these routines, there is a 'reward' that the promoter has got accustomed to receiving, like his broker giving him good news regarding his stock portfolio (reward = 'wealth trip'), or his CEO giving him good news regarding how the competition is being pulverized (reward = 'power trip').

Such routines—either cued by TV, email or social media—form a large part of the working lives of many decision-makers we meet. Much of the remainder of their time is taken up by meetings (which themselves become another habit). As a result, very little of the corporate lives of many senior decision-makers is actually used for thinking and contemplation.

A small minority of promoters have no TVs in their offices; many of these promoters also don't seem to be making active use of mobile phones. Such people arguably have more time to think and read, i.e. more time not spent spinning on a habit loop. Such promoters are often able to see their industry from unusual angles. Unsurprisingly, there is a strong correlation between such promoters and the wealth they generate for their shareholders. To quote from Saurabh's book *The Unusual Billionaires*[19]:

> 'Most Indian companies tend to focus on short-term results and hence that makes them frequently do things that deviate away from their articulated strategy . . . these deviations take them away from the path they have to travel to achieve their long-term goals . . . the willingness to resist the temptation of short-term "off strategy" profits for long-term sustainable gain is not there in most leading companies,' writes Rama Bijapurkar, a leading market strategy consultant . . .
>
> The typical promoter profiled in [*The Unusual Billionaires*] is patient and persevering, even bordering on the boring. He ignores short-term thrills based on flavour-of-the-month ideas. He consciously rejects aggressive forays into unrelated businesses . . . Such behaviour requires tremendous patience and a willingness to ignore the stock market's proclamations regarding prevailing fads and fashions.

Asian Paints, Berger Paints, Marico and HDFC Bank are among the companies covered in detail in *The Unusual Billionaires*. It is, we think, safe to say that the habits of the people running these firms have contributed substantially to the success of the companies.

How great minds simplify their working day

So how do successful people construct their working day so that their habits—by themselves—would become one of the foundations of their success. At the outset, we have to say that those looking for shortcuts should stop reading this chapter because, as V.S. Pritchett said in 1941, 'Sooner or later, the great men turn out to be all alike. They never stop working. They never lose a minute. It is very depressing.'[20]

So other than working non-stop, what exactly do the legends do habitually which entrenches their greatness? In 2013, American journalist Mason Currey summarized the working habits of nearly 200 great minds in an interesting and entertaining book called *Daily Rituals: How Great Minds Make Time, Find Inspiration, and Get to Work.* Currey's book (which itself draws from more than 400 sources) and our reading of the biographies of other great minds give us a pretty good idea of the life one would have to lead to have a high probability of doing original, path-breaking work:

1. **Reading**: Reading extensively and almost non-stop seems to be a prerequisite for producing path-breaking work. As Charlie Munger says, 'In my whole life, I have known no wise people . . . who didn't read all the time – none, zero.'[21] In fact, apart from a few painters, almost all the great minds seem to spend a large part of the day reading, sometimes at the expense of maintaining a normal social life. Indeed, almost all of the experts we interviewed for this book are voracious readers.

2. **Intense, focused work in solitude:** The vast majority of the legends whose lives are described in Currey's book spent at least three hours each day (almost always immediately after breakfast) focused on intense, hard

work. Most locked the doors of the studies, forbade anybody from disturbing them and sought peace and silence so that they could push themselves to the limit. Needless to say, they did not take phone calls or read emails or WhatsApp during these hours of intense, focused work. In Ernest Hemingway's words:

> When I am working on a book or story I write every morning as soon after first light as possible. There is no one to disturb you and it is cool or cold and you come to your work and warm as you write. You read what you have written and you always stop when you know what is going to happen next . . . You write until you come to a place when you still have your juice and you know what will happen next . . . You have started at six in the morning and you may go on until noon. When you stop you are as empty, and at the same time, never empty but filling . . .[22]

3. **Rewarding oneself after working hard:** Since one cannot work without a break and since even the legends need an incentive to push themselves through three to four hours of hard work, many of them not only take a break at around lunchtime, they ensure that the break contains something that they can look forward to. For example, as Currey writes in his book, Gustav Mahler, one of the leading composers of the twentieth century, '. . . worked until midday, then . . . walked down to the lake for a swim. Once he was in the water, he would whistle for his wife to join him on the beach. Mahler liked to lie in the sun until he was dry, then jump into the water again, often repeating this four or five times, which left him feeling invigorated and ready for lunch at home. The meal was,

to Mahler's preference, light, simple, thoroughly cooked and minimally seasoned.'

4. **Seeking high-quality input and criticism:** For many great minds, getting regular feedback from high-quality critics, who were often friends or relatives, was often a part of the daily routine. This feedback improved the quality of their work, sharpened their focus and their thinking. For example, as Currey writes in his book, Jane Austen would read out her work-in-progress on a daily basis to her mother and her sister. Gustave Flaubert would begin the day with a long, intimate chat with his mother. French author Simone de Beauvoir's daily routine hinged around her fifty-year intellectual partnership with the philosopher Jean-Paul Sartre. Each would spend the morning working alone. They would then meet for lunch and work together in the afternoon. Then, over dinner, they would critique each other's work.

5. **A well-defined daily routine:** 'Routine, in an intelligent man, is the sign of ambition,' wrote the English poet W.H. Auden in 1958. The vast majority of great minds have a clearly laid out routine which they followed day-after-day for the majority of their creative lives. Even artists, who one would imagine led bohemian, unstructured lives, were creatures of habit and routine. As Currey writes in his book, the Japanese author Haruki Murakami, for instance, '. . . wakes at 4:00 A.M. and works for five to six hours straight. In the afternoons he runs or swims (or does both), runs errands, reads, and listens to music; bedtime is 9:00. "I keep to this routine every day without variation," he told the *Paris Review* in 2004. "The repetition itself becomes the important thing; it's a form of mesmerism. I mesmerize myself to reach a deeper state of mind."'

Essentially, what the legends are doing is by forcing the majority of the quotidian decisions taken in a typical day (when to rise, when to eat, what to eat, etc.) into a rigid template, they are freeing up mental processing power for higher-value tasks.

Simplification Type 2: Simplify through principles/rules

As mentioned earlier in the chapter, creating simple powerful rules or principles is not easy. However, our professional experiences, along with our reading of the works of people wiser than us, suggest that there is a three-step path via which you too can create simple rules that will help you. The three steps are: (1) specialization—which we discussed in the preceding chapter; (2) originality—which we discuss in brief in this chapter and then in detail in Chapter 6; and (3) deep thought—which comes from steps (1) and (2) combined with your ability to simplify and declutter your daily life and your mind.

The path to simple rules is therefore: originality + specialization + deep thought.

Tip 1: Be different or have the courage to deviate from the norm

Born in 1907 in Warsaw, Polish psychologist Solomon Asch migrated to the USA in 1920. In the early 1950s, Asch conducted a series of groundbreaking experiments[23] which redefined our understanding of how profoundly peer pressure influences us.

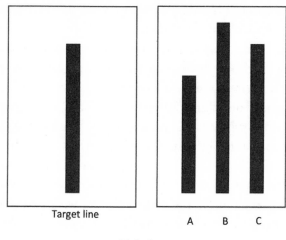

Exhibit 2

Imagine the following scene: you and seven other people are seated at a table in a small room. Everyone seated around the table is given two cards (as shown in Exhibit 2). The experimenter asks all of you, one at a time, to choose which of the three lines on the right card matches the length of the line on the left card. The task is repeated several times with different cards, and you are always the final person the room called up to answer.

If you were involved in this experiment how do you think you would behave? Would you go along with the majority opinion, or would you 'stick to your guns' and trust your own eyes (that the correct answer is clearly 'C')?

Just to make things a little difficult for you, on some occasions, the other 'participants' unanimously choose the wrong line. It is clear to you that they are wrong, but they have all given the same answer. Do you feel tempted to go along with the consensus opinion or are you independent enough to have a view which is anti-consensus?

What Asch found is that when other participants unanimously choose the wrong line, you too often give in and go with the mass opinion. To be precise, Asch found that 'on average, about one third (32 per cent) of the participants who were placed in this situation went along and conformed with the clearly incorrect majority on the critical trials. Over the twelve critical trials, about 75 per cent of the participants conformed at least once, and 25 per cent of participants never conformed.' On the other hand, 'in the control group, with no pressure to conform to confederates, less than 1 per cent of the participants gave the wrong answer.'

The Asch experiment shows us the perils of being plugged into consensus thinking (via mass media, colleagues and our friends and family). In order to view issues originally, in order to see things from first principles (i.e. reimagine a problem by breaking it down to smaller and simpler parts to solve each part and then solve the overall problem), we first have to pull ourselves away from mainstream thinking. It is hard to question conventional wisdom if you are immersed all the time in the same information stream that everyone is drinking from. In fact, as Asch's experiment shows, it is all too easy to start believing in nonsense just because everyone else believes in it.

The rise of smartphones has amplified this problem further. Former Google strategist James Williams has explained eloquently in his book *Stand Out of Our Light: Freedom and Resistance in the Attention Economy*[24] how social media and smartphones are eroding our ability to think for ourselves. He explains that our smartphones work at three levels to damage our mental health. Firstly, they distract us and thus produce 'attention scarcity'. Secondly, they make us impulsive with regards to our intentions, i.e. they make self-regulation and self-control harder. Thirdly, they not only soak up our attention but also persuade us in subtle but powerful ways (for example, to reflexively respond to messages, notifications and posts). Tormented by his years in Google, Williams makes a heartfelt plea in the book to all of us to redirect our thoughts and actions away from social media, away from smartphones. He pushes us towards 'rejecting attentional serfdom'.

Tips 2 and 3: Adopt deliberate practice and deep thought

If pulling away from what the masses are saying and thinking is the first step towards simplicity and clarity of thought, the second step is developing one area of specialized, deep expertise. Such expertise is your best chance of overcoming the 'knowledge illusion' that tends to afflict all of us (and which makes us believe that we know far more about complex things, such as global warming, the economy, GM foods, the business models of popular companies, than we really do). Specialized, deep expertise—as popularized by Malcolm Gladwell in *Outliers*—also allows us to deal with the fact that our mental processing power is limited.

We have highlighted in the previous chapter that developing your special area of expertise with deliberate practice and then diving into this area with detailed thinking forms the next step to achieving simplicity.

Once you get into the groove of deliberate practice, you need to become a more reflective, detail-oriented thinker, i.e. someone who pushes himself to think deep. At the vanguard of the movement towards specialization and focus are Cal Newport, with his hugely influential book *Deep Work: Rules for Focused Success in a Distracted World*[25], and Daniel Goleman, the man who popularized the term 'emotional intelligence'[26].

Newport's book is a must-read for anyone who wants to professionally excel as a knowledge worker. He writes:

> Deep work is the ability to focus without distraction on a cognitively demanding task. It's a skill that allows you to quickly master complicated information and produce better results in less time. Deep work will make you better at what you do and provide a sense of true fulfilment that comes from craftsmanship . . . And yet, most people have lost the ability to go deep—spending their days in a frantic blur of email and social media . . .

Goleman's book, *Focus*,[27] was published two years prior to Cal Newport's book. While both authors emphasize the positives of concentration, meditation and cutting out the distraction caused by emails and phones, Goleman makes a further point which is relevant for us. He says that as we get distracted by the inane chatter around us, we become less self-aware and our 'inner rudder' starts conking off. That in turn compromises our self-control and our ability to self-regulate our minds. As our emotional intelligence starts getting compromised, our relationships with colleagues, friends and relatives suffer. Therefore bringing 'focus' back on our lives is not just essential for our mental well-being and for professional success, it is a prerequisite for a fulfilling family/social life.

To think originally, to be different, we need to first take a step back and believe in our own decisions. And then, we need to block out as much of the noise as possible. Once we do this, there are various methods to develop original thinking. For instance, organizational psychologist Adam Grant in a TED talk highlighted the following surprising habits of original thinkers[28]:

a. Procrastinate: Between people who rush to finish things first and those who wait until the last minute, lies a sweet spot. Spending long periods of time to develop an idea or solve a problem might not be a bad thing. Obviously, this doesn't waste your time. Grant quotes a study where first movers had a failure rate of 47 per cent, compared to only 8 per cent for improvers.

b. Doubt the default: Grant speaks of people who take initiatives to doubt the default and look for better options, thereby opening up oneself to looking at the same thing with a new set of eyes and perspective.

c. Fear of not trying: Everyone feels fear, but what sets original thinkers apart is not the fear of failure but the fear of failure to try. Trying and failing then opens a new area of learning and improving. But not trying at all prevents one from even learning.

Though we delve into this subject in more detail in Chapter 6, we will cite an example here to illustrate. Say, you are fearful of water. The original thought would be to learn swimming and thus completely challenge the default setting that is coded into your mind. Not trying is worse than trying and failing. Go to a swimming pool, pay a trainer (even pay the lifeguard if you want) and force yourself to wade in the water. Then comes deliberate practice. So keep at it. Once you learn to float, slowly learn to swim, then learn the various styles. Do this at least three to five times a week—a non-negotiable target. Be strict with yourself and be disciplined. Finally, deep thought: focus on your strokes, on how your hand moves while pushing the water and gliding ahead, how your feet kick to power your movement. This might sound ridiculously easy to practised swimmers, but the fear of water is a real thing as both Anupam and Saurabh can testify.

Overcoming that fear bit by bit and learning to swim can be a liberating experience.

From the building blocks to the simple rules of thumb

And finally, the practical aspect of living a simple life— developing a framework of simple rules to live by. And these rules will change as you learn; we don't believe in permanent rigidity. So how do you develop these rules? Here are five steps.

In his seminal 1967 book *The Effective Executive*[29], management guru Peter F. Drucker laid out a five-step generic process for creating such rules. Drucker says: 'All events but the truly unique require a generic solution. They require a rule, a policy, a principle. Once the right principle has been developed all manifestations of the same generic situation can be handled pragmatically; that is, by adaptation of the rule to the concrete circumstances of the case.'

Therefore, the five key elements of the decision process are as follows:

Step 1: 'The clear realization that the problem was generic and could only be solved through a decision which established a rule, a principle . . .'

Step 2: 'The definition of the specifications which the answer to the problem had to satisfy . . .'

Step 3: 'Thinking through what is "right," that is, the solution which will fully satisfy the specifications before attention is given to the compromises, adaptations and concessions needed to make the decision acceptable . . .'

Step 4: Taking action on the basis of the rule.

Step 5: 'The "feedback" which tests the validity and effectiveness of the decision against the actual course of events . . .'

All of the above lead to simple rules of thumb which are like a Lakshman Rekha, i.e. a line in the sand which you do not cross. These play a simple but powerful role, forcing us to stay within our narrow circle of competence (and rely upon the expertise of others for matters outside that).

Simplicity case study: Marcellus Investment Managers' Consistent Compounders portfolio

How do we use these steps to make rules of thumb? Saurabh works at Marcellus Investment Managers, where his colleagues' only area of expertise is analysing Indian companies and then buying shares in outstanding companies with clean accounts and robust franchises. Given this very specific ambit of expertise, the team at Marcellus has implemented its own Drucker-like set of rules, wherein:

Step 1 is straightforward enough. Marcellus has to set up a framework of rules which determine which stocks the firm will invest in. Marcellus's rule of thumb is to look for companies which in the preceding ten years have grown their business at a certain rate (say, their revenue growth has been at least 10 per cent per annum each year) while delivering a certain minimum rate of profitability (say, return on capital employed of 15 per cent).

Step 2 for the team at Marcellus is to understand their client's needs and ascertain whether buying the sort of stocks thrown up by Step 1 is appropriate for that client. If, for example, the client says that he expects to see returns in the vicinity of 30 per cent per annum, then Marcellus might be better off not applying Step 1 on the client; the said client might be better off investing in a private equity or venture capital fund, neither of which falls within Marcellus's narrow area of expertise.

Step 3 is to implement the rule (from Step 1) for the client with necessary adaptations. So, for example, if the client does not want to invest in cigarette companies, Marcellus has to take ITC out of the portfolio even though it satisfies the rule from Step 1.

Step 4 is the ongoing management of the client's portfolio taking into account his specific financial circumstances. So if, for example, the client's primary residence has been damaged by a cyclone, Marcellus has to help the client encash part of his portfolio to pay for the reconstruction of her residence.

And, finally, **Step 5** is taking feedback from the client as to whether he is satisfied with what Marcellus is doing for him. If, for example, several clients say that they would like to talk to the team at Marcellus every month, then it would make sense to hold a monthly webinar wherein all clients can log in and pose their questions to Marcellus's investment professionals.

Focused repetition of these five steps should help Saurabh and the team at Marcellus improve and hopefully cause their brains to develop like those of the London cabbies we met in the previous chapter.

The intent of this rule-bound investment process is to reduce subjectivity and make the whole process of investing in Indian stocks as rule-based as possible. This rule-based approach to investing is laid out in more detail in two bestselling books—

The Unusual Billionaires and *Coffee Can Investing: The Low-Risk Road to Stupendous Wealth*[30].

* * *

Key takeaways from this chapter

- Both in the context of business and in the world of investing, simple strategies are easy to understand, easy to implement, easy to sell to others and easy to course-correct from. But as easy as simplicity sounds, it is anything but. Most simple systems are in fact the results of complex processes.

- How can we achieve simplicity? First, simplify through habit/process/method. Habits work in cycles of routines and rewards. Studies of the lives of great minds tell us that there are five specific habits that simplify life: reading; intense focused work in solitude; rewarding oneself after working hard; seeking high-quality input and criticism; and a well-defined daily routine.

- Second, simplify through principles/rules by a) specializing, b) being original, and c) combining originality and specialization into deep-focused thought. Develop these rules by being different and having the courage to deviate from the norm. Put in deliberate practice to improve your performance.

Professor Sanjay Bakshi's Framework around Simplicity

Professor Sanjay Bakshi is an adjunct professor at Management Development Institute (MDI), Gurugram, where he teaches two popular papers on behavioural finance and business valuation, and forensic accounting and corporate governance. He is also the managing partner at ValueQuest Capital, a Securities and Exchange Board of India (SEBI)-registered investment advisory firm.

Sanjay is regarded as one of the most popular Indian professors in the fields of finance and investing. He has a large following on social media, fuelled in part by his hugely popular *Fundoo Professor* blog. He is a BCom (Honours) from the University of Delhi, a chartered accountant and an MSc in Economics from the London School of Economics.

We met Sanjay at the Lodhi hotel in New Delhi, where he hosted us for a sumptuous breakfast. Then over several cups of coffee and plates of cookies, we discussed how many of the behavioural finance ideas today go back to Indian religious and philosophical texts such as the Gita and the Upanishads. Sanjay's voracious reading habits are well-known, and he shared many reference materials at our meeting.

As a professor of behavioural finance, Sanjay believes that in the past few years, a cottage industry on biases has mushroomed partly on the back of rising awareness around this topic and partly due to the popularity of Nobel laureate Daniel Kahneman's mega bestseller, *Thinking, Fast and Slow*[31]. However, if you have read old Indian scriptures, Sanjay believes that the entire discourse around behavioural finance would look like old wine in a new bottle. For example, the idea of risk or loss aversion, he says, has been around for more than a thousand years from the concept of *upekkha* (equanimity) in the Dhammapada, a collection of Buddhist scriptures. Similarly, the endowment effect is another way of describing detachment which goes back to the most famous dialogue in the Mahabharata—between Lord Krishna and Arjuna—which also emphasizes the importance of process over outcome.

Sanjay is a big believer in the idea of intense focus and cutting off all distractions to spend quality time on a single simple idea. He shows his iPhone, which has a blank home screen and no notifications. Throughout our two-hour conversation, his iPhone doesn't ring, beep or light up even once. Emphasizing the importance of focus, he quotes from Swami Vivekananda (finding an idea and making it your life) and Charlie Munger (extreme specialization is the way to succeed), and takes us through the eight stages of yoga: yama, niyama, asana, pranayama, pratyahara, dharana, dhyana, samadhi. 'For our purposes, three of those eight—pranayama (breath control), pratyahara (withdrawing from our senses), dharana (concentration and focus) are the important ones,' he tells us.

Sanjay is a fan of Swami Sarvapriyananda, minister and spiritual leader of the Vedanta Society of New York, and during our breakfast he showed us many of his videos. In a video[32] titled 'The Mind of a Yogi', Swami Sarvapriyananda explains the difference between the mind of a worldly man (turbulent, muddy, messy) and the mind of a yogi (simple, clear, still). 'It is so powerful in our own context. We get so distracted with things that are irrelevant. We create so much of clutter and noise and distractions. Like our eager anticipation every year for the Union budget. But how does the budget matter? In the whole scheme of things over the really long term, it is a non-event,' he told us.

Sanjay advises that in any profession, for achieving excellence, you have to get away from noise and clutter and move into a world of clarity and focus. 'You have to be careful about what gets inside your head. And to avoid things that shouldn't get inside your head, you have to shut your mind, physically and mentally,' he tells us and shows us a video[33] of the Tibetan Buddhist teacher Mingyur Rinpoche on how to train your monkey mind.

Sanjay illustrates this by taking an example of analysing a cash-flow statement to emphasize the power of focus. 'When you look at the cash-flow statement, just singularly focus on that and not on, say, management quality, growth potential, leverage, etc. For example, focus on just one thing, or one question, the answer to which is in the cash-flow statement read along with the other two statements—the balance sheet and the earnings statement. The question could be: Are earnings converting into operating cash flow? Does this business need external financing to grow or to even survive? Is the intensity of competition increasing or decreasing?' he advises.

Sanjay is a big fan of Warren Buffett and Charlie Munger and quotes extensively from the Berkshire Hathaway giants. To illustrate the importance of focusing on just a few priorities in life, Sanjay quotes the following from a 2015 blog post:

Buffett wanted to help his employee get ahead in his working life, so he suggested that the employee list the twenty-five most important things he wanted to accomplish in the next few years. He then had the employee circle the top five and told him to prioritize this smaller list. All seemed well until the wise billionaire asked one more question: 'What are you going to do with the other twenty things?' The employee answered: 'Well the top five are my primary focus but the other twenty come in at a close second. They are still important so I'll work on those intermittently as I see fit as I'm getting through my top five. They are not as urgent but I still plan to give them dedicated effort.' Buffett surprised him with his response: 'No. You've got it wrong . . . Everything you didn't circle just became your "avoid at all cost list."'[34]

We asked Sanjay, 'What does a young student of Prof. Bakshi who wants to succeed in life learn from our conversation?' 'Financial independence and the thrill of frugality,' came the answer.

'Focus intensely on becoming financially independent,' he tells his students. In order to achieve this, he advises them to underspend their income by not buying branded clothes, by not getting a mortgage and by not even carrying a credit card. He tells them to reorganize their P&L. Whatever salary they earn is revenues of an 'operating business'. Then there are expenses. He tells them to keep these to a bare minimum in the initial years of their careers. He tells them that they are entitled to spend whatever is left after a large part of the disposable income is invested into other great operating businesses at reasonable valuations. This is not the way people think of their P&L. They invest whatever is left over after taking care of all expenses. Sanjay asks his students to flip the P&L. They are only entitled to *spend* whatever is left after investing much of the disposable income. This should be the method for many, many years and that is how one gets to be financially independent.

He says, 'You don't know how much thrill I get when my students tell me that his or her saving rate is 50 per cent, that he or she didn't buy a house, that he or she is buying second-hand clothes or unbranded clothes, and that all the money that is not spent to such frivolous temptations is being invested in wonderful operating businesses that will keep compounding their capital.'

He cites Buffett's inspirational quote—'If you don't find a way to make money while you sleep, you work until you die'—to underscore the importance of saving aggressively, starting early in life and building a portfolio that works even when his students sleep. If they do this, then that pool of savings, combined with the power of compounding, becomes their primary source of income in their lives instead of the salary from their jobs. Of course, wealth is for enjoyment and one can loosen the purse strings a bit when one is financially independent, he says, but in the initial years, the focus must be on building a significant pool of capital that will lead to financial independence.

He tells us, with a lot of pride, how some of his students who took the lessons seriously have become dollar millionaires in just a few years of passing out of MDI and how they are now in a position to say that they don't work for money. Rather, money works for them. That cliché from *Rich Dad Poor Dad*[35] really works, he says.

Those ex-students, says Sanjay, are truly financially independent, and can look at the world as *it is*, and not as some employer will have them look at it, because they do not have to depend on a monthly salary any more. 'If you don't need a monthly salary, then you can be truly independent. True wisdom comes from financial freedom,' he tells us. And that is the most important lesson he learnt from his idol Charlie Munger.

CHAPTER 4

Connecting with Your Inner Self[1]

'We're the middle children of history, man. No purpose or place. We have no Great War. No Great Depression. Our great war is a spiritual war.'

—*Fight Club*[2]

What is spirituality?

Yoda, Gandalf, Master Shifu, Jiddu Krishnamurti, Kahlil Gibran, Eckhart Tolle[3]—there is a long list of gurus. But why did Luke need Yoda? Why did Po need Shifu? Because all of Luke's and Po's knowledge and experience was incapable of taking them through the challenge that lay ahead. All of us need to develop our inner strength and inner peace (which is what the various gurus ultimately represent) in order to balance our emotions and help us through difficulties. Rationality just isn't enough. We need more. Which is where spirituality comes in and helps us live simpler, happier and more fulfilled lives.

We can almost hear you groaning. We did too when we were in our teens and twenties. At that stage of our lives, as ambitious young students fed on high adrenaline, testosterone-charged movies such as *Wall Street* (1987), *Top Gun* (1986), *Agneepath* (1990) and *Hum* (1991), we subscribed to the late, great Khushwant Singh's view[4]:

> A modern fad which has gained widespread acceptance amongst the semi-educated who wish to appear secular is the practice of meditation. They proclaim with an air of smug superiority, 'Main mandir-vandir nahin jaata, meditate karta hoon (I don't go to temples or other such places, I meditate).' The exercise involves sitting lotus-pose (padma asana), regulating one's breathing and making your mind go blank to prevent it from 'jumping about like monkeys' from one (thought) branch to another. This intense concentration awakens the kundalini serpent coiled at the base of the spine. It travels upwards through chakras (circles) till it reaches its destination in the cranium. Then the kundalini is fully jaagrit (roused) and the person is assured to have reached his goal. What does meditation achieve? The usual answer is 'peace of mind'. If you probe further, 'and what does peace of mind achieve?', you will get no answer because there is none. Peace of mind is a sterile concept which achieves nothing. The exercise may be justified as therapy for those with disturbed minds or those suffering from hypertension, but there is no evidence to prove that it enhances creativity. On the contrary it can be established by statistical data that all the great works of art, literature, science and music were works of highly agitated minds, at times minds on the verge of collapse.

In fact, the Indian cricket team in the 1990s appeared to have taken Singh's advice to heart, with talented batsmen entertaining the crowds briefly before the entire batting lineup collapsed unceremoniously, especially when we were up against strong sides such as Australia, England and South Africa.

Then, as Indian cricket came of age in the twenty-first century under more level-headed leaders such as Sourav Ganguly, Rahul Dravid and Anil Kumble, we too matured and realized that if we wanted to play the long game, if we wanted to utilize our talent more efficiently we would have to get a grip on our minds.

What follows in this chapter is our attempt to a get a grip on our minds. That being said, we are not going to delve into religion and the philosophical and scientific debates on the nature of the human soul. Those are separate, vast discussions, and we doubt whether we have the competence to opine on subjects as profound as these.

Spirituality means different things to different people. But in a broad sense, we can say it involves acknowledging that there exists an inner self—you could perhaps call it a soul—separate from the material or the physical one. Spirituality then is not a specific practice, but rather a way of looking at things that can form the basis of a way of life.

Again, this is a highly personal outlook, but we are believers in spirituality and its connection with simplicity. So, in this chapter we simply discuss our experiences, the practices we have built on the back of our version of spirituality, and what works for us and hopefully helps you too.

Balancing the emotional and the rational

In business and in investing, we have to make decisions and choices from a sea of possibilities. To make these decisions, we usually have information and data on hand to analyse and consider. And then we have to make a probabilistic call about the future which is as much emotional as it is rational.

It is impossible to make a decision which is just based on numbers, because for tomorrow's world we have no numbers, no 'future facts'. Our decisions, therefore, have to balance the emotional and the rational.

For example, when you see the sunset from a beach shack in Goa, a part of you absorbs the facts about the natural phenomenon (time, temperature, etc.). But another part of you appreciates the beauty of the spectacle and loves the changing mood of the day as night falls on the beach.

Similarly, in our professional lives too, whether we like it or not, we react to most events (the performance of Saurabh's portfolio, his annual appraisal, his bonus, the financial statements of a company in which he has invested in, etc.) at both a factual/rational level and at an emotional level. Our academic and professional training, for the most part, is geared to help us deal only with our rational responses to such stimuli.

Just as we can experience sunsets and deal with corporate results, we can read people both rationally and emotionally. The American physicist Leonard Mlodinow, in his superb book *Subliminal: The New Unconscious and What it Teaches Us*[5], points out that humans—from as early as the age of four—have a unique ability to understand what other people are like and how they are likely to behave. Our emotional response to people often dominates our rational response. Spirituality helps us balance both.

More specifically, here are three areas where, in our experience, adopting a more spiritual approach works:

1. Dealing with clutter

Our manic obsession with buying things we don't need has cluttered our physical spaces with useless items. And mentally, we are no better off, with the clutter of distractions from cat videos to checking our social media when we know we have a fast-approaching deadline. And finally, there is the clutter of fruitless relationships and the time we spend with people that draw down our energy reserves. The more you pack into your day, the greater the risk that you suffer from cognitive overload; your intellectual abilities are then compromised regardless of how hard you work.

The spiritual approach to this is to place greater value on the well-being of our inner self, prioritizing those possessions and relationships that truly matter to you. It is a philosophy that has been espoused by many over the ages. Chuck Palahniuk famously wrote in his book *Fight Club*[6]: 'The things you own ending up owning you.' Stoicism, a school of ancient Greek philosophy, speaks of frugality. And there is even scientific evidence to wake us up to meaningful relationships.

'The Harvard Study of Adult Development' is one of the world's most comprehensive studies of adult life, spanning nearly eighty years. The study's findings are startling. Robert Waldinger, director of the study, summarizes these as follows:

> The surprising finding is that our relationships and how happy we are in our relationships has a powerful influence on our health. Taking care of your body is important, but tending to your relationships is a form of self-care too. That, I think, is the revelation. Close relationships, more than money or fame, are what keep people happy throughout their lives, the study revealed. Those ties protect people from life's discontents, help to delay mental and physical decline, and are better predictors of long and happy lives than social class, IQ, or even genes.[7]

2. Dealing with emotions

'Men are not afraid of things, but of how they view them,' the Greek philosopher Epictetus said centuries ago. We have to deal with our fears and our anxieties in a constructive, practical, clear-headed manner. For example, if as an equity analyst, Anupam is anxious about his firm's exposure to the pharma sector, he needs to get to the bottom of his anxiety. Is it because he doesn't understand the science behind these companies? Or is the anxiety driven by his inability to understand the regulatory regime around pharma products? Or is it simply because he hasn't invested time and effort in understanding the industry properly?

Ray Dalio, founder of Bridgewater Associates—one of the largest hedge funds in the world—says in his book *Principles*[8] that 'the most valuable habit I've acquired is using pain to trigger quality reflections. If you can acquire this habit, you will learn what causes you pain and what you can do about it, and it will have an enormous effect on your effectiveness.'

And the Roman emperor Marcus Aurelius wrote in *Meditations*[9]: 'If you are pained by external things, it is not they that disturb you, but your own judgement of them. And it is in your power to wipe out that judgement now.'

3. Achieving deep focus

Achieving peak performance is pure joy; it also involves deep, almost extreme focus and overcoming huge challenges (and hence pain). From intense physical training to long hours of focused work, almost any goal that is worth achieving will require inhuman effort.

In the end, hitting this peak is immensely rewarding. In our experience as equity analysts, the work we put into researching a company requires deep focus—and it is not always rewarding. While we spend hours toiling away analysing annual reports and travelling to gather primary data, the market might just not care for our effort. As a result, for many years, the stock price of that company might not go anywhere. This is the pain and self-doubt that we have to endure. But when one of our investments finally proves us right, our reward is more than just the profits we make—it is also the emotional pay-off that comes from having weathered the pain and reached our goal.

Principles and practices

Connecting with your spiritual side, as it were, is easier said than done. The biggest question we need to ask ourselves is 'What is my purpose?' It might make us sound like hipster gurus, but we believe that connecting with your purpose is what connects productivity with spirituality. It is what eventually led Luke to confronting his father and becoming a Jedi knight; it is what eventually led Po to becoming a Kung Fu Panda. One of the most famous scenes in the Indian epic tale Mahabharata is where Krishna awakens Arjuna to his purpose.

Arjuna's famous dilemma—which is the fulcrum of the Gita—arises in Kurukshetra as the Pandava and Kaurava armies line up against each other armed and ready for combat. Upon seeing his kinsmen on the other side of the battlefield, Arjuna lays down his famous bow—the Gandiva—and refuses to engage in battle. Krishna, his charioteer, first tries to reason with Arjuna. When that does not work, Krishna resorts to his authority as God and impresses upon Arjuna that his dharma is to be a warrior, whether he likes it or not. He cannot escape his dharma and he must fulfil it. Arjuna has to be a warrior for what is right and just. While your and our goals in life might be more prosaic, all of us have to understand and fulfil our dharma.

Mythology and movies apart, here are the principles and practices that work for us.

Principle 1: Frugality

Frugality is a concept common to a range of spiritual philosophies, from the Buddha to Socrates, from Rousseau to Thoreau. Not buying or owning things that add very little to your life not only saves you money but also frees up mind space for more useful activities. We don't believe in buying the latest smartphones every year and we don't believe in stocking up on clothes and shoes in sales.

Saurabh has, at any point in time, only one suit, six shirts (one for each working day in the week) and only one pair of plain black shoes. As a result, not only is his closet very empty, his decision of what to wear to work requires no application of mind. Furthermore, he wears these items until they wear out, regardless of what the latest trend in men's fashion might be.

The late Steve Jobs had almost no material possessions at home until he got married. Saurabh aspires to Jobs's ability to understand good design but can confidently say that even after marriage he has very little by way of material possessions, other than a lot of books and a big collection of songs in his decrepit phone, which has a cracked screen and a cheap plastic cover.

Principle 2: Positivity

We are hardcore believers in positivity. When dealing with our emotions, especially our fears and anxieties, we try to follow a constructive, level-headed approach. Research tells us that the brain (a) is incredibly sensitive to positive suggestions, and (b) suffers from 'confirmation bias' with regard to our preconceived notions about ourselves. This wiring of the human brain is a potent driver of self-improvement.

For example, in one study, Harvard professor Ellen Langer divided a group of hotel housekeeping staff into two groups. Phil Dobson described the study in *The Brain Book: How to Think and Work Smarter* thus: 'One group was told their levels of daily activity met the definition of an "active lifestyle"; the second group was told nothing. One month later, the first group had experienced a significant decrease in waist-to-hip ratio, and a 10 per cent drop in blood pressure.'[10] That is the power of positive suggestion in changing not just behaviour but actual health outcomes of people.

This approach has worked for us. Before he became an investment manager, Saurabh, for instance, set up a successful stockbroking business in Mumbai on the principles of honesty and transparency. This was not easy. Saurabh and his colleagues worked long hours and wrote detailed notes regarding the long-term prospects of clean, well-managed Indian companies. However, some of their recommendations went wrong, leading to anxiety and a fear of client anger.

As a response, Saurabh's team decided to declare upfront to their clients that their stock recommendations were made on the strength of the company's franchise and corporate governance. And that some of these recommendations might not make money in the near term. Clients understood that that is the way even the best portfolios perform. Eventually, the stockbroking business rose up the rankings and became a market-leading franchise, proving the efficacy of the approach.

Beyond these broad principles, though, there are two specific practices that form the foundation of the spiritual side of the Simplicity Paradigm.

Practice 1: Meditation

Meditation is a practice where an individual trains her attention to achieve a clear, calm and stable state of mind. The Dalai Lama believes that meditation and prayer have similar benefits. However, our reading on the subject suggests that there are two differences between meditation and prayer. Firstly, meditation is, in general, a more advanced form of concentrating and focusing the mind than prayer. Secondly, while prayer has as its focus either a god or a deity, meditation—especially in its more advanced forms—can be about completely blanking out the mind.

Jason Voss, a successful investor, says in his book *The Intuitive Investor: A Radical Guide for Manifesting Wealth*[11]: 'Meditation is a natural state of mind that occurs when the egoic mind is diminished or turned off.' According to Voss, 'egoic mind means the state of mind where a sense of "I", or a sense of separateness from the interconnectedness of the universe, exists.' In other words, by subduing your ego and your sense of self, meditation allows more creative thoughts to bubble up to the forefront of your mind.

The recorded origins of meditation are usually traced to the Chinese and Indian civilizations around the fifth century BCE, although it also appears highly likely that people elsewhere in the ancient world had also clocked on to the benefits of this simple but powerful practice. As John Selby says in *Seven Masters, One Path*[12]:

> Several thousands of years ago, among the . . . Taoist culture of ancient China, the judging, analytical thinking mind was already correctly identified as the perpetrator not only of our particularly human blessings in life, but also of our particularly human curses. They understood clearly that . . .

we humans have gained vast powers to think logically, reflect upon past experiences, and manipulate the world to our advantage. However, because thinking is a past-future function of the mind, we have tended to lose touch with the vital experience of participating spontaneously in the present moment.

Meditation aims to resolve this 'lost in thought' dilemma as we temporarily distance ourselves from the constant barrage of thoughts from our inner virtual reality, and shift into a deeper consciousness. By learning to calmly watch thoughts flowing through our minds without being attached to those thoughts, we liberate ourselves from chronic identification with our ego's limited notion of what life is all about . . . In the Taoist tradition, when we quiet our thoughts in meditation, we let go of trying to manipulate the world based on our inner fantasies of how things should be.

What are the work-related benefits of meditation? Dalio and Voss have written extensively about how meditation has helped them become better investors. When we asked Voss how meditation had helped him, he pointed us towards Selby's excellent book, which is referenced above. What follows in this section is a summary of what we have learnt from these three books[13] and from our chats with Voss. The benefits of meditation—going from the most basic to the most advanced—appear to be:

- **Stress relief and recovery from difficult experiences:** This is the most commonly cited benefit of meditation. Normally, mental and physical stress causes increased levels of cortisol (also called the primary stress hormone). Cortisol in turn promotes depression and anxiety and disrupts sleep. Scientific studies show that meditation reduces stress and cortisone. Effectively, meditation has the opposite effect—on the body and the mind—as an adrenaline rush (which increases your heart rate, elevates your blood pressure and boosts energy levels). As a result, meditation plays a dual role of not only providing relief from a stressful experience but also helping in the rejuvenation and recovery process (via lower cortisol, less anxiety and better sleep).

- **Clarity of thought and greater focus:** Uncluttering our mind so that we can think more clearly, even if we are facing time pressure and/or financial pressure, is clearly a valuable skill to have. Psychologists are increasingly of the view that one of the best ways to regulate your body and your emotions is through meditation. In fact, research shows that meditation not only improves your health, it also strengthens your mental muscle, especially your ability to focus and concentrate. A brain imaging study by Massachusetts General Hospital found physical changes in the brain after an eight-week meditation course[14]. Researchers identified increased activity in parts of the brain associated with learning, memory, self-awareness, compassion and introspection as well as decreased activity in the amygdala.

- **Higher level thinking and creative ideas:** According to Voss, meditation allows you 'access to creativity, intuition and wealth manifestation. Exploration of this topic opens up an entirely new world, one rich with skills for making you richer.' To quote from Dalio's book *Principles*, 'I also came to understand that while some subconscious parts of our brains are dangerously animalistic, other are smarter and quicker than our conscious minds. Our greatest moments of inspiration often "pop" up from our subconscious. We experience these creative breakthroughs when we are relaxed and not trying to access the part of the brain in which they reside, which is generally the neocortex. When you say, "I just thought of something", you noticed your subconscious mind telling your conscious mind something.'

- **Greater ability to work co-operatively:** Regardless of how talented we might be, successful professional endeavour almost always involves working in collaboration with other people. Unfortunately, our education system and the general ethos of capitalism focus on our identity as individuals. That in turn inhibits the extent to which we are voluntarily willing to collaborate with others. Life, especially in the financial services profession, seems to hinge on chasing greater pay and perks. Meditation helps you de-emphasize your own role and what rewards you will get from your efforts. That in turn makes it easier for you to work with others for their benefit. Ironically, that is a far more efficient way to move forward in the world rather than barging forward Gordon 'Greed is Good' Gekko-style[15].

So how does one meditate in the midst of a packed schedule? The beginner's format for meditation simply focuses on using a basic technique to either distract or relax your conscious mind (where your ego resides). Here is Saurabh's basic technique to meditate on flights and car journeys: close your eyes and count backwards from 100 to zero while trying to visualize each number as you call the number out in your mind. The reverse counting is a way of distracting the ego and thus letting the mind enter a more relaxed mode. Practising this technique on a daily basis for even ten minutes allows you to gain control of your mind to such an extent that soon you will be able to meditate at a time and place of your choosing.

The more advanced formats involve concentrating in one or more long sessions (of an hour or more) each day. This often involves using chanting as the technique being used to distract the egoic mind. The effort then is to focus the mind on the mantra that you are chanting and hold that focus for very long periods of time. It is hard to do but Dalio and Voss swear by these advanced meditation techniques and the way these techniques have helped them become better investors and better human beings.

When it comes to meditation, there are a wide variety of techniques and approaches, and what we have given here is just one of those. Feel free to search and try out different methods; our only advice would be to keep it simple.

Practice 2: Relentless focus

Focus helps us connect our practice with our purpose and our execution with our vision. We declutter with zeal. Especially on weekdays, we strip away everything that diverts our attention from our work. For example, we avoid 'networking events' where people whose own objectives of attending the event are fuzzy meet others with equally fuzzy objectives in a noisy setting. Instead, we use this time to meet a list of people directly related to our investment research—for example, dealers, distributors, company promoters, etc. Similarly, we avoid industry conferences in five-star hotels with a rambling cast of speakers and time-consuming schedules.

We also ruthlessly control what we consume. For example, we use social media with heavy discretion. Saurabh is manic obsessive—he has no Twitter or Instagram accounts. He does not even have WhatsApp on his phone. He wants to make it difficult for people to contact him and for himself to contact other people.

Anupam, on the other hand, has specific limits on his Twitter usage, uses Facebook only occasionally and restricts himself to mere sentences on WhatsApp (which he uses only for coordinating and setting up meetings and not for long or life-changing conversations). Neither of us is obsessed with social media and both of us are aware of its danger as a weapon of mass distraction. We leave it to users to find their balance.

Ultimately, these two practices tie into the idea of deliberate, focused, deep work—a concept central to the Simplicity Paradigm. As computer scientist Cal Newport says in his book *Deep Work: Rules for Focused Success in a Distracted World*, 'The ability to perform deep work is increasingly rare at exactly the same time that the work is becoming increasingly valuable in our economy. As a consequence, the few who cultivate this skill, and then make it the core of their working life will thrive.'

In fact, a quarter of a century before Newport gave us the concept of deep work, American psychologist Mihaly Csikszentmihalyi's concept of 'flow'—and immersing yourself deeply both in work and in leisure—captured the essence of the same idea. Csikszentmihalyi, in his book *Flow: The Psychology of Optimal Experience*[16], says that 'flow' is a state you achieve when you lose yourself in a specific activity (whether for work or otherwise) and typically experience deep enjoyment, creativity and total enjoyment with life. This positive state can be controlled, not just left to chance. He writes:

> First, the experience usually occurs when we confront tasks which we have a chance of completing. Second, we must be able to concentrate on what we are doing. Third and fourth, the concentration is usually possible because the task undertaken has clear goals and provides immediate feedback. Fifth, one acts with deep but effortless involvement that removes from awareness the worries and frustrations of everyday life. Sixth, enjoyable experiences allow people to exercise a sense of control over their actions. Seventh, concern for the self disappears, yet paradoxically the sense of

self emerges stronger after the flow experience is over. Finally, the sense of the duration of time is altered; hours pass by in minutes, and minutes can stretch out to seem like hours.

At the core of this, Csikszentmihalyi says, is the idea of autotelic, or self-contained, activities. That is, 'one that is done not with the expectation of some future benefit, but simply because the doing itself is the reward.' He gives the example of investing in the stock market—doing it just to make money is not autotelic. However, 'playing it in order to prove one's skill in foretelling future trends is—even though the outcome in terms of dollars and cents is exactly the same.'

He writes: 'Teaching children in order to turn them into good citizens is not autotelic, whereas teaching them because one enjoys interacting with children is. What transpires in the two situations is ostensibly identical; what differs is that when the experience is autotelic, the person is paying attention to the activity for its own sake; when it is not, attention is focused on its consequences.'

In the end, this concept of 'flow' can be applied to all aspects of our lives—whether professional or personal, tasks or relationships. For example, for both Saurabh and Anupam, the main driver of writing this book is that it pushes us to absorb new concepts, to understand the implications of these concepts for our own lives and then to convey them to the readers in as lucid a manner as we can.

We find this process satisfies the vast majority of the conditions that Csikszentmihalyi has laid down for what constitutes 'optimal experience'. For us learning, understanding and writing are autotelic experiences. In a way, this builds up to the ultimate goal of our approach to spirituality: a meaningful life with a sense of purpose.

* * *

Key takeaways from this chapter

- Spirituality involves acknowledging an inner self separate from the material or the physical one. Spirituality is not a specific practice but rather a way of looking at things that can form the basis of a way of life. Spirituality helps us in balancing the emotional and rational parts of ourselves.

- Spirituality can help us in dealing with clutter (both mental and physical), in dealing with emotions and in achieving deep focus. We should prioritize those possessions and relationships that truly matter to us. Fear is natural, but we should deal with our fears and our anxieties in a constructive, practical, clear-headed manner.

- What are the specific practices which help us connect with our purpose? Meditation: distinct from praying, meditation is when an individual trains her attention to achieve a clear, calm and stable state of mind. Relentless focus: it helps us connect our practice with our purpose and our execution with our vision. So strip away everything that diverts attention from your work, and ruthlessly control what you consume in terms of time.

- What are the benefits of meditation? For us, they are stress relief and recovery from difficult experiences, clarity of thought, higher-level thinking and creative ideas, and greater ability to work co-operatively (as opposed to obsessing about our place in the world).

Jason Voss's Spiritual Journey from Wall Street to Sarasota

Jason Voss has a multifaceted background. He has a BA in Economics and an MBA (with an emphasis on finance and accounting) from the University of Colorado, and holds the chartered financial analyst (CFA) charter. Jason is the CEO of Active Investment Management (AIM) Consulting, LLC, which helps small to medium-sized active investment management firms create and deliver long-lasting alpha. Prior to this, Jason was the global content director at the CFA Institute, and the author of *The Intuitive Investor*. Over the course of his investment career as co-portfolio manager of the Davis Appreciation and Income Fund (DAIF), the fund bested the Nasdaq by 77 per cent, the S&P 500 by 49.1 per cent, and the DJIA by 35.9 per cent[17]. In 2005, Jason switched tracks and stepped out of active fund management on Wall Street.

On 23 May 2019, we had a long call on Skype from Saurabh's home with Jason, who is based in Sarasota, Florida, USA. Jason is a firm believer in the power of spirituality and in the practice of meditation. As he writes in his book *The Intuitive Investor*, 'Meditation is a natural state of mind that occurs when the egoic mind is diminished or turned off.' According to Voss, '. . . egoic mind means the state of mind where a sense of "I", or a sense of separateness from the interconnectedness of the universe exists.' But given that investment is a rational, rules-based exercise, how did a successful fund manager on Wall Street find his way into mediation and spirituality? Meditation was always a part of Jason's life, from the time he was a kid right up to his teenage years. But it was during a painful divorce in his late twenties—which coincided with Jason's promotion to a portfolio manager—that Jason returned to meditation as a formal practice. As both Saurabh and Anupam can testify, the world of investments is a high-stress one where, as Jason puts it, 'all of a sudden the burden of the world and other people's fortunes are on your shoulders.' Within a few months of making meditation a part of his daily routine, Jason started having creative realizations about how his own inner mechanisms were not serving him as an investor.

He gave us two specific examples. The first was the realization that he had grown up poor and really wanted to be successful in his life. However, that desire was driving him to prove himself and demonstrate how smart he was. In the process he ended up hurting people and negatively impacting his career. 'So when I made the realization that so much of my decision-making is born of insecurity and has nothing to do with the underlying performance of the security, or the prospects of the securities, or the composition of the portfolio, or how I value a business, I stopped doing those things,' he told us.

The second realization was that the most important relationship we all have is with ourselves. And only we get a vote in the nature of this relationship—we can be forgiving or unforgiving of our faults; we can be quite a terrifying adversary to ourselves. Once Jason realized how he was an adversary to himself and ended that practice, he learnt to wear the mantle of portfolio manager as it truly should be worn—that of a guardian, a fiduciary in the truest sense of the word. 'That realization of loving yourself freed me, because I no longer had to please other people. I could then focus on what I should really be focused on, which is taking care of and being the guardian of the reputation of my firm,' he told us.

We spoke about the debate between spiritualism and materialism, and religion versus science. Jason believes that religion and science are both the same in that they are both explorations of the truth. On spiritualism versus materialism, Jason believes that: (a) we are all interconnected; and (b) consciousness is primary to materialism. 'Once you realize consciousness is prime and you realize meditation is a technique to discover these insights, then all of a sudden, the conversation is no longer about how science and spirituality are related; you see them as the exact same endeavour—the pursuit of truth. Science has never really discovered consciousness in the way that a meditator can,' he told us. He doesn't see meditation and spirituality as separate from science and scientific method. Is it possible to be spiritual without being religious? 'Absolutely. I believe that institutions (such as economic institutions, scientific institutions, or the institution of family) exist because of a profound realization of universal values. Spirituality—that we are all interconnected—is the source of values and religion is the institution,' he told us.

If spirituality and meditation are such powerful tools, then why are we not seeing hordes of youth flocking to gurus and ashrams? Or even have more lunchtime meditation sessions across organizations? Jason believes that centuries of materialism and objectivity as mental models have meant that most people struggle to see beyond these mental models. But these mental models are also broken. In quantum mechanics, objects exist in varying and hazy states as against classic mechanics, which places objects at specific places and times. Indeed, scientists have proved that objectivity is an illusion.[18] Add to this the idea that capitalism is seen as the pre-eminent institution of competition—whereas capitalism is actually as much about co-operation as it is about competition. 'All of this is hardcoded in us like a program. I would say it is a software programme that is in need of an upgrade,' he told us.

We conclude with the thought that spirituality is the bridge connecting your practical state of knowledge to where you want go in the world. 'The advice I have given to the young, mostly men and a few women that I've mentored over the years, is that you must first know yourself exceptionally well in the investment business and discover what makes you unique,' he told us.

Jason thinks of personalities as lenses that have to be polished. Old mental models create a fog on the lenses that prevents the light from shining as beautifully as it could. Meditation practices are the polishing techniques that help you be the best. 'You need to find the tools and techniques that exalt your consciousness. I love that word 'exalt', because it is just that. Once you discover what makes you unique and your unique talents—and that's only found through spirituality—then all of a sudden magic happens,' Voss ends our discussion on a magical note.

Section 3

Desirable Behaviours
(The Three C's)

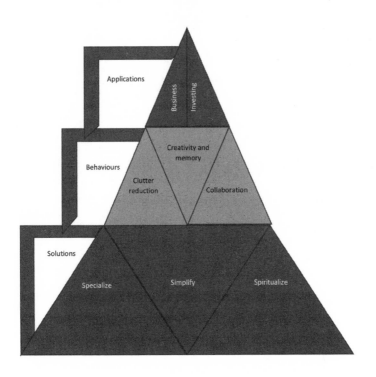

CHAPTER 5

Reduce, Reduce, Reduce: Getting Rid of Clutter

'Nothing contributes so much to tranquilize the mind as a steady purpose—a point on which the soul may fix its intellectual eye.'

—Mary Shelley[1]

'Facebook is the new cigarettes . . . You know, it's addictive. It's not good for you. There's people trying to get you to use it that even you don't understand what's going on. The government needs to step in. The government needs to really regulate what's happening.'

—Marc Benioff, CEO of Salesforce[2]

Introduction

Both of us are refugees from the large corporate world where our life was a daily blur of meetings, targets, budgets, travel, deadlines, networking, etc. We walked away from that world partly because we realized that no matter what our abilities were, if we couldn't control our working environment, we wouldn't be able to function effectively. As Phil Dobson says in *The Brain Book: How to Think and Work Smarter*, 'Even if you meditate every day, if you can't manage your tasks and your projects, your system will go back into stress due to cognitive overload.' So, we have made a conscious attempt to focus on what is important.

Beyond workplace pressures, there is another force operating in most of our lives which is exponentially increasing our stress and mental-clutter levels—our smartphone. As Cal Newport explains in his book *Digital Minimalism: On Living Better with Less Technology*[3], beyond the obvious distraction caused by checking your phone eighty-five times a day and spending three hours of screen time per day (statistics for the average phone user in the USA), smartphones are insidiously harming our minds and our lives in three ways:

- **Loneliness:** Citing research conducted by psychologist Matthew Lieberman, author of *Social: Why Our Brains Are Wired to Connect*[4], Newport highlights that thanks to evolutionary adaptation, our brains are wired to be social— to read other people's emotions, their minds, their feelings and then to connect with them and interact with them. What smartphones and social media appear to be doing is damaging our ability to cognitively connect with the world around us in two ways: (a) by reducing the time available for such interactions because of the amount of time we spend on our smartphones; and (b) reducing the need to have such interactions by persuading us that we can interact with our friends, our colleagues and our suppliers over the phone rather than talking to them in person. Newport says,

'The loss of social connection . . . turns out to trigger the same system as physical pain . . .' What is the result of this? Citing a study of young adults led by Brian Primack (of the University of Pittsburgh), which appeared in the *American Journal of Preventive Medicine*[5], Newport reports: '. . . the more someone used social media, the more likely they were to be lonely. Indeed, someone in the highest quartile of social media use was three times more likely to be lonelier than someone in the lowest quartile.'

- **Extremism:** Around the world, in large and seemingly mature democracies, the political discourse seems to be becoming increasingly polarized. Americans saw this in the run-up to Donald Trump's election; Britons saw this in the run-up to Brexit; and Indians see this whenever a General Election is around the corner. The way social media is designed, says Newport, contributes to this: '. . . online discussion seems to accelerate people's shift towards emotionally charged and draining extremes. The techno-philosopher Jaron Lanier convincingly argues that the primacy of anger and outrage online is, in some sense, an unavoidable feature of the medium: In an open marketplace for attention, darker emotions attract more eyeballs than positive and constructive thoughts. For heavy internet users, repeated interaction with this darkness can become a source of draining negativity – a steep price that many don't even realize they're paying . . .'

- **Anxiety:** All of us need peace and solitude to do high-quality work on difficult, complex subjects. The digital world robs us of this peace and solitude, not just in our offices, not just in our homes but also when we are at the playground with our kids, when we are on holiday and when we are relaxing with friends. Newport says, 'Eliminating solitude also introduces new negative repercussions that we're only now beginning to understand. A good way to investigate a behaviour's effect is to study a population that pushes the behaviour to an extreme . . . these extremes are readily apparent among young people born after 1995 . . . a 2015 study by Common Sense Media found that teenagers were consuming media . . . nine hours per day on average . . . If persistent solitude deprivation causes problems, we should see them show up here first . . .' So is there any evidence of widespread mental issues associated with those born post-1995? Newport cites research conducted by Jean Twenge, a professor of psychology at San Diego State University and renowned expert on generational differences in American youth: 'As Twenge notes in her September 2017 article for *The Atlantic*, she has been studying these trends for over twenty-five years. But starting around 2012, she noticed a shift in the measurements of teenager emotional states . . . Young people born between 1995 and 2012, a group Twenge calls "iGen", exhibited remarkable differences as compared to the Millennials that preceded them . . . "Rates of teen depression and suicide have skyrocketed," Twenge writes . . . "It's not an exaggeration to describe iGen as being on the brink of the worst mental-health crisis in decades . . . Much of this deterioration can be traced to their phones," Twenge concludes.'

Not all of this bad news though. There are some advantages to using social media as well, provided you control your usage. Says Jeff Hancock[6], a psychologist who runs the Social Media Lab at Stanford University, 'Using social media is essentially a trade-off . . . You get very small advantages for your well-being that come with very small costs.'

An article in *Scientific American* summarized the results from Hancock's research as: 'Hancock and his team found that more social media use was associated slightly with higher depression and anxiety (though not loneliness) and more strongly associated with relationship benefits (though not eudaemonic or hedonic well-being). (The largest effect, at 0.20, was the benefit of stronger relationships.) He and his colleagues also found that active rather than passive use was positively associated with well-being.[7]

While the debate on exactly how damaging social media is continues, it is difficult to argue with the point that any form of distraction when you are trying to do high-quality work reduces your effectiveness. We are fighting a battle with mental clutter and stress on two distinct but interrelated fronts—in our workplaces and in our digital world. And while we sometimes struggle with the definition of what is important in our personal lives, it has become easier to declutter our professional lives. As mentioned in the preceding chapter, we find that 'networking events' and rambling day-long conferences in swanky hotels are not a good use of our time. Hence, pulling out of work-related events where no work really gets done is a relatively straightforward way to reducing mental clutter.

As we gradually seek to reduce mental clutter, we find that it is becoming easier to focus longer and deeper on the sorts of things we like to do. For example, Saurabh likes thinking about which companies are better than others and why they are better than others. He then spends days on end reading up more on these companies, meeting knowledgeable people who know more about these companies than he does and then thinking further about what helps these companies make money. It is the sort of work that he enjoys doing, and an added bonus is that this sort of focused work makes him better at what he does.

Similarly, Anupam left the corporate world in 2013 to become a writer and podcaster. He has decluttered his daily schedule by dedicating large chunks of time to a few activities, instead of multitasking many activities in small time slots. For example, he listens to podcasts during his fitness routines and shuts off all emails and smartphone distractions when he is writing, reading or carrying out research work. During his podcast recordings, he has to perforce switch off his mobile phone. During his four-year stint as a consultant for Ambit Capital, Anupam helped write more than twenty high-quality research reports which were instrumental in Ambit Capital being voted as the most independent research brokerage in India by the Asiamoney Global Brokers Polls in 2017. Anupam and IVM's podcast, *Paisa Vaisa*, was voted the Best Business Podcast at the Asia Podcast Awards in 2019.

Why bother reducing clutter?

Most of us are now so habituated with being swamped by digital media that we can't even contemplate breaking out of these digital jails. Life in a digital jail entails relentlessly checking and responding to emails and WhatsApps all day long. The rest of the time goes into checking social media notifications. After that, if there is any downtime left in the evenings, it is spent on web surfing, ranting on social media sites and watching streaming media. What is the point of breaking free of this digital jail especially in a country like India where most cities have no parks, no beaches and no community areas where the public can relax and recuperate?

In *Deep Work*, Newport says that the free market—on a global scale—rewards people who master hard skills (eg. the ability to write high-quality prose in the English language) and then produce consistently at an elite level (eg. writing Harry Potter novels, which is what J.K. Rowling did to rise from poverty to become a dollar billionaire).

Newport points out that Rowling habitually locks herself up in a hotel in downtown Edinburgh when she is working on her novels. In a similar vein, he highlights that the young Bill Gates worked non-stop for two months to produce the first version of the programming language BASIC. During this period of frenetic programming to write the code that would ultimately form the foundation of Microsoft's dominant operating system, Gates would fall asleep in front of his computer while coding. He would then wake up an hour later and continue coding.

In contrast, the vast majority of the cooking, sports, politics and make-up videos on social media are easy to replicate. In fact, that is exactly what millions of teenagers around the world—including Saurabh's children—are doing. That is an interesting hobby for them to have but it is unlikely to be the path they take to build their name and fame.

Even if you believe that there are other drivers to Rowling's and Gates's success, it is hard to rebut Newport's key point: deep work—i.e. 'professional activities performed in a state of distraction-free concentration that push your cognitive capabilities to their limit'—creates value, improves your skills and helps create output which is hard to replicate.

If we look back at our journey over the past five years, reducing clutter in our lives and in our minds was a step-by-step process. It wasn't always easy for us to keep moving forward on this journey—the easy thing usually is to let the clutter rebuild—but we reckon the path would have been easier if someone had given us the sort of route map which we have provided in the rest of this chapter.

Six sequential steps to reducing mental clutter

Step 1—Start with your goals: Each of us has to figure out what we want from our lives. Over the years, we have watched with envy people wiser than us lay out their goals with great clarity. A friend, who also manages a fund, recently told Saurabh, 'In an ever more complicated world, I have sought to simplify my life and focus on fewer things—starting with my family, my investors and closest colleagues.'

Another helpful way to figure out what to focus on comes from Greg McKeown in his outstanding book *Essentialism: The Disciplined Pursuit of Less*[8]: 'If it isn't a clear yes, it's a clear no.' What McKeown is saying is that eliminating all the 'maybes' from our life allows us—perhaps forces us—to focus on the stuff that we know we really want to focus on.

A very different philosophy to use when seeking to settle upon what to do with your life comes from Jeff Bezos, the founder of Amazon. Before he started Amazon, Bezos was a trader in the New York offices of the investment manager D.E. Shaw & Co. Not only was Bezos highly paid, the founder of the firm—D.E. Shaw—liked him and seemed to have earmarked him for a promotion. To leave all this behind him and start an online bookstore in the early 1990s—at a time when few people had heard of the Internet let alone understand what an online bookstore would be—was a massive deal for Bezos. Most people around him—including his boss and parents—urged caution.

So how did Bezos convince himself to take the plunge and chart a course which not only reset his goals in life but changed the way the world shops? In a beautiful book on how maths can help us optimize our goal-seeking in everyday life, the authors Brian Christian and Tom Griffiths[9] recalled how Bezos used regret as a powerful motivator at this critical juncture. They quote Bezos as follows: 'The framework I found, which made the decision incredibly easy, was what I called – which only a nerd would call – a "regret minimization framework". So I wanted to project myself forward to age 80 and say, "Okay, now I'm looking back on my life. I want to have minimized the number of regrets I have." I knew that when I was 80 I was not going to regret having tried this. I was not going to regret trying to participate in this thing called the Internet that I thought was going to be a really big deal. I knew that if I failed I wouldn't regret that, but I knew the one thing that I might regret is not ever having tried. I knew that that would haunt me every day, and so, when I thought about it that way it was an incredibly easy decision.'

Our goals don't always have to be profound life goals hinging upon our family or our careers; they can be practical goals, such us saving money for retirement or becoming the best drummer in the country or training to become a marathon runner. Whatever they might be, goals are the foundation of mental decluttering. Goals give our life purpose and, as highlighted in the Mary Shelley quote at the beginning of this chapter, that plays a major role in decluttering our mind.

Step 2—Prioritize: Even a basic to-do list helps us declutter our minds and frees up mental space. For most of us, if we don't write things down, the chances are high that we will forget that action point. Saurabh uses the memo function available on his smartphone to create a to-do list which can easily be turned into a prioritized list of action points. When it comes to prioritizing, the most useful principle is to do the 'tough things first'. Ray Zinn, CEO of Micrel and the longest serving CEO in Silicon Valley, wrote a famous book with this title[10] and with the management philosophy that leaders need to tackle the most difficult problems first.

But suppose you were to say that your goals are not profound but mundane, that you are trying to achieve something as practical as, say, buying a flat or getting a well-paid job or finding a life partner. How should you prioritize?

In *Algorithms to Live By*, the authors make the case that these decisions are variants of the 'optimal stopping' problem, i.e. problems where, faced with a range of possible choices (which usually appear to you in sequential form such that once you have rejected an option, that option never reappears), we need to decide when to stop looking and grab the first best option which appears thereafter. The answer to these sorts of problems is usually 37 per cent.

If, for example, you are planning to sell your house over the next 100 days, you should wait to see what offers you get until day 37 and then take the best offer you get on any day thereafter. It is worth Googling on this subject (of optimal stopping) to see how high school probability calculations can help us reduce mental clutter and improve clarity of thought.

Step 3—Use checklists for planning and execution: Thanks to Atul Gawande and his bestselling book *The Checklist Manifesto*[11], millions of professionals have understood the power of this seemingly simple process. Gawande highlighted that checklists break down complex tasks while ensuring consistency and efficiency, especially if more than one person is working on a project. Everybody—from ambulance crews to airline pilots to architects—can benefit from checklists.

In fact, as Gawande highlights, there are two very different purposes for which checklists can be created. A 'do-confirm' checklist allows more freedom to complete tasks from memory before consulting the checklist. Once the tasks are completed, a checkpoint occurs and at this juncture the checklist can be consulted to confirm that no tasks have been overlooked. An example of this is a pilot preparing a plane for take-off—he goes through a list of checks which confirm that the aircraft is in an appropriate condition to fly and then and only then he starts taxiing towards the runway. While it is possible for the pilot to memorize all of the checks, that is a risk no airline wants to run. Hence there is a clearly laid out printed checklist that every pilot has to go through before getting ready to fly.

The second type of checklist is the 'read-do' kind. These checklists are more like recipes—you start by reading each item on the list, then you complete it before moving on. An obvious example is a recipe for baking a cake. Another example of a 'read-do' checklist is the influential and life-saving WHO Surgical Safety Checklist, which is actually segmented into three separate checklists: (1) steps that surgeons have to take before the induction of anaesthesia; (2) steps that surgeons have to take before skin incision; and (3) steps that surgeons have to take before the patient leaves the operating room.[12]

At Marcellus Investment Managers, Saurabh and his colleagues have turned the investment process of assessing a stock into a 'read-do' checklist (step 1: check accounting quality; step 2: check consistency of return on capital employed over the last decade and revenue growth over the past fifteen years; step 3: read the last fifteen years of annual reports to assess capital allocation; step 4: assess sustainable competitive advantages, etc.).

Step 4—Build a 'cache' for memories you need to retrieve frequently: In 1879, Hermann Ebbinghaus, a psychologist at the University of Berlin, began a series of experiments on himself to understand how memory works. As Christian and Griffiths describe in *Algorithms to Live By*: 'Each day, Ebbinghaus would sit down and memorise a list of nonsense syllables. Then he would test himself on lists from the previous days. Pursuing this habit over the course of a year, he established many of the most basic results in human memory research. He confirmed, for instance, that practicing a list multiple times makes it persist longer in memory, and that the number of items one can accurately recall goes down as time passes. His results mapped out a graph of how memory fades over time, known today by psychologists as the "the forgetting curve".'

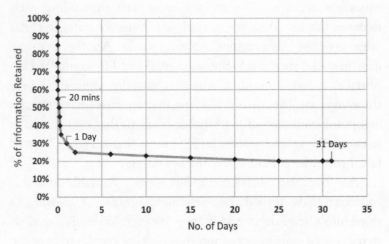

Exhibit 3: Ebbinghaus's forgetting curve[13]

As we get older, all of us suffer from the tyranny of the forgetting curve. For each of us, every year adds half a million minutes of lived experience. If you assume that on each working day of the year, we meet on average two new people, by implication we end up meeting around 500 new people each year. Each of those meetings brings information (during the course of the meeting) and memories (post the meeting). Add to that material we have read, audio clips we have heard and videos that we have watched, it is not surprising that our ability to retrieve information from the database in our brain slows down as we grow older. This is no different from how travelling from point A to point B takes more time as a city gets bigger, or how retrieving books from a library becomes more time-consuming as the library gets bigger.

An essential element of reducing mental clutter is aimed at addressing this problem of memory retrieval on demand. The most effective way to address this challenge has come from computer scientists—they use 'caching' to structure the memory in your computer in a tiered structure. In your smartphone, tablet or laptop, there are at least two layers of memory. The main memory chip which stores the overwhelming bulk of the data in your machine and can accommodate several gigabytes of data but is slower to access. Therefore, to help you access the most useful bits of information in your machine quicker, computer scientists have created a smaller memory chip called 'cache memory'. Also called CPU memory, this is a smaller, faster memory, closer to a processor core, which stores copies of the data from frequently-used main memory locations.

We can use the same principle and apply it to the human mind and build for it a cache memory of items which we need to remember, recall and use most frequently. Items such as your phone password, your PAN number, your life partner's and children's birthdays, your wedding anniversary, where you keep your car keys, the best parking spot in the local shopping mall, etc. are part of the cache memory of most people. But beyond these obvious items, is there another way to use the principle of caching?

The answer is an unequivocal 'yes' and the method to figure out what else to commit to cache memory has come from two different sources. Firstly, American computer scientists figured out in the 1970s that items which are least recently used (LRU) should be the first to be evicted from the cache memory. Then, in the 1990s, Yukio Noguchi, an economist at the University of Tokyo, hit upon a filing method which is similar to LRU. Noguchi started by creating files (physical files) for each bit of useful information he received and then, after he had labelled and dated the file, he would put the latest files to the extreme left-hand side of his filing cabinet. He followed this 'left insertion' rule for old files as well as new ones, i.e. every time he pulled out a file to use its contents, he would return it to the filing cabinet as the leftmost file. This turned out to be one of the most efficient filing systems ever created.

We can use this principle to reduce clutter in our lives and in our minds. So, that first generation iPod that Saurabh hasn't used for ten years has to exit his cupboard even though he believes it to be a historically significant electronic device. Ditto for the Bermuda shorts which he hasn't worn in the past five years. Similarly, memories of his driving test in Mumbai from a decade ago can also be removed from his caching memory. In contrast, Saurabh's running gear and car keys should be kept at the front of his cupboard. Since managing an investment management firm requires Saurabh to understand securities market law, the SEBI Act, 1992 has to become a part of his cache memory. In other words, the principle of caching allows us to understand how we can organize our mind, our memories and our possessions. Only the most centrally essential items are kept; everything else is abandoned.

Step 5—Use a jotter for thoughts and ideas: Clearly, our mind is much more than a glorified database; it is also an ideas engine and often a whirlpool of creativity. So if the caching of memories described in Step 4 pertains to the database aspect of our minds, how can we optimize the mental clutter associated with the creative and imaginative aspects of our mind?

More often than not, many of us get our best ideas not when we are at our desk trying to solve a problem. Instead, the breakthrough ideas often arise when our brain is relaxed, say, in the shower or during the morning run. Rather than merging these ideas with the to-do list or with the execution plan, it is usually better to create a separate repository for such creative ideas. Save your best ideas in your chosen repository so that you do not lose them and they do not take up valuable mental real estate.

Is there an optimal way to create your personal repository of ideas? Effective methods include sending yourself an email or just keeping a small notebook handy. Some of Saurabh's colleagues use Evernote, a tool loved by productivity gurus. Others use Google Docs or just spreadsheets.

Far more important than the specific tool being used to capture the ideas is the frequency with which you revisit your repository of ideas. Therefore the best method for storing your ideas is one that encourages you not only to keep them but also makes it easy for you to revisit them. After all, keeping track of your best ideas is only useful if you have a plan to revisit them and put the best ones into action. In that regard Step 5 and Step 4 become similar insofar as your best ideas become a part of your cache memory. That in turn allows them to percolate in your mind and see connections between these ideas that others can't. In other words, the human mind's database function is intimately linked to its creative function. Memory and creativity are both manifestations of intelligence and this is a topic we return to in the next chapter.

Step 6—Reduce the time spent on the smartphone: Most smartphones allow you to track how much time you are spending staring at the screen. Given that many professionals now end up having to do fifty- to sixty-hour weeks (including commuting time), if over and above that you are spending any more than a couple of hours a day on your smartphone, it will be hard for you to think straight. (Until a year ago, Saurabh was doing well over three hours of phone screen time per day on average.)

Radically reducing the time spent on the phone is the first step towards developing greater clarity of thought. Three different books—*Deep Work*, *Focus* and *Peak*—point in the same direction. These books contend that if you want to come up with simple but powerful insights you have to specialize and focus—focus on deliberative practice, focus on reflective thought. Running from meeting to meeting while WhatsApping and emailing is unlikely to be a productive way to work in a world where penetrating insights are the key source of value and hence wealth. While we highlighted Rowling and Gates at the beginning of the chapter as 'deep work' success stories, if you refer to the habits of the great men and women cited in Chapter 3—Asimov, Munger, Hemingway, Flaubert, etc.—it becomes apparent that in every era and in every profession, the ability to concentrate, to go deep is a necessary condition for professional success.

Thanks to the runaway success of *Deep Work*, Newport's prescriptions for creating ninety-minute slots for solid, uninterrupted work (without Internet or emails or colleagues disturbing you) are now well-known. Newport says that you should begin by trying to do this for an hour each day and then gradually build up to four hours of deep work every day. As you do so, you will develop myelin—a white tissue which develops around neurons—in the relevant areas of your brain. This allows your brain cells to fire faster and cleaner. Effectively, you are upgrading your brain and this should allow you to come up with new ideas and solutions quicker.

But you can only do this sort of work if you get rid of your craving for social media, for text messaging, for constantly checking your emails and answering phone calls through the day. How can we break all these nasty habits that we have acquired from years of shallow work?

In his book *Digital Minimalism*, Newport asks you to first quit social media[14] and then undergo a form of digital detox wherein for a month you abandon all forms of optional digital media (basically abandon everything which is not essential for your family's life safety and well-being). Since most of us are totally hooked to our phones, Newport gives us a few tips on how we can get ready for our one-month digital sabbatical:

1. **Build up your social life:** Before you begin your digital detox, you need to understand how you will fill the void left by digital media in your life. For many people compulsive phone use fills up the void created by a well-developed social and family life. The itinerant life of the typical Indian professional—who moves cities almost every other year—makes it even harder to build relationships in the local community. If you are such an individual—and truth be told, many of us are—you need to plan in advance which classes or community groups you will join or activities you will do with your family in the time freed up during your digital detox.

2. **Partial phone deprivation:** During weekdays, start leaving your phone behind on your desk when you go for meetings or when you go for your lunch break. On holidays, start leaving your phone at home when you go out for dinner or for a movie or—better still—for a long walk in the park. As you do this you will gradually get accustomed to staying away from your phone. That in turn will make you less prone to picking up your phone and peering at it repeatedly.

3. **Put your phone on DND:** Even when you are with your phone, learn to put in on 'Do Not Disturb' (DND) mode so that you don't get notifications for anything and you don't get incoming calls. You can adjust your DND settings such that near and dear ones can reach you but no one else can.

Then in specific chunks of time which you have set aside each day—ideally during your evening commute—get your phone calls done.

4. **Scheduled digital dosing:** Just as with your phone calls, minimize your use of the Internet, social media and text messaging; have pre-scheduled time slots each day in which you access the Internet and do your emailing and text messaging. For the rest of the day, stay away from the Internet and from messaging. If through the day you keep responding to every message which crops up on your screen, you are giving yourself no chance to do deep work, which also means that you are giving yourself no chance to develop your myelin.

5. **Digital downtime every evening:** When you are done with work for the day, try to shut down for the day completely. So no emailing, text messaging and Internet surfing once you have shut shop for the day. That necessarily implies that you: (a) focus on your family and your social relationships and yourself after you have wound up work for the day; and (b) have a clear plan for how you will spend your evening. (If you don't have a plan, chances are that you will drift back to digital media for entertainment.)

6. **Remove social media apps and use website versions:** Social media platforms such as Facebook and LinkedIn have a multitude of uses and while some of these features have become addictive for millions of users (this seems to be particularly true for Facebook), you might not want to throw out the baby with the bathwater. Hence, one way to hold on to the best features of these platforms (eg. the ability to find like-minded people, the ability to recruit the right people or find the right suppliers, etc.) while jettisoning the worst (eg. notifications, 'likes') is to delete these apps from your phone and install the website versions

on your desktop. You will find that the time it takes to boot up your desktop, open your web browser and then fire up Facebook kills a big part of the impulse-driven behaviour which characterizes our use of social media.

Effectively what Newport is saying is that we need to try to build a routine for our workday wherein Internet use takes place within pre-specified time slots and ditto for phone calling. As a result, the rest of our schedule is freed up for deep work.

Saurabh has implemented bullets 2, 5 and 6. With a bit of help from his better half, he reckons, he will be able to implement bullets 1 and 5. Then he will be ready for Newport's digital detox. When Saurabh begins his month-long digital detox, he will be conscious of Newport's warning that the first two weeks will be painful and there are no tips or tricks that can mitigate that pain. But as Saurabh consciously pulls back from all optional forms of digital media over the course of the month, he will find that things will settle down. Saurabh knows that his friends and clients won't abandon him because he has abandoned his smartphone. Gradually, Saurabh will find that the quantum and quality of interactions with friends and family improving. He will become less stressed, less anxious and less fidgety. After a month of full digital detox, Saurabh can then add back a small number of carefully chosen online activities that he believes will provide massive benefits for activities or goals which he deeply values, eg. posting his blogs on LinkedIn (using the website version of LinkedIn), reading his emails and visiting the three websites where he finds high-quality commentary on finance, economics and psychology. These websites are ft.com (*The Financial Times*); the family of sites that ritholtz.com has built; and Farnam Street (fs.blog).

It helps that among his colleagues, Saurabh can already see a wide spectrum of behaviours in terms of smartphone usage.

Two of his colleagues are super disciplined in terms of phone and Internet use, and they have no trouble working in a focused manner for ninety-minute intervals. Unsurprisingly, these two gents produce outstanding investment insights.

At the other end of the spectrum tend to be bright young interns who work for Marcellus Investment Managers; they belong to the iPhone generation and Saurabh can see that they find it hard to read an annual report in one sitting. It takes them a few months before their minds settle down, their phones switch off and they start learning that concentrating for long periods of time is 50 per cent of the skill required to be an analyst.

Observing the youngsters in his team grow up, Saurabh remembers his teenage years when his dad used to sit next to him as he struggled with algebra and calculus. Saurabh's dad would lock the door of his room, sit himself down next to his desk and say the same thing again and again: 'Concentrate . . . concentrate . . . learn to concentrate.' Saurabh used to hate his dad for doing this, but with the benefit of hindsight he realizes that the years his dad spent at IIT Kharagpur had taught him the value of deep work.

Clutter reduction: The link between specialization and simplicity

It is highly unlikely that you will be able to execute the preceding six steps if you are not able to exhibit the behaviours discussed in the three preceding chapters of the book. So, for example, if you have not chosen to specialize in a specific field, it is going to be hard for you to settle upon your goals. Similarly, if you have not begun simplifying your working day, it is unlikely that you will be able to use checklists for prioritization or execution.

Clutter reduction is therefore linked inextricably to the three preceding chapters. In a way clutter reduction opens the doors for you to reap the benefits of the three preceding chapters, i.e. if you have already specialized, simplified and spiritualized, it is highly likely that clutter reduction will help you become more creative.

Clutter reduction case study: Planning the day at Marcellus

Given that the USA is the largest market in the world for books, most business books are written with an American audience in mind. That in turn creates some peculiar challenges for readers elsewhere. So, for example, if you read books on the mega successful companies of the past three decades—Amazon, Google, Microsoft, etc.—you will hear about how the founders and the staff worked long hours year after year to build these zillion-dollar enterprises. Saurabh learnt the hard way that if you try to replicate this culture of long hours of intense work in Mumbai—where the transport infrastructure is not what it is in San Francisco or Seattle and where people don't have easy access to parks, beaches and the countryside to recharge their batteries—you end up physically and mentally hurting your colleagues.

Similarly, in a noisy, hyperactive city such as Mumbai, if you create Silicon Valley-style open-plan offices with beanbags and foosball tables, you are not helping anyone, because intense, focused work requires quiet, clutter-free environment.

Realizing that the way most open-plan offices are organized is not conducive to high-quality work, the employees at Marcellus Investment Managers have sought to organize ourselves in a better manner. The team has effectively segmented itself into three:

- The operations team sits in an open-plan office which is a beehive of activity and noise thanks to clients' phone calls, the operations team's chats with Marcellus's custodians, brokers and fund accountants, etc.
- The investment management staff sit in a smaller room which is very quiet (phones are on silent, noise-cancelling headphones are used by some) unless a debate is taking place about the merits of a specific investment. Noise is frowned upon in this room and using the internal rating system, analysts are quick to highlight the names of colleagues who have disturbed the peace and calm in the 'research room'.
- The salespeople are, as you would expect, never in the office unless they are pulled away from their client meetings for a weekly internal team meeting. When the salespeople are in the office, noise is a given and everybody plans their day accordingly.

The entire company comes together on Monday morning at 8.30 a.m. for the weekly team meeting where progress is reviewed and action points are agreed upon. However, beyond that one team meeting per week, each of the teams works during different work hours. The operations and trading teams reach the office at 8 a.m. so that their commute is done before Mumbai's roads are clogged by rush-hour traffic. An early arrival also helps the traders to get ready for the stock market, which opens at 9.15 a.m. The investment analysts often work from home if they want to focus entirely on reading, say, the last fifteen years of annual reports on a given company that they are researching. Finally, the salespeople—since they often have dinner with clients in the evening—start the day later and head straight for the client's office rather than coming to the Marcellus office. Building a successful business is hard work. However, decluttering people's minds and their lives makes it easier for them to deliver outstanding results.

* * *

Key takeaways from this chapter

- Workplace pressures tend to occupy most of our mind space. On top of that, smartphone addiction with constant exposure to messaging apps, email and social media adds another layer of stress and mental clutter. The harmful effects of this include loneliness, extremism and anxiety.
- Once you have chosen a field for specialization, simplified your working day and taken up spiritualization, the next logical step is to declutter your life.
- Steps to declutter: start with your goals, prioritize them, then use checklists, build a cache for memories, use a jotter for thoughts, reduce the time spent on the smartphone.
- Cal Newport's recipe for a digital detox: build up your social life, go through partial phone deprivation, put your phone on DND, adopt scheduled digital dosing, enforce on yourself digital downtime every evening and then remove social-media apps while shifting to their website versions.

How Harsh Mariwala Cuts through Clutter

Harsh Mariwala is the founder and chairman of Marico Limited. He is also a rarity among Indian businessmen. In keeping with his simple, uncluttered approach, Harsh built Marico around two major brands—Parachute and Saffola—both of which are market leaders in their respective segments. In contrast to the typical Indian promoter who after succeeding in his main business falls for the ego trip of empire building, Harsh has steadfastly refused to diversify in unrelated areas. Unlike the typical Indian promoter who holds on to his company until his last breath, Harsh relinquished day-to-day operations to Saugata Gupta in 2014 (Saugata is now managing director and CEO of Marico). Harsh is a billionaire at ease with himself and yet full of energy to help entrepreneurs fulfil their own dreams as part of his Ascent Foundation. Marico is in the original list of 'coffee can' companies profiled in depth in *The Unusual Billionaires*.

We met Harsh on 3 September 2019 on a rainy morning at Marico's headquarters located at the edge of Mumbai's Bandra Kurla Complex. Harsh loves reading and we spotted business classics (Stephen R. Covey's *The 7 Habits of Highly Effective People*[15]; Jim Collins and Jerry I. Porras's *Built to Last: Successful Habits of Visionary Companies*[16]) as well as relatively newer books (Daniel Goleman's *Focus*[17], Navi Radjou and Jaideep Prabhu's *Do Better With Less: Frugal Innovation for Sustainable Growth*[18]) on Harsh's well-stocked bookshelf. We spoke about grit, passion, simplicity, focus, turning points in Marico's history and much more.

Harsh keeps a diary with printouts stuck on the pages. He showed us two such pages[19] (see Exhibit 4), both of which reflect Harsh's clarity of thought. The first is titled 'Role of Chairman, Marico Limited', and it is a list of nine specific areas with a list of duties in each area. The second is titled 'The Marico I would like to leave behind' and it defines Marico's legacy.

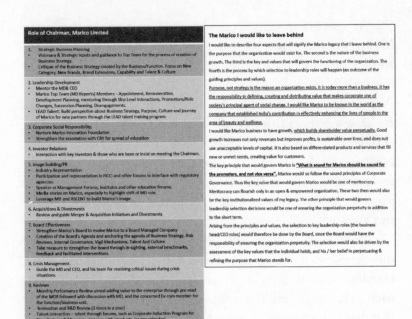

Exhibit 4: Pages from Harsh Mariwala's Diary

Harsh is a big believer in simplicity and focus. The first phase of building Marico involved moving out from a family-run commodity business (Bombay Oil) to a professionally run FMCG firm (Marico) in the 1990s. This was followed by building both brands with an intense focus backed by insights. Harsh says, 'I strongly believe that focus will lead to depth and depth will lead to excellence.' He gives us the example of hair oil in the 1990s. While hair oil's use was going down internationally, there was a huge market in rural India, which was using unbranded hair oil. 'I saw the opportunity to convert them to branded hair oils. I took a big bet, acquired a few brands, started new brands, entered the amla oil segment. The clarion call was given internally that we have to get market leadership,' he told us. Marico backed this with its memorable *'Champi kiya kya?'*[20] campaign to drive the message of the benefits of hair oil. Harsh was always clear that he would not take on the giants head-on. 'We didn't want to get into the hair wash category which is heavily competitive with Hindustan Unilever Limited (HUL), Procter and Gamble (P&G), and L'Oréal. But we were focused on hair oil, and over time our vision changed from being leaders in hair oil to being leaders in pre- and post-wash haircare. After that change in vision, we acquired Set Wet and Livon and those bets paid off,' he told us.

The deepening and widening of brands continued in edible oils as well. Marico positioned Saffola as the 'good for heart' cooking oil and then launched food products around that, such as Saffola Oats. But Marico's consumer insights revealed that Indians preferred savoury breakfast over sweet ones (such as cornflakes). 'We didn't have a differentiator compared to Kellogg's and Quaker in terms of the plain oats. And Indians like savoury breakfast—in the south, they like idlis, in the north, parathas etc. So then we launched the range of savoury oats based on the taste preferences in different parts of the country. In that segment, we have 70 to 75 per cent market share. We built the market,' he told us.

Harsh built Marico's brand strategy around a simple question—how can they be the market leader? Because if you're not the market leader, then you don't have the pricing power and will always be vulnerable to the market leader's price actions. Selling small packs at low prices was another way to maintain leadership so that even if a competitor launches a cheaper brand, people will not easily shift away for a few rupees in price difference.

Having built a successful FMCG franchise, Harsh could easily have bid for licences for coal mines or telecom or banks—

all fashionable things for Indian promoters to do in the opening decade of this century. But Harsh studiously avoided the clutter of unrelated diversifications. 'Discipline is very important. Be focused. I like to leverage my strengths not my balance sheet,' he told us.

Marico is also well-known for high standards of corporate governance—for example, a top-notch board of directors. Harsh believes that a great board of directors also attracts brilliant professionals from all fields, and that allows the company to have top-quality people at the top, guiding the company forward. Harsh is a big believer in building a great working culture, personally setting high standards of conduct from the early days of building Marico by, among other things, paying very high rates of tax. 'If I evade taxes, the culture goes down in the organization,' he told us. This is exactly the advice he gives the entrepreneurs at Ascent Foundation. 'Be fully compliant from day one. It is not about size but about building a culture of good governance. If the top starts taking shortcuts then people down the line will start taking shortcuts,' he told us. A good, honest work culture also attracts talented employees who want to work in such companies.

How did Harsh let go of the day-to-day management of the company he built over decades and holds a 60 per cent stake in? 'The organization doesn't belong to me. Who am I to say that I should be giving this to my children? What is good for the organization comes first and not what is good for the promoters,' he tells us in a matter-of-fact manner. But if Harsh was so detached, he could have sold off Marico to any MNC giant (for example, HUL, when Keki Dadiseth, then chairman of HUL, offered to buy Harsh out in the 1990s) and started a new business. When we asked him about this apparent paradox, Harsh explained, 'I have very strong pride in what I do. It is not about wealth; it is about legacy. Why should I sell out to an MNC when I've built this organization that is bigger than I am?'

Finally, we ask him for his advice for a twenty-five-year-old starting off his or her career. 'I am a big believer in grit. Passion combined with perseverance is grit. I'm a big believer in leveraging your strengths, rather than improving your weaknesses,' he tells us. So find your strength yourself and through people who know you well. Strengthen areas that need improvement and then leverage your career based on your strengths.

For those who want to become entrepreneurs, Harsh recommends that they start with smaller organizations where they can learn across many functions and work with an entrepreneur. For those who want to work in big companies, he recommends that they work with start-ups and small entrepreneurs.

And what about the forty- to forty-five-year-old who wants to start a second career? Harsh believes that everyone should reinvent themselves every ten to twenty years, just as he has. 'I'm doing a lot of new things, which I would never have been able to do if I was managing the company,' he told us. 'A mid-career professional who has built up his or her finances can become an entrepreneur, look at helping other entrepreneurs, or they could also take up corporate social responsibility while staying in a larger company.'

6

Develop Your Creativity and Memory[1]

'The reasonable man adapts himself to the world; the unreasonable man persists in trying to adapt the world to himself. Therefore all progress depends on the unreasonable man.'

—George Bernard Shaw[2]

In a market such as Mumbai, there will be at least a hundred professional coders who can write algorithms that can spot moneymaking opportunities in the stock market. Now imagine this: You come up with a piece of software that can make even 3 per cent more money than the typical cash-futures arbitrage algorithm used by other fund houses. What happens? You become the hottest property in town. Every fund house will bend over backwards to hire you.

The same would be true if you were an interior designer, a cricketer, journalist or civil engineer. In a highly competitive free-market economy, even if your ideas are only marginally better than those of your peers, you are very much in demand. What we are talking about, as you might have guessed from the chapter title, is the power of original thinking—arguably the greatest source of value and wealth in a competitive free-market economy.

There is no disputing that originality is a valuable characteristic. But just what does thinking originally entail?

There is no standard definition as such, but when we say original thinking, what we are referring to is actually a spectrum or a range. At the peak, you have the radical thinkers, those who come up with truly revolutionary ideas. But you also have people who reimagine existing concepts or apply them to new fields or problems. And then you also have incremental innovation, where you take something old and improve it or further build upon it.

Another, more personal, example is Saurabh's adaptation of Rob Kirby's investing approach to Indian conditions. The adaptation is inspired by a 1984 article written by Kirby (a celebrated investment manager of the Capital Guardian Trust Company). The investment construct of leaving a high-quality portfolio untouched for very long periods of time, suggested by Kirby, works beautifully in India and delivers benchmark beating performance year after year. We shall return to this construct in Chapter 9 of this book.[3]

The key to success in a competitive field is 'thinking differently'—as opposed to blindly following established or conventional wisdom. It is a core concept of our Simplicity Paradigm. Without further ado, let us dive right into how to think differently.

What is your deep, driving desire?

The Upanishads, a set of ancient Sanskrit texts, say, 'You are what your deep, driving desire is. As your desire is, so is your will. As your will is, so is your deed. As your deed is, so is your destiny.' While we are rather sceptical of 'destiny', we do have desires and motivations in our lives. Saurabh wants to build a world-class investment firm; Anupam wants to reach out to the world with his podcast. These are what drive us.

We see two broad motivations driving the people around us: (a) striving to achieve new heights within an existing system; and (b) challenging the existing system and being a force for change. Succeeding in these motivations is not easy but when one does succeed, fame and (sometimes) fortune are natural outcomes.

For instance, India's cricket superstar Virat Kohli is clearly driven by the need to become the best in his sport. He has worked very hard to achieve his goals, and his success has brought him wealth and recognition from an early age. We encounter people with similar personalities in the boardrooms of India's largest companies and in Mumbai's investment banks—clever, hard-working, ambitious people who are driven to constantly achieve more.

The celebrated author Arundhati Roy, on the other hand, is driven by a need to speak out against what she sees as an establishment that is oppressive. Roy is fundamentally driven by the need to challenge the status quo because of her belief that the status quo gives a raw deal to many groups in Indian society.

Roy's views on the exploitative nature of the Indian state and the unrestrained descriptions of sexuality in her books have made her the target of abuse by many. But that does not frazzle her, largely because she did not set out to seek popularity in the first place. She is neither a consensus hugger herself nor does she seek the approbation of all. Most people in our social circle in Mumbai do not like Roy, and their scorn and disapproval define her identity.

Kohli strives for excellence within a pre-existing system (for elite cricketers). Roy strives to bring about change in the system. Both of them think differently from others around them. Kohli's deliberate practice and his approach to physical fitness give him an edge and set him apart from other cricketers who might be as talented as him. Roy's resolute fight for the underdog and refusal to seek validation from the Indian establishment speaks of her determined nonconformity. Both approaches are equally valuable.

Before anything else, you need to find your own motivation. It need not be a world-changing aspiration—just something you find worthwhile. Something you can devote your energies to. That is the first step to originality.

Beyond that, there are a few practices we think can help.

Six ways to help drive original thinking

Can you really reinvent the wheel? No, it is made and it is done. Can you find a way to connect taxis to users via an app? Yes, we have Uber. Can you develop simple, easy-to-understand investment products that only track indices and don't have complicated and high-fee structures? Yes, they are called exchange-traded funds (ETFs).

How and to what extent can original thinking be cultivated? We don't see any easy answers to this question. As we have said, we believe that the spectrum of original thinking encompasses innovations, improvisations and tweaking existing ideas, all the way to reimagining and inventing new concepts. Original thinking may not and should not be a universal prescription. Often enough, original ideas flop. Nevertheless, herd mentality is a very real danger. Thinking differently—however nebulous the term 'original' may be—can help avoid that trap.

So how can we nurture new ideas? How can we stay creative? Here is what has worked for us. This is a list in progress. It is by no means exhaustive and will keep changing as we keep learning.

1. Read widely alongside your deep specialization

Every single expert interviewed for this book turned out to be a voracious reader. More generally, most successful writers that we have met have turned out to be avid readers. Beyond writing, seeking out other people's ideas, wisdom and original thinking is almost always a good idea because before you can come up with well-developed ideas, you need to understand the best ideas of others.

The easiest way to access other people's ideas is through reading. Read columns, read articles and, most importantly, read books. More than other formats, a book gives the author more space to articulate their idea clearly—to go 'deep'.

Reading also becomes an experience, and as we are going to see in more detail a little later on, varied memories/experiences can help drive original and imaginative thinking. Creative people are usually those who seek out the broadest perspective.

Saurabh, for one, asks almost everyone he meets what their favourite books are, and he has on his phone a long list of varied book recommendations from people he has met. Then once a week, usually on a Saturday morning, with a steaming cup of filter coffee in hand, he orders a few of these titles and then spends most of his free time reading one book after another. As a result, ever so often Saurabh ends up with a big pile of recently acquired books and then his wife forces him to gift several of these titles to friends in order to keep the house uncluttered.

Having said all of that, it is unlikely that your average newspaper reader or typical social media junkie will be bursting with fresh ideas; such people are more likely than not to parrot the fashionable ideas in circulation at a given point of time. Instead, creativity, it would appear, arises from gaining mastery of one's discipline by using a very specific style of reading/education. We call it the 'T-shaped' model of brain development—the creative masters read around extensively while educating/training themselves intensively in a specific field. We saw in Chapter 2 how the martial arts icon Bruce Lee used this technique to map his path to stardom.

In a completely different field, Einstein used this model of mastery to generate the insight which ultimately led to his 'special theory of relativity, a monumental achievement . . . [for] a single scientist working alone and out of the academic mainstream'[4]. Experts who have sought to understand how Einstein cracked this puzzle have broken his problem-solving into two parts.

Step 1 was a thought experiment that Einstein conducted when he was just sixteen years old. This thought experiment contained the seeds to cracking the problem of special relativity. In Einstein's own words from his *Autobiographical Notes*[5]: '. . . a paradox upon which I had already hit at the age of sixteen: If I pursue a beam of light with the velocity c (velocity of light in a vacuum), I should observe such a beam of light as an electromagnetic field at rest though spatially oscillating. There seems to be no such thing, however, neither on the basis of experience nor according to Maxwell's equations. From the very beginning it appeared to me intuitively clear that, judged from the standpoint of such an observer, everything would have to happen according to the same laws as for an observer who, relative to the earth, was at rest. For how should the first observer know or be able to determine, that he is in a state of fast uniform motion? One sees in this paradox the germ of the special relativity theory is already contained.'[6]

Einstein's thought experiment highlighted a paradox with utmost simplicity: either I am moving with the beam of light with velocity c or I am at rest. I cannot be in both states at the same time.

Step 2 is Einstein proceeding to crack this paradox over the next eleven years, thus helping the world understand how light travels and more generally, how objects—including celestial bodies—move in a world where gravitational effects are negligible.

Einstein's ability to hit upon the novel thought experiment in Step 1 was greatly helped not just by his (fairly conventional) schooling in Germany and then Italy, but also by: (a) his extensive discussions with his uncle, Caesar Koch, who would spend hours discussing complex maths problems with his teenage nephew; and (b) his special schooling in Switzerland in a *Kantonsschule* which specialized in *Anschauung*, i.e. intuition or 'apprehension or immediate perception that involves fewest elements of rational insight'.[7]

Einstein's success in Step 2 was also underpinned not just by his conventional university education at Zurich Polytechnic but also by the inputs he received on his scientific papers from his uncle. Furthermore, through his teenage years, Einstein absorbed the philosophy of Immanuel Kant, the father of *Anschauung*, who propounded that all of us possess not just intellect but also intuition. Kant famously argued that the objects we see around us are just 'mere representations and not . . . things in themselves'[8]. Kant's exhortation to think about the world in abstract terms and nail down truths which are independent of what we have experienced in our day-to-day life had a direct influence on Einstein's intellectual development.

2. Explore the world

Seek out experiences in life which take you out of your comfort zone. So rather than going to Goa for a weekend break for the hundredth time, venture out into a wildlife resort or visit a different country. Anupam will never forget his solitary night in a tent in Hunder, Ladakh, for the silence almost drove him deaf.

As far as your finances allow, seek out varied experiences in your professional life. Doing the same thing year after year will give you in all likelihood a more linear career growth path, but if you want to become an original thinker, you might want to make multiple lateral moves to learn new skills or work in multiple industries.

By the time Saurabh was twenty-five he had worked as a newspaper boy, a bathroom cleaner, a cashier in a betting shop, a clerk in a bank, an economist for the financial regulator in the UK and a management consultant. Each stint, while challenging in its own way, provided him with insights into how the world works. Each job enhanced Saurabh's skill set and allowed him to move forward a few more steps.

For example, as a betting shop cashier in London, Saurabh saw that the clients who bet the least frequently and spent the least amount of time in the betting shop typically took home the most amount of money. Almost twenty years later that insight helped him create a distinctive and highly effective style of equity investing in India which is detailed further on in this book. As an economist on secondment to the UK financial regulator, Saurabh saw first-hand how the smartest British financial services firms used lobbying to build competitive advantages. That perspective helped him identify firms in India that excel at using the legal and regulatory system to building competitive advantages for themselves. As a newspaper boy in his mid-teens, Saurabh used to deliver the newspaper to around a hundred shops in the high street near his residence in London. Over the next four years, Saurabh saw how most of these shops were first disrupted by the rise of large-format supermarkets and then by the rise of the Internet. That perspective entrenched in his mind the conviction that no business—regardless of what sector it is in—is free from disruption unless it is constantly strengthening its competitive advantages.

More generally, the exposure to different types of jobs and people helped Saurabh learn how to work collaboratively in diverse environments. As a teenager working in a high-stress environment like a betting shop or a bank, you are not going to last very long in the face of pushy customers unless your colleagues are there to help you and you, in turn, have their backs when they are faced with difficult situations.

These vastly different experiences not only gave him life skills which later helped him become a serial entrepreneur across two countries; it also helped him understand that the only real source of value in the business world is a worker's ability to break a business problem into constituent tasks and get the job done.

The psychologist Adam Grant in his book *Originals: How Non-Conformists Move the World*[9] cites a study 'comparing every Nobel Prize-winning scientist from 1901 to 2015 with typical scientists of the same era'. It found that while both groups attained deep expertise in their respective fields of study, the Nobel laureates were 'dramatically more likely to be involved in the arts than less accomplished scientists'. Varied experiences, anyone?

In Exhibit 5, we take inspiration from a table in the book *Originals: How Non-Conformists Change the World* (2016), by Adam Grant, to show the chances of a Nobel Prize winner with varied experiences being interested in the arts (relative to a typical scientist).

Hobby related to the arts	Greater chances of the Nobel Prize winner enjoying the hobby as compared to the typical scientist (number of times)
Related to music. For example, playing a musical instrument or composing or conducting music, etc.	Two times
Related to the arts such as painting, sculpting, etc.	Seven times
Related to the crafts. For example, woodworks, mechanics, electronics, glass-blowing, etc.	Seven and a half times
Related to writing, in forms such as essays, poetry, novels, books, etc.	Twelve times
Related to the performing arts at amateur or professional levels, as an actor, dancer, musician, etc.	Twenty-two times

Exhibit 5

3. Enhance your memory

One of the most fascinating aspects of creativity is how dependent it is on memory. Beethoven wrote: 'I carry my thoughts about with me for a very long time, often for a very long time before writing them down. I can . . . be sure that . . . I shall not forget [a theme] even years later. I change many things, discard others and try again and again until I am satisfied; then in my head I begin to elaborate the work . . . the underlying idea never deserts me. It rises, it grows. I hear and see the image in front of me from every angle . . .'[10]

Psychologists have demonstrated that memory is a type of intelligence; in fact, intelligence is nothing more than a specialized bank of memories. Nobel laureate Daniel Kahneman famously said that intelligence is 'not only the ability to reason; it is also the ability to find the relevant material in memory and to deploy attention when needed'.[11] That in turn leads us to delve into how creative people enhance their memories so that their recall is richer and deeper than that of the average person.

Henry Roediger, who runs the Memory Lab at Washington University in St Louis, has found that 'memory champions' have high cognitive ability. He says: 'We found that one of the biggest differences between memory athletes and the rest of us is in a cognitive ability that's not a direct measure of memory at all but of attention.'[12]

Simply put, people who have developed their memories to a very high level have learnt how to focus their attention on essential information. They have highly developed 'attentional control', i.e. the ability to maintain heightened focus on essential information for long periods of time. In other words, a side effect of the effort that these champions put into memorizing stuff is that they learn to concentrate for extended periods of time. This ability can be then usefully applied to any task requiring deep concentration.

How do we develop these skills? We know a few basic ones such as mnemonics. Our favourites are 'How I wish I could calculate pi' (the length of each word denoting the first seven digits of π, i.e. 3.141592), and 'My very educated mother just served us nine pizzas' (the initial letters of the words

MVEMJSUNP symbolizing the order of planets orbiting the sun). But what about a broader way to improve your memory and learning power?

The Internet is full of memory-strengthening resources. On Coursera, 'Learning How to Learn', an extremely popular massive open online course, has a dedicated section on procrastination and memory. We have done this course and can vouch for its effectiveness. In this chapter we will focus on two popular ways to boost your memory.

Tip 1: The mind palace: Fans of the hit British TV series *Sherlock* will remember this ancient Greek technique being used by the titular detective in the finale of the third season. After being shot dead at point-blank range, Sherlock discovers the answers to staying alive within his brain by going into his 'mind palace', where he has stored a vast collection of memories.

This is a dramatized version of what is called the method of loci, a technique that uses visualization of familiar locations to quickly recall information. Nelson Dellis, four-time USA Memory Champion, explains it thus: 'You want to turn information you're trying to memorise into something that your brain naturally prefers to absorb. Once you have that picture, the next step is to store it somewhere—somewhere in your mind you can safely store it and retrieve it later.'[13]

Dellis used the mind-palace technique to memorize two decks of playing cards for the USA Memory Championship. He used a strategy to assign cards to people, for example, the king of hearts was his father, the queen of hearts was his mother, nine of hearts was his wife, etc. And then he visualized these people along a path through one of his old homes as a proxy to remember the cards.

Ron White, a two-time USA Memory Champion, had set an American record for the fastest time to memorize a deck of cards—one minute twenty-seven seconds (Dellis would go on to beat that record in 2011). White's process involves two steps, namely, creating a mental map and creating a substitute image for each playing card. He then places ten items of furniture (e.g. desk, TV, cupboard, bed, mirror) in five rooms of his house. Then, he looks around each room in a clockwise direction and memorizes each of these fifty items inside his house. These items have to be memorized to a point where you can repeat them flawlessly. Finally, add two more furniture items in a new room or two items in your yard. That is fifty-two items for fifty-two cards. Now that the map has been created, each card becomes one item.

To get to the point where you can use the method of loci takes time and, you have guessed it, practice. Even if you don't really master it, the very act of practising this technique can help shape the way you think and remember. In fact, a study[14] found that using the method of loci can cause lasting changes to the brain itself.

Tip 2: The SQRQS model: Can you remember how this chapter began? We don't blame you if you can't. We struggle to remember details of a long article or a book, often forgetting vital parts. And this lapse of memory is one of the biggest hurdles to our goal of achieving deep focus in our chosen fields.

In fund management, for instance, we have to remember key portions from annual reports of companies. Annual reports can run into hundreds of pages, with many tiny details hidden among them. Let us say a company changes an accounting policy or faces an auditor's qualification. What if we forget that many years ago, the company faced the exact same situation? We miss what could be a pattern. This could be a serious lapse while choosing a stock to buy or sell.

Dobson's *The Brain Book* has a neat technique which could help us remember the material contained in the books that we read. The technique is called SQRQS:

Step 1: Scan: Before you start reading, scan the book. Decipher the length and how the information is presented.

Step 2: Question: Now ask yourself, 'What do you know about this already? What do you hope to find out?' This helps establish a context and find meaning. Remember, you learn by associating new information with what you already know.

Step 3: Read: Now read the book. If you pause between sections, you will increase your recall even further.

Step 4: Question: Put down the book and test yourself. What specifically do you remember? How would you explain it to someone else? What do you think about it? Did you disagree with any of it?

Step 5: Scan: If Step 4 highlighted things you hadn't remembered but wanted to, one last scan will fill in the blanks.

4. Work hard and produce lots of ideas

Stanford professor Robert I. Sutton writes in his book *Weird Ideas that Work: How to Build a Creative Company* [15]: '[O]riginal thinkers . . . will come up with many ideas that are strange mutations, dead ends and utter failures. The cost is worthwhile because they also generate a larger pool of ideas—especially novel ideas.'

The renowned Bengali film director Satyajit Ray directed thirty-six movies in a thirty-five-year career stretching from the mid-1950s to the early 1990s. In addition to that, he published more than two dozen books in Bengali (short stories, novels and poetry) and three books analysing cinema (in India and around the world). From this phenomenal body of work emerged a few masterworks that have defined filmmaking in the twentieth century and garnered accolades at home and abroad.

Ray's career is not dissimilar to William Shakespeare's. Many of us will remember from our high school days his most famous plays—*King Lear*, *Othello* and *Macbeth*—but most of us don't realize that he wrote at least thirty-seven other plays that we know of: a similar rate of productivity to Ray's.

Take your time to come up with an idea but then don't dawdle; keep the tempo of idea creation high. If you produce lots of good ideas, it is but inevitable that some of them will be great ones. In fact, Wallace and Gruber[16]—experts who have studied in detail how intellectual giants such as Charles Darwin, Michael Faraday, Einstein and William Wordsworth produced a stream of path-breaking work—say that a hallmark of creative people is the willingness to have lots of creative projects on the go at the same time:

> We use the term enterprise to stand for a group of related projects and activities broadly enough defined so that (1) the enterprise may continue when the creative person finds one path blocked but another open toward the same goal and (2) when success is achieved the enterprise does not come to an end but generates new tasks and projects that continue it.
>
> Enterprises rarely come singly. The creative person differentiates a number of main lines of activity. This has the advantage that when one enterprise grinds to a halt, productive work does not cease. The person has an agenda, some measure of control over the rhythm and sequence with which different enterprises are activated. This control can be used to deal with needs for variety, with obstacles encountered . . .

A second outstanding characteristic of enterprises is their longevity and durability. To take only one example, Milton began the work that led to 'Paradise Lost' in 1640 but did not complete it until 1667. It was the major project within the enterprise of writing epic poems; that enterprise was one among several – politics, prose pamphlets, and the shorter poems.

5. Don't worry about being late

Procrastinating can be good. It is a question of balance, and of careful decision-making. Alongside being a hard worker, you should be happy to be late, to delay things until you have hit upon an idea/created something which is fresh and original (rather than a copy-paste job). You have to let your mind meander for the original idea to hit you.

Some of the most creative equity analysts we have worked with routinely produced research notes late, regardless of what carrots and sticks were waved at them. They are not driven to seek the approval of others and the reward which comes from that. For them, their work first and foremost is its own reward. As it is for all creative people.

Take, for example, the poems of William Butler Yeats: 'Lest it be thought that liberation "from the pressure of will" produced outpourings of untrammelled spontaneity, be it noted that Yeats was an extremely deliberate writer. He "followed a pattern of composition which was to vary very little for the rest of his life: prose draft, rough verse drafts, fair copy, magazine publication and then further revisions for the first printing in book form." . . . one of his biographers stresses "the tremendous organisation that informs the poems and the poet; every crisis is mastered and every poem comes out of years of preparation".'[17]

Leonardo da Vinci started painting the *Mona Lisa* in 1503 and then left it incomplete. He completed the masterpiece just before his death in 1519. As art historian William Pannapacker explains: 'Leonardo's studies of how light strikes a sphere, for example, enable the continuous modelling of the 'Mona Lisa' and 'St. John the Baptist'. His work in optics might have delayed a project but his final achievements in painting depended on the experiments . . . Far from being a distraction like many of his contemporaries thought—they represent a lifetime of productive brainstorming, a private working out of the ideas on which his more public work depended . . . You cannot produce a work of genius according to a schedule or an outline.'[18]

6. Jam with other creatives and find allies

It is extremely rare for creative people to work in a void. Such people have a range of associates around them to provide emotional support (especially encouragement in the face of setbacks), intellectual support (especially thoughts on how to see the same idea differently) and practical help (money, meals, etc). *Creative People at Work* has a riveting chapter on how the English poet William Wordsworth wrote his poems with the help of others—particularly his sister, Dorothy, and the poet Samuel Taylor Coleridge. More specifically, the composition of one of Wordsworth's most famous poems—'Daffodils' (also called 'I Wandered Lonely as a Cloud')—relied heavily on inputs from his sister. As described in Chapter 4 of *Creative People at Work*:

> Wordsworth's living arrangements facilitated bringing others into the process of reworking . . . This was true of his collaborative relationship with Coleridge and more pervasive . . . in his relationship with his sister Dorothy.

Dorothy was an extremely sensitive observer and recorder of the Lake District's landscape scenes where she and her brother lived and walked. Wordsworth's famous poem 'Daffodils', composed in 1804, finds its source in the vocabulary and images of Dorothy's 'Journal' where she describes the daffodils she and her brother had seen on a walk together . . . Wordsworth's poem begins:

> 'I wandered lonely as a cloud
> That floats on high o'er vales and hills
> When all at once I saw a crowd,
> A host of golden daffodils;
> Along the lake, beneath the trees,
> Ten thousand dancing in the breeze . . .'[19]

Dorothy had described the scene in her 'Journal' in April 1802:

> 'I never saw daffodils so beautiful they grew upon mossy stones and about them, some rested their heads upon these stones as on a pillow for weariness and the rest tossed and reeled and danced and seemed as if they verily laughed with the wind that blew upon them. . .'

Thus one of the best known poems in English begins with a joint experience, a scene observed by William and Dorothy . . .

Even for those of us who are working in more prosaic fields such as finance, marketing or HR, brainstorming and discussing with groups of thinkers can be a very powerful driver of creativity. Saurabh has three close friends who work in the investment management industry, all of whom read widely and hold strong points of view on a range of topics (from politics to restaurants and music). The four of them meet once every other month for dinner and hold forth on various topics. Saurabh comes out of these dinners with not only suggestions on what books to read but with new ways of seeing the world, new ideas which he can play around with in the subsequent weeks. Some of his most creative investment ideas have emerged from these bimonthly dinners with friends.

Creativity is a continuous, multistep endeavour

After everything we have said so far, we have to admit that there is no standard method which works when it comes to a subject as open-ended and fluid as creativity and original thinking.

As Ed Catmull, the president of both Pixar and Disney Animation Studios and a pioneer of animation, writes in *Creativity, Inc.*[20], there are no set rules for being creative or keeping creativity alive. Anything that can be listed as a rule is already halfway to becoming obsolete.

Arguably, the two most accessible studies on creativity over the past twenty years are Grant's *Originals*, and Wallace and Gruber's *Creative People at Work*. Both books stress that there is no cut-and-dried recipe for creativity. Nor is there a fixed set of personality traits which indicates whether one person will be more or less creative than her neighbour. Both books stress that creativity is the result of purposeful, determined and sustained effort rather than being the result— as the popular preconception goes—of a light bulb going off in the head of a genius.

Creativity requires constant self-examination (to understand your own biases, prejudices and set ways of thinking) and relentless pursuit of self-discovery, renewal and trying things in new ways. In Catmull's words: 'Often finding a solution is a multi-step endeavour. There is a problem you are trying to solve—think of it as an oak tree—and then there all the other problems—think of these as saplings . . . Even after all these years, I'm surprised to find problems that have existed right in front of me . . . For me, the key to solving these problems is finding ways to see what's working and what isn't, which sounds a lot simpler than it is. Pixar today is managed according to this principle, but in a way I've been searching all my life for better ways of seeing.'

Our experience of life has been that while quitting well-paid jobs in Mumbai's financial services sector was a nerve-wracking experience for middle-class professionals like us, the pay-off of being able to do new things, learn new skills and enjoy new experiences (such as writing this book) is more than worth the generous monthly pay cheque that we used to get from our erstwhile employers.

In fact, in mid-2018, when Saurabh began building Marcellus Investment Managers, he consciously looked around not just for the smartest people he knew in the investment management profession but also for people who love to read extensively, to discuss ideas for hours on end and—at the same time—know how to work hard. In fact, for most of the team which founded Marcellus, the very decision to leave behind the world of broking, investment banking and wealth management in order to build Marcellus hinged on such considerations, i.e. they wanted to spend lots of time reading and discussing ideas rather than chasing targets, budgets, deadlines and other such ephemera from the conventional business world. Marcellus continues to hire people who enjoy reading, at length and in depth, while having the maturity to bounce half-formed ideas off colleagues. Saurabh has repeatedly seen that from the seeds of such protean ideas great investments are born.

Creativity case study: How great investigative writers excel

Investigative journalists are paid to uncover undiscovered facts and perspectives. The best investigative journalists have the mental agility to deal with complexity and detail alongside the courage to acknowledge unpleasant realities. In this section we outline how four outstanding investigative writers —Robert Caro, Steve Coll, Ramachandra Guha and Manu S. Pillai— pursue excellence in their craft. For those who haven't come across their work, here are short bios of these four writers:

Robert Caro: A two-time Pulitzer Prize winner, Caro is famous for his biographies of Robert Moses, the powerful but racist civil servant who built most of the expressways, bridges and parks around New York City, and of former US President Lyndon B. Johnson. Caro began his career as a newspaper journalist but the seven years which took him to write his book on Robert Moses—a book which won him his first Pulitzer—resulted in him becoming a full-time historian. Such is Caro's reputation for exhaustive research and detail that he is sometimes invoked by reviewers who call writers 'Caroesque' for their extensive research.

Steve Coll: Another two-time Pulitzer Prize winner, Coll is currently the dean of the Columbia University Graduate School of Journalism. The first Steve Coll book we read was *On the Grand Trunk Road: A Journey into South Asia*[21], a book written while Coll was living in India as the *Washington Post*'s South Asia bureau chief. Coll cemented his legendary status with remarkably well-researched books: on the Securities and Exchange Commission's (SEC) battle against Wall Street during the 1980s (co-authored with David A. Vise[22]); on the history of the Central Intelligence Agency (CIA)[23]; on how Al-Qaeda is run and how Pakistan's Inter-Services Intelligence (ISI) makes a fool out of everybody else[24]. So deep is Coll's knowledge that the US government turns to him for guidance on some of these matters.

Ramachandra Guha: A versatile intellectual, Guha is arguably contemporary India's most famous historian. He is best known for his epic trilogy of books which capture India's evolution over the past 150 years—*India After Gandhi*[25], *Gandhi Before India*[26], and *Gandhi: The Years That Changed the World*[27]. His research into the social history of Indian cricket culminated in an award-winning book—*A Corner of a Foreign Field: The Indian History of a British Sport*[28].

Manu S. Pillai: By far the youngest of this quartet of great writers, Pillai is arguably the brightest young historian in India. In 2015, the BBC appointed him as a research assistant to help Sunil Khilnani with his outstanding book-cum-radio show *Incarnations: India in 50 Lives*[29]. Subsequently, in the last three years, Pillai has published three well-researched books: *The Ivory Throne: Chronicles of the House of Travancore*[30], *Rebel Sultans: The Deccan from Khilji to Shivaji*[31], and *The Courtesan, the Mahatma and the Italian Brahmin: Tales from Indian History*[32]. We can safely say that these books are riveting tales of intrigue and conflict that would hold your attention for hours on end.

So what marks out these great writers?

1. Question received wisdom: Although Mark Twain said that 'whenever you find yourself on the side of the majority, it is time to pause and reflect', most of us live in an echo chamber surrounded by people who are culturally and economically similar to us. We tell them what they like to hear and, for the most part, they return the favour. Great researchers buck this trend by having a more sceptical mindset. For them the natural thing to do is to question the status quo rather than accept things as they are.

For example, in his five-volume biography of President Johnson, Caro dismantles the conventional narrative built around Johnson by his previous biographers—that he rose from a dirt-poor Texan background and worked his way up to the presidency courtesy of his intelligence and industriousness. Caro shows how money from the Texan construction company Brown & Root underpinned Johnson's ascent. Thanks to Caro's research, we now know that Johnson was the first modern-day American president to cut deals with firms that benefit from government contracts. Brown & Root provided money to Democrat politicians who needed election campaign finance. In return, these politicians supported Johnson, who in turn saw to it that Brown & Root got the government contracts it sought.

2. Absorb the detail but see the big picture: Before they hit the 'eureka moment', great researchers learn to keep digging. And in order to avoid getting lost in the detail, they learn to keep the big picture in mind. Coll provides a masterly demonstration of this in *Directorate S: The C.I.A. and America's Secret Wars in Afghanistan and Pakistan, 2001–2016*. The book is based on 550 interviews (conducted over 2007–17 across the USA, Pakistan, Afghanistan and Europe by Coll and his four researchers); hundreds of WikiLeaks cables; court documents from seven cases fought in US courts; twenty sets of documents from the US government; around thirty reports published by a variety of bodies (eg. the US Army, the London School of Economics, Atlantic Council, etc.); and more than 200 other books and news reports.

And yet through all of this, Coll keeps his and the reader's focus on the central narrative, namely: (a) Osama bin Laden and Al-Qaeda used the Taliban and Pakistan's ISI to create a base in Afghanistan from which to attack US interests; (b) the ISI made extensive use of US money to fund terrorists in Afghanistan who eventually turned their guns and bombs on the USA itself; and (c) the US intelligence agencies persistently underestimated the threat posed by bin Laden and the ISI in spite of the considerable body of evidence available to the CIA about the same.

3. The courage to question your own hypothesis: Outstanding researchers have the willingness to continue researching even when the facts suggest that their own initial hypothesis is incorrect. While most biographers of Mahatma Gandhi have typically relied on the great man's account of his own life (which runs into 5,000 pages) along with Richard Attenborough's 1982 movie, *Gandhi*, Guha takes a different approach in his two-volume biography of the Mahatma.

Guha repeatedly digs out contemporaneous sources and cites them in his books even when they contradict the Mahatma's own account of his life. For example, in Chapter 35 of the second volume of the biography, Guha cites a letter written in the mid-1940s by Horace Alexander, a close friend of Gandhi's. The letter dealt with the chastity tests that Gandhi was subjecting himself to. To quote Guha: 'The goal of the experiment was his old, continuing, obsession with the goal of brahmacharya—the instrument, his grand-niece, Manu. Sometime in late December 1946, Gandhi asked Manu to join him in the bed he slept in. He was seeking to test, or perhaps further test, his conquest of sexual desire.'[33]

Guha then quotes from Manu's own diary about what she thought of these experiments. Then he concludes, 'So, contrary to what has become the received wisdom on the subject, there may have been, as it were, two sides to the story. Both Gandhi and Manu may have wanted to go through this experiment, or ordeal. To be sure, there was a certain amount of imposition— from his side.' Guha knows that for him and for other devotees of the great man, this isn't an easy conclusion to reach. However, he does not flinch from doing the research and telling us what he makes of the situation.

4. Communicate by simplifying complexity: The oldest book on human communication is Aristotle's *Rhetorica*[34]. Aristotle believed that an effective communicator must use compelling logic to make his point. Great researchers are adept at this. In India today, more than any other writer, Manu S. Pillai is communicating Indian history to a contemporary audience with a short attention span. He says, 'The books I read made it clear to me that the typical (and I daresay tedious) linear narratives which masquerade as history in popular imagination are highly limited, unable by their very nature to do justice to the magnificence of India's story . . . it was work on my first book, *The Ivory Throne*, that really got me questioning received wisdom and notions—my protagonist, Sethu Lakshmi Bayi, was the last female Maharajah of Travancore . . . I wanted to resurrect her because she deserved to be more than a passing footnote in the story of Kerala. The themes I tried to weave around her tale—the matrilineal system, the invention of "tradition", and the constant intermixing of cultures, in ways that would amaze and perhaps even shock some of us today— challenged elementary concepts I had learnt in school, based as they were on patriarchal standards and viewed through historically limited lens. As soon as my eyes were opened, I wanted to combine solid research with appealing language—

after all, what is the point of discovering the past in all its glory, if it cannot be disseminated to a larger audience?'[35]

* * *

Key takeaways from this chapter

- Identifying your deep driving desire is the first step towards original thinking. Then ask yourself whether you want to strive for excellence within the pre-existing system or whether you want to change the system. Both are valid avenues for doing something worthwhile.

- How can you develop original thinking and creativity? Read widely alongside deep specialization, explore the world, enhance your memory, work hard and produce lots of ideas, don't worry about being late, jam with other creatives and find allies.

- Memories play a vital role in building perceptions and hence influencing and shaping life thereafter. Regular practice of the method of loci (which uses visualizations and familiar information about one's environment to quickly and efficiently recall information) and the SQRQS Model (Scan–Question–Read–Question–Scan) can help shape your thought process and retention power.

Sanjeev Bikhchandani: The Billionaire Who Broke All the Rules

Sanjeev Bikhchandani is the founder of Info Edge, which owns portals such as Naukri, 99acres, Jeevansathi, as well as stakes in large start-ups such as Zomato and Policybazaar. Sanjeev is a maverick of sorts. Not only has he rejected softer options repeatedly in life (for example, he opted for entrepreneurship over a cushy job very early on), he has time and again gone for the more painful options and persevered with them for long periods of time (for example, building Naukri.com after the collapse of the tech bubble).

Although he does not have a formal venture capital background, Sanjeev takes contrarian calls when it comes to investing early in start-ups (for example, Zomato, Policybazaar). And despite staying in a city like Delhi, he does not have a high-flying, publicity-hogging, page-three lifestyle, even though he is a billionaire. Sanjeev's ability to think differently goes well with his in-your-face, frank personality. We met Sanjeev on 20 July 2019 at his home, in an affluent neighbourhood in south Delhi on a drizzly Saturday afternoon. Our meeting was in the basement of Sanjeev's home where he has a large office. Sanjeev regaled us with the story of his life and his investment decisions over many cups of coffees and *nankhatais*, and over many laugh-out-loud moments.

We began by asking him if the entrepreneur bug had bitten him early in life. 'When I was ten years old I wanted to be Rajesh Khanna; when I was eleven years old I wanted to be Sunil Gavaskar; when I was twelve years old in 1975, somehow it came in my head that I should think of being an entrepreneur. There are kids who will do what their fathers did. And there are other kids who just won't. So I'm in the latter category. My father was a doctor in the government. So I said two things—I won't become a doctor, and I won't join the government. I wasn't a very obedient child. So I didn't like to do what we all do,' he told us plain-faced even as we looked on in amazement because as kids—especially in 1975—we did what our parents told us to do, no questions asked, especially when you are academically brilliant, as Sanjeev clearly was. After his schooling at the prestigious St. Columba's School in Delhi, Sanjeev went to the hallowed St Stephen's College for his BA in Economics. After a three-year stint at the advertising major Lintas, Sanjeev completed his postgraduate diploma in management from IIM Ahmedabad.

Sanjeev was a St Stephen's graduate and an IIM-A alumnus, and one would think that the world was his playground. But instead of taking a cushy job at a Citibank or HUL or leaving for greener pastures overseas, Sanjeev chose to remain in Delhi and work for Hindustan Milkfood Manufacturers (HMM, which eventually merged with GSK Consumer Healthcare). His reason for staying on in Delhi was interesting: 'I wanted to stay at home and save money for my start-up. I was very clear from my teenage days that I would build my own firm.'

While at HMM, watching his colleagues look for opportunities in the 'Jobs' sections of magazines, Sanjeev got the idea of a jobs portal. No one would leave an MNC job with GSK but everyone in the firm seemed interested in knowing about the opportunities in the market. Convinced of the business opportunity around a jobs listings directory, Sanjeev quit his job in 1990.

From 1990 until 1997, Sanjeev slogged hard in pursuit of his idea. When we asked him about giving up an MNC job to chase what seemed like a wild idea, Sanjeev calmly attributed it to ego: 'It is about persistence and sheer stubbornness because I refused to go back to a job branded as a failed entrepreneur. If you're struggling, no matter how long you struggle, you're simply not successful yet. You're not a failure, you're just not a success yet. The moment you quit entrepreneurship and go back to a job you're declared a failure. You have nothing, you have no victory to declare. I couldn't stomach being branded a failure.'

Sanjeev's ego was backed by huge amounts of toil. Through the 1990s, he held down three to four jobs to sustain an income. He taught at management institutes such as Delhi's Institute of Management Technology (IMT), trained MBA-entrance exam aspirants at coaching classes and was even the consulting editor for the 'Jobs' page at the *Pioneer* newspaper. 'I lost the fear (of not having a salary) and actually began to enjoy the independence,' he told us, remembering the early days of struggle. Seven years after quitting his job, Sanjeev and his co-founders started Naukri.com in 1997. Within four years, the dot-com bubble had burst but Sanjeev was extremely lucky to get funding from ICICI Venture in 2000, just before the collapse of the bubble. Knowing how lucky they were, Sanjeev put most of the funds into fixed deposits to protect the money.

But the real effort was in keeping his start-up alive in a post-bust world. By 1997, as India's tiny Internet base started picking up, job-seeking firms went the online route. Learning from his work experience at Lintas, Sanjeev demanded a 100 per cent advance for job listings, and it worked. Despite these revenues coming in, Sanjeev was burning money rapidly. 'I was clear about one thing—that I will never run after money. So the DNA comes from there. But the task becomes to create a product or service which is so wanted that people are willing to pay you a 100 per cent advance. So, we kept raising the bar,' he told us.

The venture capital money could only last him so long. Hitesh Oberoi (the current CEO of Info Edge), who joined Sanjeev in 2000 to head sales and marketing, suggested that they use the direct sales model. Sanjeev and Hitesh crunched their numbers and saw that their average salesman was selling Rs 50,000 per month of advertising inventory at a total cost of Rs 22,000 per month. The salesman thus became a profit centre. 'Any successful company to scale needs what I call a repeatable profitable unit. In the case of McDonald's, maybe it is a burger or an outlet. So within two years we had 240 salespeople across eleven branches across eleven cities in India—and the company had turned around. That was how we survived the meltdown,' Sanjeev told us.

By the time it listed in November 2006, Info Edge reported revenues of Rs 84 crore and profits of Rs 13 crore for the year ending March 2006. The IPO got a huge response, getting oversubscribed more than fifty times and the stock price closing at Rs 593, compared to the IPO price of Rs 320[36]. Upon listing, Info Edge's market cap was Rs 1,618 crore, and Sanjeev—after sixteen years of toil—owned 43 per cent of the company (as of

31 March 2007). At the time of this book going to press in 2020, Info Edge's market cap (as per the Bombay Stock Exchange[37]) is Rs 28,287 crore, implying a growth rate, between 2006 and 2020, of 24 per cent CAGR.

CHAPTER 7

Teaming Up with the Best

'It soon became clear, however, that Abraham Lincoln would emerge the undisputed captain of this most unusual cabinet, truly a team of rivals. The powerful competitors who had originally disdained Lincoln became colleagues who helped him steer the country through its darkest days.'

—Doris Kearns Goodwin[1]

Abraham Lincoln was the underdog among the Republican nominees for the 1860 presidential elections in the USA. Lincoln, then a former representative from Illinois was, on paper, no match for the candidates in the fray for the nomination, namely: William Seward, senator from New York; Simon Cameron, senator from Pennsylvania; and Salmon P. Chase, governor of Ohio. And yet Lincoln went on to win the Republican nomination and then the election.

After he won the election, Lincoln could have chosen his senior team like any other leader—from his allies and people who shared the same views and opinions as him. However, Lincoln did something extraordinary. He chose the same distinguished people who were his rivals for the Republican nomination. Thus, he made Seward the Secretary of State, Cameron the Secretary of War and Chase his head of treasury. As if this wasn't enough, he chose former Democrats as well. Edward Bates from Missouri became attorney general, Gideon Welles became Secretary of the Navy and Montgomery Blair was made postmaster general. This became the team of rivals that went into the presidency as the US Civil War was entering its final phase. Lincoln then pushed through the historic Thirteenth Amendment to the US Constitution which outlawed slavery across the country. Unfortunately, his career was cut short when he was assassinated in April 1865.

Lincoln's strength of character is legendary, and he is regarded as among the greatest US presidents ever. In her book *Team of Rivals: The Political Genius of Abraham Lincoln*, Goodwin quotes Leo Tolstoy, 'Washington was a typical American. Napoleon was a typical Frenchman, but Lincoln was a humanitarian as broad as the world. He was bigger than his country—bigger than all Presidents put together.'

Lincoln's team of rivals speaks of a very highly evolved leader who consciously chooses not to surround himself with sycophants. Instead, he chose highly qualified rivals. Why did he do that? And how did that experiment pan out? This story lies at the centre of collaboration.

Humans and collaboration: Made for each other

Aristotle famously said, 'Man is by nature a social animal; an individual who is unsocial naturally and not accidentally is either beneath our notice or more than human. Society is something that precedes the individual.' While we might want to believe in our uniqueness, identity, individual beliefs and values as being the core of our being, scientific research and evolution show that we are wired to be social animals. In his book *Social: Why Our Brains Are Wired to Connect*, psychologist Matthew Lieberman, who is a professor and director of the Social Cognitive Neuroscience Laboratory at UCLA, focuses on three major adaptations in our brains that lead us to become more connected to the social world.

First, there is a neural overlap between social pain (say, the loss of a loved one) and physical pain. Functional magnetic resonance imaging (fMRI) scans of the brain show that our brains treat social and physical pain in a similar manner (a point which we discussed in Chapter 5 when talking about clutter reduction). Second, our brain has a network devoted for social networks. Lieberman writes: 'The greatest ideas always require teamwork to bring them to fruition; social reasoning is what allows us to build and maintain the social relationship and infrastructure needed for teams to thrive.' And third, our sense of self is malleable and this leads us to help others more than ourselves.

Interestingly, Lieberman writes that humans have evolved in three stages, each of which are repeated as we grow up:

Stage 1: Connection and the desire to stay connected.

Stage 2: Mind reading, which makes us form and maintain groups that we connect with.

Stage 3: Harmonizing, i.e. neural adaptations that allow group beliefs and values to influence our own. Thus, our connection with a larger social group is both evolutionary and part of our neural make-up.

In fact, collaboration and co-operation also have deep evolutionary origins. As Yuval Noah Harari notes in *Sapiens: A Brief History of Humankind*[2]: 'Ants and bees can also work together in huge numbers, but they do so in a rigid manner and only with close relatives. Wolves and chimpanzees cooperate far more flexibly than ants, but they can do so only with small numbers of other individuals that they know intimately. Sapiens can cooperate in extremely flexible ways with countless number of strangers. That's why Sapiens rule the world, whereas ants eat our leftovers and chimps are locked up in zoos and research laboratories.'

Collaboration is the simple task of working with others towards a common goal. Thus, collaboration is everywhere. Our parents, teachers, mentors are all collaborators in ensuring we get the best that they can give. We work in organizations with teams sharing common targets and goals. In the apartment blocks and neighbourhoods where we stay, we collaborate to ensure a harmonious environment.

There is only so much that an individual can achieve in life by herself. But a team that collaborates can not only bring the best of out of each team member but collectively the sum of the parts can be greater than the whole. Almost every product that we see and use—even our relationships—are born of collective effort. A single brilliant woman might be a visionary leader. But organizations that develop great products are the result of teams working in collaboration, and great institutions outlast great individuals.

Co-operation is hardwired in humans. As Harari notes in his book, social co-operation is key to our survival and reproduction. Whether it involves sitting around a fire in a cave or—as is more likely these days—using a collaboration tool such as Slack, collaboration is an important element of a life well-lived. As we train ourselves to specialize in our chosen area of knowledge and simplify our lives, we should also learn to work with diverse talents. A team of members with different perspectives working towards common goals should enrich every team member's life.

Collaboration is a soft edge

In his book, *The Soft Edge: Where Great Companies Find Lasting Success*[3], US journalist Rich Karlgaard outlines a triangle of long-term company success. The base of the triangle is the strategic base (fundamental attributes) and the two sides are the hard edge (precise execution) and the soft edge (expression of your deepest values). The soft edge consists of the following pillars: trust, smarts, teams, taste, and story. Collaboration and teamwork are critical parts of the soft edge, given that teams are one of the five pillars of the soft edge.

While most successful companies eventually develop successful strategies and efficient execution, developing the soft edge is what takes these successful companies even further. Great strategy and execution can be copied but maintaining a soft edge is a key differentiating factor, especially in the present era when technology erodes competitive advantages much faster. Karlgaard writes: 'a) Great, enduring organizations are masters at both the hard and soft edges b) top performance depends on finding the right balance of hard and soft skills for any given situations and c) on balance, the soft edge is gaining currency. In this tough, global Great Reset economy, mastery of the oft-neglected soft edge will become as critical as (or even more critical than) mastery of the hard edge.'

HDFC Bank is India's largest bank based on market capitalization (as per the Bombay Stock Exchange on 4 Jan 2020). The origin of the first team at HDFC Bank, when Aditya Puri built an elite team of bankers from diverse backgrounds, is an apt example of collaboration. Puri is well-known for getting conflicting teams to contribute towards a common organizational goal. Several banking industry veterans told us of regular meetings and conference calls with team leaders that were helmed by Puri. These meetings weren't for the faint-hearted, especially when the targets hadn't been met. As veteran banking journalist Tamal Bandyopadhyay writes in *HDFC Bank 2.0: From Dawn to Digital*[4] (a follow-up to his original 2013 book on HDFC Bank, *A Bank for the Buck*[5]): 'If he wants to, Aditya can be really abrasive too. In a meeting, if you haven't prepared something despite him telling you to do it or you have missed something right under your nose, he can be brutal and cut you to pieces.' Tamal's book has a section dedicated to Puri's legacy where he describes how Puri keeps politics out of work. He quotes Abhay Aima (group head, equities and private banking at HDFC Bank) as follows: 'He [Abhay] thinks the key to Aditya's leadership is being able to deal with different people differently. "You can't have one fixed rule; you have to be flexible. Aditya does that. If I and X colleague of mine were handled the same way, either I would have left by now or my colleague."'

A leader's importance is not that he does everything. The reason a leader is central to the fortunes of a company is because the leader plays the role of coordinating various parts of the company at tricky junctures where various teams seem to be locked in conflict with each other. It is this ability to manage conflicts seamlessly that separates the great leaders from the good ones. Puri is a great example of a leader with an uncanny ability to manage conflicts within his team. In this regard, a leader resembles an air traffic controller with a very high level of emotional intelligence whose critical ability is to manage many aircraft and pilots with precision by making it apparent that if everyone remains calm, things will be normal and if anyone panics, there will be consequences. A CEO's primary job is thus managing the entire team of leaders.

India's former cricket captain Sourav Ganguly's great skill—other than his own batting talent—was getting a talented and diverse team, which included the likes of Yuvraj Singh,

Harbhajan Singh, Zaheer Khan, Sachin Tendulkar, Virender Sehwag, Rahul Dravid and V.V.S. Laxman, to work together as one unit. Ganguly's job was also to get team politics out of cricket. This requires a great deal of maturity and emotional security because you will get attacked by hot-headed, high-achieving leaders who will accuse you of taking sides.

Puri knows that the 'risk' and 'lending' functions at HDFC Bank cannot be allowed to fight with each other if the bank is to deliver the steady growth it is famous for. Although superficially it appears that the risk and lending functions have conflicting goals (wherein the risk function is supposed to act as a check and balance against the lending function), Puri's job is to make people realize that they are ultimately shooting for the same goal: greater profitability for HDFC Bank. The resolution of conflicting goals is a tough job that no business school can teach you.

Looking beyond HDFC Bank, we find in Amul another example of a very evolved leadership collaborating with a diverse set of stakeholders. Amul is India's legendary dairy company, and the man who engineered this remarkable enterprise's rise to glory is Verghese Kurien. Born into an affluent Syrian Anglican family in Kerala in 1921, Kurien excelled in academics and sports first in Loyola College in Chennai, then in the College of Engineering (Guindy) and, finally, in Michigan State University (where he was sent on an elite scholarship sponsored by the government of India). Upon his return to India in 1949, the Government sent him to work at a run-down creamery[6] in Anand in what was then part of Bombay State and is now Gujarat.

Kurien hated his government job in Anand and when he quit a few months later, Tribhuvandas Patel, a prominent political leader of local farmers, persuaded Kurien to stay and help run the Kaira District Co-operative Milk Producers' Union

Limited, which came to be known popularly as Amul dairy). Twenty-five years later this co-operative was merged into other co-operatives to create the now legendary Gujarat Co-operative Milk Marketing Federation Ltd (GCMMF).

Arguably, the most striking example of sustained co-operation on an epic scale in India, GCMMF generated revenues in FY19 of Rs 33,000 crores (nearly $4.5 billion). That is three times as much as its closest competitor Nestlé India's revenues, and only 20 per cent shy of HUL's revenues. On this measure, GCMMF is India's second largest FMCG company. Not only is GCMMF big, it grows much faster than its rivals. Over the past decade, GCMMF has grown revenues at 17 per cent CAGR compared to Nestlé's 10 per cent and HUL's 9 per cent. Over the last five years, the growth gap between GCMMF and its two largest rivals has got even bigger! In key FMCG-product categories such as butter, cheese and packaged milk, Amul has been the long-standing market leader in the face of sustained efforts by MNCs to break its dominance. GCMMF is also India's biggest exporter of dairy products.[7]

Growth aside, the scale on which GCMMF operates is astonishing. GCMMF's daily procurement of milk is 2.3 crore litres from more than 18,700 village milk co-operative societies (which include 36 lakh milk producer members). The way GCMMF aggregates the milk produced by these members into the village co-operative dairy, and then further aggregates that into the district co-operative, which in turn feeds into the mother dairy has been studied by numerous management experts. So how does GCMMF give a fair deal to its farmers, its management team, its 10,000 dealers, its one million retailers and its hundreds of millions of customers? At the core of this pioneering co-operative's success appear to be four factors:

Careful cultivation of the brand: Its sixty-year-old brand, with its distinctive imagery of the little girl in the dress with the red polka dots, has been central to Amul's success. Cultivated with great effort and patience, numerous surveys have shown Amul to be one of the most trusted brands in the country. As Kurien says in his autobiography *I Too Had a Dream*[8]:

> ... we had to make the products as attractive as possible to the market ... We sought help from advertising professionals ... In 1966 ... the Amul account was given to the Advertising and Sales Promotion Company (ASP) with the brief that they should dislodge Polson from its 'premier brand' position in Bombay. That was when Eustace Fernandes of ASP created the Amul mascot – the mischievous, endearing girl. The image of the Amul girl went down so well with consumers that very soon it became synonymous with Amul ... Together, the team at ASP gave Amul butter its memorable and catchy campaign tagline 'Utterly, butterly, delicious' – which broke all records to become the longest-running campaigns in Indian advertising history.

Sustained alignment with stakeholders' interests: The practical concept which underpins GCMMF's functioning is that of a fair deal for the farmer and the linked idea of the disintermediation of the middleman. As Harish Damodaran explains in *India's New Capitalists: Caste, Business, and Industry in a Modern Nation*[9]:

> A farmer pouring buffalo milk with 6% fat content to a Gujarat co-operative 2004-05 would receive Rs 13-14 per litre, which is 25-30% more than the corresponding farmgate prices paid by dairies elsewhere in the country ... Taking an average rate of Rs 13, the GCMMF dairies would in 2004-

05 have pumped in around Rs 2,800 crore to their farm members, constituting 70% of their aggregate turnover of Rs 4,000 crore. By contrast, milk purchase costs are less than half of the value of product sales for a company like Nestle India, marking the essential difference between a farmer controlled co-operative and an investor owned concern.

Political and regulatory buy-in: GCMMF and Kurien were able to co-opt almost every single politician of note in independent India to help them promote the cause of Gujarati farmers. As Kurien's autobiography shows, Sardar Patel, Jawaharlal Nehru, Lal Bahadur Shastri, Morarji Desai, T.T. Krishnamachari, Y.B. Chavan, Indira Gandhi—basically anyone who mattered in New Delhi or in the politics of western India—was brought to Anand, wowed by the scale of the miracle in Anand and converted to the cause of promoting Amul. Kurien explains in his autobiography how he repeatedly used his political clout to hurt his competitors by getting bans, embargoes, tariffs, etc. imposed on them. An interesting incident[10] dates to 1962, when, upon the Indian Army's request, Kurien stopped supplying butter to the open market and instead diverted all his output to the army. When a rival company, Polson, took advantage of this by increasing the prices of its butter, Kurien simply went to the government and had Polson's butter output frozen. When Polson's aggrieved promoter complained to the relevant minister in Ahmedabad, Kurien told him in front of the minister, 'You bloody bastard. You come here and speak lies to the Minister. I will castrate you.'

Calculated risk-taking on a consistent basis: With a clear goal of helping farmers earn more from their produce, Kurien repeatedly took major risks to open up new opportunities for Amul. For example, in the 1950s, in the flush season, Amul's farmers were producing twice as much milk as was required by the Bombay market (Amul's main market at that point). The logical thing to do was to convert this surplus into skimmed milk powder and condensed milk. However, at that point of time, the received wisdom the world over was that buffalo milk, which was Amul's main output, could not be used to make skimmed milk powder and condensed milk. In a 'world first' demonstration of its kind, using a machine made by Larsen and Toubro (L&T), Kurien's colleague and college friend H.M. Dalaya demonstrated to the Bombay government that buffalo milk could be used to make skimmed milk powder. A few years later, Amul made cheese from buffalo milk, another world first. Kurien's autobiography *I Too Had a Dream* contains several examples of audacious risk-taking on a pan-India level, including the launch of 'Operation Flood' in 1970—the scheme which took the Amul model pan-India and catapulted India from a milk powder importing beggarly nation into a surplus milk exporter. If, like us, you grew up in the India of the 1970s and 1980s, you owe your physical development to Operation Flood milk and hence to Kurien!

Diversity makes for more effective collaboration

While the ideas of collaboration and teamwork are as old as mankind, workplace diversity is relatively new, especially in the Indian context. In Western countries, the concept of diversity in teams is better understood due to the cultural context in which Western companies have to operate. Management consultant giant McKinsey & Company's 2018 report titled *Delivering through diversity* reinforced the link between diversity (measured on gender and ethnicity) and company financial performance.[11] Companies can develop better inclusion strategies to develop a competitive edge. McKinsey's study expanded on their 2014 research: 'In the original research, using 2014 diversity data, we found that companies in the top quartile for gender diversity on their executive teams were 15 percent more likely to experience above-average profitability than companies in the fourth quartile. In our expanded 2017 data set this number rose to 21 percent and continued to be statistically significant.'

In his book *The Soft Edge*, Karlgaard extends the concept of diversity beyond gender and ethnicity and into cognitive diversity—or differences in mental process, perception and judgement. Apple stands apart in this regard in merging technology with design. At a time when none of the computing greats of that era thought about distinctive design being a differentiating factor, Steve Jobs partnered with industrial designers such as Hartmut Esslinger in the 1980s and with Jony Ive in 1997. Where did Jobs get the idea of simple, clean designs? This is what Walter Isaacson, the author of Steve Jobs's biography, wrote: 'Jobs' love of simplicity in design was honed when he became a practitioner of Buddhism. After dropping out of college, he made a long pilgrimage through India seeking enlightenment, but it was mainly the Japanese path of Zen Buddhism that stirred his sensibilities.'[12]

Collaboration with groups of people outside of our own backgrounds can be a deeply enriching experience. These groups should consist of people from diverse backgrounds—i.e. where the members have varied experiences, different types of expertise and a diversity of beliefs. Groups like these can come together around a shared, simple and uplifting goal. A diverse set of people working towards a common goal will avoid pitfalls such as groupthink and echo chambers. How can you achieve this? Helen Lee Bouygues of the Reboot Foundation and a former partner at McKinsey & Company provides the following tips: 'It's crucial to get outside your personal bubble. You can start small. If you work in accounting, make friends with people in marketing. If you always go to lunch with senior staff, go to a ball game with your junior colleagues. Training yourself this way will help you escape your usual thinking and gain richer insights.'[13]

Both Saurabh and Anupam have worked in the institutional equities business (colloquially referred to as 'broking'), which is known to be extremely competitive. India's broking business has evolved over time. Back in the 1990s, the Indian broking industry was dominated by Bachelor of Commerce (BCom) graduates and chartered accountants (CA) who formed the first generation of Indian brokers (research analysts and salesmen). Equity research was still in its formative years and for recommending a stock, an analyst would mainly need to know the balance sheet inside out.

Post-1991, as the financial services sector slowly opened up to foreign brokerages, the second generation of brokers consisted mainly of IIT graduates and IIM MBAs, especially since the multinational brokers visited these hallowed educational institutions and hired the best talent money could buy.

When Saurabh came to India in 2009, he reckoned he needed people from both talent pools so that the diversity in his team could lead to outstanding results. What led Saurabh to this idea? Saurabh knew that almost two decades since liberalization, two things had changed—first, the Indian economy was now large and diverse enough to warrant a deep understanding of manufacturing processes, supplier and distributor networks, end-user markets, etc.; and second, the quality of accounting in India remained shoddy and hence astute CAs were necessary to understand fabricated and cooked books. So Saurabh blended these two diverse talent pools, such that for each sector he had a sector expert with elite educational qualifications and/or relevant industry expertise, and to support these sector experts, Saurabh placed CAs recruited through a rigorous interview process which zeroed in on forensic accounting skills. In the process, Saurabh achieved diversity in subject matter experts and blended very different ethnic communities—chartered accountants from India's great mercantile communities alongside doctors, engineers, IIT-IIM graduates from middle-class backgrounds.

Here is an example of how this research team could potentially work together. The pharmaceutical sector analyst could be a doctor with many years of experience and deep industry knowledge. He would, therefore, have a better grasp of, say, the efficacy of a newly launched oncology drug than an analyst who is, say, a chartered accountant who probably depends on management commentary to understand the future potential of the same drug. However, the doctor would not be as well-versed with the intricacies of a balance sheet as the CA, whereas the CA might just underestimate or overestimate the revenue potential of the drug. But by combining both the doctor and the CA, you are combining diversity and collaboration to create a higher level of creativity.

Tips for more effective collaboration

Conventional thinking and our collective war stories typically revolve around the cult of the 'great leader'. Numerous tomes have been written about the genius of iconic CEOs and their methods. The reality is that these founders built institutions and groups of people that worked collectively and cohesively to achieve a common goal. These collaborations helped their companies achieve superior levels of performance. The individual brilliance of a founder/promoter/CEO can only get a company so far. While the skills and visions of a founder are critically important at the start-up stage, as a company grows large, the ability of that leader to bring together diverse teams working towards common goals determines the future of the company. Here are two tips for achieving effective collaboration:

1. Workplace design: Jobs's individual brilliance and creativity is well-documented. But Jobs built an institution that has survived and, arguably, thrived even after his death in 2011. What even fewer seem to appreciate is that Jobs was a master at getting diverse groups of people to work together for the common goal. And he knew this very early on. Jobs insisted that computer engineers worked together with artists and designers, i.e. at the intersection of technology and humanities. And Pixar was a great example of this intersection. In 2000, Jobs scrapped a plan to design Pixar's campus into three buildings—one each for computer scientists, artists and executives. He chose, instead, a single vast space with an airy atrium at its centre. As Ed Catmull told Jonah Lehrer: "'The philosophy behind this design is that it's good to put the most important function at the heart of the building," Catmull said. "Well, what's our most important function? It's the interaction of our employees. That's why Steve put a big empty space there. He wanted to create an open area for people to always be talking to each other.'"[14]

Jobs's legacy is evident in the construction of Apple's new headquarters—Apple Park. Jobs was clear that Apple's HQ needed to focus on facilitating collaboration. As Ive said, 'While it is a technical marvel to make glass at this scale, that's not the achievement. The achievement is to make a building where so many people can connect and collaborate and walk and talk.'[15]

But what about a post-Jobs Apple, especially one without Jony Ive (who resigned in 2019)? We believe that the departure of Ive does not really negate Jobs's achievement. Jobs passed away in 2011 while Ive left Apple in 2019. Ive arguably stayed with Apple for most of his high-calibre productive career and this itself is testimony to Jobs's ability to balance beauty in design with commercial interests without disrupting the company by pulling it in either direction. Apple never rested on its laurels, delivering one blockbuster product after the other, starting with the iPod. In its post-Jobs avatar, Apple has created a successful franchise of its Smart Watches and AirPods, and this shows that the spirit of innovation Jobs created still sustains after his era. The ability of Jobs's successor, Tim Cook, will be tested in the future to see if he can do the air traffic controller's role of balancing, and like with flights, sequencing conflicting priorities of Apple's designers and its sales and commercial arms.

Closer home, HUL's Andheri headquarters in Mumbai was starkly different from the behemoth's previous office in south Mumbai. While the older office had hierarchy, structure and seniority written all over it, the newer campus in Andheri embodied a different version of HUL. As Shashank Shah recounts in his book *Win-Win Corporations: The Indian Way of Shaping Successful Strategies*[16]: 'Employees literally cut across all levels as they traverse the facility's length and breadth. Doug Baillie, the CEO of HUL when this new facility was envisaged, was deeply involved in the space plan. He wanted that all employees park their cars in the basement and walk into the reception and the main atrium every day, rather than having separate routes to their floors from the basement, which could minimize interaction.'

2. Incentive design: So, how do you create the perfect team? The typical response would be to say that one should hire brilliant people and pay them well. That might work for a while but as companies get bigger, managing teams gets far more complicated. Google ran Project Aristotle in 2012 to understand team dynamics. The results were astonishing and yet simple. Writing for the *New York Times Magazine*, Charles Duhigg, a Pulitzer Prize-winning author, reported two behaviours that all good teams shared: 'First, on the good teams, members spoke in roughly the same proportion, a phenomenon the researchers referred to as "equality in distribution of conversational turn-taking." . . . Second, the good teams all had high "average social sensitivity" — a fancy way of saying they were skilled at intuiting how others felt based on their tone of voice, their expressions and other nonverbal cues.'[17]

Thus, a high level of trust is vital in bringing together people in teams to work towards common goals. How does a leader achieve high levels of trust? By developing emotional intelligence (EI). Yes, this might be a worn-out cliché, but it remains essential to a team's success. *Harvard Business Review* lists three conditions to developing EI: a) make time for team members to appreciate each other's skills; b) surface and manage emotional issues that can help or hinder the team's progress; and c) celebrate success and positive emotions.[18]

Striking a balance between the 'team' and the 'leader'

Given what we know about the power and potential of groups working with common purpose, founders/promoters must resist the urge to enforce their personalities on their teams. The cult of the heroic leader militates against the creation of collaborative groups. They must encourage creativity and collaboration. The Marwari community in India serves as a case study of durable and extensive collaboration without the need for a dominant leader to oversee such an endeavour. So, what are the broader societal values/qualities which lead to some teams/companies/ societies pulling together so cohesively so that the end result is much greater than the sum of the parts? We look for answers in the rich literature that has sprung up around India's small (there are fewer than nine million Marwaris in India) but spectacularly successful Marwari business community. From the perspective of collaboration, we highlight four such hints gleaned from books about the highly successful community:

1. Alignment of interests: Over a hundred years ago, and long before agency theory was developed by academics in US business schools, the great Marwari firms which controlled trade in India's Ganga-Yamuna floodplains had created a system of incentives which aligned their managers' interests with the promoters'. As Thomas A. Timberg writes in *The Marwaris: From Jagat Seth to the Birlas*[19]:

> Until the First World War, the Tarachand Ghanshyamdas office or gaddi at 18, Mullick Street in Calcutta took up an entire floor... There were 89 clerks working there. The head manager, Chhaganlal Bhavsinghka, was paid the princely sum of Rs 250 a month . . . Besides their pay, the managers often received a share in the profits of the firm. Jainarain Poddar, the chief manager, testified in court that he received Rs 2-3 lakhs annually over a period of several years, probably his share of profits. Other branch managers had variously defined share of profits. The exact arrangements differed from firm to firm.

2. Complementarity of skill sets/interests: For a team to collaborate over an extended period of time to achieve a common goal there has to be avoidance of duplicating skill sets and responsibilities within the team. As soon as two people in a team realize that they have similar skill sets and responsibilities, politics kicks in to vitiate the atmosphere in the team. Long before HR managers had discovered 'strength finders' and skill maps, the great Marwari firms had figured out a unique solution to this problem. As Timberg writes: 'Managers and clerks in 1914 were mostly Shekhawati

Aggarwals like the Poddars themselves . . . Some other Great Firms preferred Brahmin clerks to those from their own caste because it was perceived that they would be less likely to enter into competition with the original firm . . . The managers were regularly rotated and promoted. Harduttrai Prahladka joined the firm in 1860 in Calcutta and moved to the Mathura and Ramgarh branches, before leaving the firm. He returned as a branch manager in 1896.'

3. Monitoring of performance alongside rules which provide rewards and punishments: In her book *Business Maharajas*[20], Gita Piramal uses a quote from the industrialist Shashi Ruia to explain why the late Aditya Birla was so successful: 'The key to Aditya Birla's success lay in his ability to organize himself and everyone around him.' She then quotes Birla himself as saying, 'What do you do to attract people? You give them tremendous powers and independence while monitoring their performance . . . Watch the financials, intervene if necessary, decide what next industry to get into, and which ones to withdraw from.'

4. Willingness to look beyond personal financial incentives: Several centuries before the term 'to network' became a verb, the Marwari community had understood the power of co-operation across vast networks, and therefore groomed their children in a specific way. Timberg describes this in detail (the parentheses and emphases in bold are ours):

> Communities and castes with a history of involvement in business orient their children . . . to the trade, applaud success and know how to help each other in business. It is for this reason that the psychological make-up of those who run businesses in crowded markets is often marked

by **n-affiliation** [N-Affil: a psychological orientation to work social networks, as politicians do] rather than **n-achievement** [N-Ach: refers to an individual's desire for significant accomplishment, mastering of skills, control or high standards] . . . In a study of small engineering shop owners in Howrah, Raymond Owens demonstrated that members of the Mahasiya caste, who were prominent among owners of shops, had high n-affiliation since their business success was dependent on networking with caste fellows. The other entrepreneurs who came from a wide variety of castes, usually upper-class 'service castes' [Brahmins, Kshatriyas, Baidyas], had high n-achievement . . . Everything in the environment of these young Marwari men assisted them in being successful in business. They had a first-class support network constituted by their traditional family firms, business groups and the community. When they arrived in a new place, they found a basa, which provided boarding, lodging and society. Their friends and relatives were already in business and could help them.

However, even the largest of Marwari groups have seen a tough transition. The Novelis acquisition taught Kumar Mangalam Birla many lessons, especially in managing people. In an essay titled 'Butter chicken at Birla', Birla had this to say about creating an emotional bond within a group that now spans diverse people across continents: 'Some Indian companies prefer to leave their foreign acquisitions to operate on their own, almost as independent outposts. But if you want all your employees to share the same values and to feel a sense of kinship with one another, as we do, you've got to work at creating an emotional bond—the kind of thing that an Indian growing up hearing the name Birla, or attending a Birla school, would take for granted.

By the same token, you have to be prepared to treat all your employees and managers, Indian and non-Indian, equally.'[21]

The important role of work culture and communication

Work culture has an important impact on collaboration. Founders/promoters define the work culture and have a large role to play in how employees work in an organization. There are many approaches to work culture, and so there is no one-size-fits-all model.

Jack Ma, the co-founder of Alibaba, famously believes in the tough, rigorous Chinese work culture of 996—working 9 a.m. to 9 p.m., six days a week.[22] For many of us in India, this might not be a big deal. Certainly, for both Saurabh and Anupam, working twelve hours a day, six days a week formed a large part of their careers. When we were in our twenties, we even had fun doing it because some of our best work was the product of long hours of work. But not everyone enjoys such a tough routine, which can also lead to burnout and disillusionment if done for long and without any evident reward.

As with most things in life, there is usually no need for extremes. There is enough path in the middle. Indeed, for young employees in start-ups, an aggressive and rigorous work culture might just backfire. Basecamp is a project management and team communication software company based in Chicago. Its founders, Jason Fried and David Heinemeier Hansson, are the authors of *It Doesn't Have to Be Crazy at Work*[23]. As the title of the book suggests, you don't necessarily have to work eighty-hour weeks to rise in your profession. Indeed, the employees at Basecamp work half that many hours a week and, in addition, take Fridays off in summer. The authors present provocative views that fly in the face of human-resource (HR) strategy. For example, in the chapter titled 'We're not family', the authors write: 'The best companies aren't families. They're supporters of families. Allies of families. They're there to provide healthy, fulfilling work environments so that when workers shut their laptops at a reasonable hour, they're the best husbands, wives, parents, siblings, and children they can be.'

Communication also plays a role in collaboration. The nature of communication itself has changed over the past few decades. Anupam and Saurabh recall a time in the post-liberalization era of expensive communication in India when research reports would be faxed to clients, international calls and trips were restricted, and team meetings would happen face-to-face. However, today, the nature of team meetings—indeed of any communication—has changed fundamentally with the shift from phone calls and physical face-to-face meetings to email and then to instant messaging platforms such as WhatsApp, Slack and Telegram. The positive impact of these platforms is that they give us the ability to truly communicate with anyone, anywhere in the world, without disturbing them. The negative impact is that increasingly we talk to people less.

Ask yourself this, how often do you actually speak to someone on your phone? An October 2019 *Wall Street Journal* article titled 'The Phone Call Isn't Dead, It's Evolving' quoted a survey by the research firm MRI-Simmons, which said that in 2012, talking was the most popular way to communicate via cellphone with 94 per cent of survey respondents having done so in the prior week. By the spring of 2019, less than half had used their phones for an actual phone call, preferring instead to use texting, emailing, posting to social media and using chat apps. Thus, over the years, things have now come to a point where an incoming phone call is seen as intrusive or potentially the bearer of bad news.[24]

This shift in communication has had an impact on collaboration as well. In an outstanding article in *The New*

Yorker, titled 'Was E-mail a Mistake?'[25], Cal Newport wrote about synchronous versus asynchronous messaging. An example of synchronous messaging is a face-to-face meeting or a phone call where two people can talk simultaneously. An asynchronous message is when you can read a message whenever you want, like a WhatsApp message.

Newport writes: 'For much of workplace history, collaboration among colleagues was synchronous by default . . . an office was usually a single space where a few people toiled.' This was disrupted first by the rise of large offices (spread across many floors), and then by email. This is how workplace communication moved from synchronous to asynchronous. We know the case for asynchronous communication—a WhatsApp ping is convenient, practical, non-intrusive, respects privacy, etc. At an organizational level, asynchronous messaging reduces costs because email is cheaper than, say, a meeting at a coffee shop. However, instant messages come with their own set of problems. At least a few of us have had 'WhatsApp fights'. In the office, what can be solved by a phone call, might take more than a few emails, leave alone the perils of 'reply all'. From the perspective of collaboration, Newport's conclusion is significant: 'We can acknowledge, with the benefit of hindsight, the reasonableness of the hypothesis that asynchrony in the office would increase productivity. We can also admit that this hypothesis has been largely refuted by experience. To use the terminology of computer science, it turned out that the distributed systems that resulted when we shifted toward asynchronous communication were soon overwhelmed by the increasing complexity induced by asynchrony.' Basically, rather than improving our productivity, emails and texts and WhatsApp messages reduce our ability to perform effectively in the workplace.

We can testify to the benefits of face-to-face meetings when it comes to collaboration, on both work-related and personal fronts. We use instant messaging simply to set up meetings and leave the actual meat of the discussion and collaboration for face-to-face communication, as far as possible.

We were born to collaborate

Our workplace and the people we work with are not social clubs. They are just a group of people working together. Their skills complement each other in such a way that as a team they work towards the same objective. Teams at work should bring together different types of personalities from diverse backgrounds. While this type of a team might not make for the most convivial gathering, it has the potential for the best team as a diversity of views and perspectives can only add depth to the overall quality of the team.

India's foundations are also rooted in a diverse, even opposing, set of people, brought together to form independent India's first cabinet. As Ramachandra Guha writes: 'India was made united and democratic by an extraordinary act of political selflessness, whereby a particular party put the interests of the nation above its own. The Congress had dominated the struggle for freedom from British colonial rule, but when the first Cabinet of independent India was constituted, crucial portfolios were assigned to those who were not Congressmen. The Madras businessman and Justice Party politician, R. K. Shanmukham Chetty, was made Finance Minister, while the Akali Dal leader, Baldev Singh, became Defence Minister.

'The most remarkable appointment to that first Cabinet, however, was that of B. R. Ambedkar. Through the 1930s and 1940s, Ambedkar had been a bitter opponent of the Congress, and had attacked Mahatma Gandhi in particular in very sharp language.'[26]

Collaboration case study: Tata Consultancy Services (TCS)

The art of collaboration among a diverse set of people towards a common purpose can be seen in many areas. Corporate life is one such area and in this case study, we show how TCS is a prime example of collaboration on an epic scale.

TCS started as a division of Tata Sons in the late 1960s and transformed itself from an in-house share registry manager to an IT services giant, first in India and then globally. With FY19 revenues of $20 billion, TCS is among the five largest IT services companies in the world. TCS is also the largest company (by market cap and profits) in the Tata Group. TCS's market cap ($118 billion as of 29 October 2019) is more than the combined market cap of its big peers—Infosys ($40 billion), HCL Technologies ($22 billion) and Wipro ($21 billion).[27]

The story of TCS is that of the exemplary leadership of F.C. Kohli, the founder of the company, S. Ramadorai, N. Chandrasekaran ('Chandra'), and finally the current CEO, Rajesh Gopinathan. Each of these leaders played an important part in ensuring that their diverse teams worked towards common goals (rather than imposing a brand new, heroic/improved 'vision' on the firm).

Under Kohli's leadership, TCS branched out from an in-house captive unit of the Tata Group to gaining external clients and specializing in software services. Kohli laid the foundations and processes of the organization. Ramadorai (CEO from 1996 to 2009) scaled TCS up for growth with initiatives such as decentralized decision-making to ensure flexibility in bagging large contracts. Then, Chandra (CEO from 2009 to 2017) pivoted TCS during the critical phase of transition from the older era of software services to the new generation of digital, finally handing over the reins to Gopinathan for the next phase of growth. To put things in perspective, under the leadership of these CEOs, TCS revenues grew twenty times in sixteen years from $1 billion in 2003 to $20 billion in 2019—a feat unmatched by any other Indian IT services firm. From our discussions with industry veterans, the role of collaboration emerges as instrumental to TCS's success.

Firstly, we note that in contrast to what happens at Infosys, all TCS CEOs are groomed internally, already having spent many years within TCS before rising to the post. By choosing an internal candidate (usually a veteran team player) as her successor, the outgoing leader sends a message of confidence that the firm itself is a 'team of leaders'.

The fact that leadership changes in TCS are organic allows the firm to retain its largest clients for longer. In fact TCS's largest clients are larger than those of other Indian IT services firms. For example, TCS's implementation of a core banking platform for the State Bank of India in 2003–04 remains the largest such project implemented anywhere in the world. In the words of specialist research provider TowerGroup: 'The implementation of the Tata Consultancy Services (TCS) BaNCS system at the State Bank of India (SBI) represents the largest core systems project ever undertaken.'[28] Successful implementation of colossal projects such as these has helped TCS become the only Indian IT services firm to rank among the world's three largest IT services firms.[29]

Secondly, employees are aligned to organizational goals as part of routine process. Unlike many IT companies that were started by first-generation entrepreneurs, TCS came from the Tata Group and therefore institution- and organization-building was in their DNA. Hiring and training practices are institutionalized to ensure that employees are aligned to common goals. In fact, every year, TCS trains or re-trains 2,00,000 employees. It is highly unlikely that any other firm in India trains even half as many people in a given year.

And thirdly, TCS has standardized processes to a very large extent and captured their application development life cycle in an institutional knowledge base. This gives the firm the ability to have the largest scale implementation among peers and in a much shorter timeframe. These processes are the result of many years of collaboration and processes laid down by top managements over the years.

Collaboration case study: Amazon Prime

Amazon launched its delivery service Amazon Prime in 2005. At that time, Amazon offered its customers two-day delivery for their orders for a one-time upfront payment of $79 per year. Amazon Prime was a first-of-its-kind service that came at a time when Amazon was facing tough competition from online rivals such as eBay and offline rivals like Best Buy. An article on *Vox* termed Prime as 'the greatest retail innovation of the internet age' and described how the idea of offering free, guaranteed two-day shipping at a prepaid price was not without risk and dissent among the inner rank and file. Yet Jeff Bezos chose to go ahead with the idea. The *Vox* article features stories from Amazon employees recalling how Prime was created. We reproduce one quote here: 'Vijay Ravindran (former Amazon director of ordering): Back then there wasn't a blind faith that every Jeff idea was going to be a home run. And so there was a lot of pushback. Very prominent people who are at Amazon today and in high positions told me, "You shouldn't be allowing Jeff to do this," and, "This is setting a bad example for the company."'[30]

But Amazon Prime had predecessors. Amazon had offered free shipping for orders of $100 and more during peak holiday seasons in 2000 and 2001. Shipping costs were among the key hurdles holding back customers shopping on Amazon.

Therefore, free shipping motivated them to buy more stuff and cross the $100 threshold. But how would Amazon convert holiday-season free shipping into an exclusive offer available to all Prime customers on an ongoing basis?

In early 2002, Bezos held a meeting to discuss this and Greg Greeley, Amazon's then vice president (worldwide retail finance) and CFO international, gave the example of airlines that reduced ticket prices for customers willing to stay at their destination through a Saturday night. Amazon could, similarly, make shipping free for customers who could wait for their delivery, while charging shipping costs to customers who wanted delivery quickly. Amazon introduced the service Free Super Saver Shipping in January 2002 for orders above $99 and dropped the limit to $25 within a few months.

However, this idea was not acceptable to everyone. In *The Everything Store: Jeff Bezos and the Age of Amazon*[31], Brad Stone wrote about that meeting: 'Not everyone was happy with this outcome. After that meeting, Warren Jenson (then the CFO of Amazon) took Greeley aside and berated him, in that moment seeing free shipping as nothing but another potential balance-sheet buster.'

Amazon's work culture (long hours, competitive and intensely driven atmosphere[32]) has drawn its set of critics, but it is still another example of having diverse people with different perspectives, even diverse and opposing views, working together towards a single goal, namely making their company a market leader and—in the case of Amazon—a giant. Colleagues don't have to be best buddies and bosses don't have to treat you as family. In the early 2000s, Amazon faced an exodus of employees leaving the firm, resulting in high attrition. Stone writes in *The Everything Store*: 'Bezos never despaired over the mass exodus. One of his gifts, his colleagues said, was being able to drive and motivate his employees without getting overly attached to them personally.'

* * *

Key takeaways from this chapter

- Co-operation is hardwired in human beings. Working collaboratively with creative and diverse minds—ideally working towards common goals—allows you to achieve more and learn more from those around you.

- Collaboration is a soft edge. While most successful companies eventually develop successful strategies and efficient execution, developing the soft edge is what takes these successful companies even further in the long run. Examples of collaboration to achieve truly outsized success include HDFC Bank, Amul and TCS. Teams with members who bring varied experiences, different types of expertise and a diversity of beliefs can avoid common corporate pitfalls such as groupthink and echo chambers.

- While the skills and visions of a founder are critically important at the start-up stage, as a company grows large, the ability of that leader to bring together diverse teams (consisting of driven, ambitious people) working towards common goals determines the future of the company. Steve Jobs was and Jeff Bezos is a master at getting diverse groups of people to work together for a common goal.

Lessons from Manish Sabharwal's Multifaceted Career

Manish Sabharwal is the co-founder and chairman of TeamLease, a vocational training firm and one of India's largest human resources companies. Beyond TeamLease, Manish has many roles which reflect his innate ability to collaborate with people from different backgrounds. Manish is an independent member on the board of the Reserve Bank of India (RBI), a member of the National Skill Mission of the Central Advisory Board of Education (Ministry of Human Resources) and of the Advisory Board of the Comptroller and Auditor General (CAG) of India. Manish also serves on various state and central government committees on education, employment and employability. He is associated with many more ventures than he lets on in his official biography. For example, he is the managing trustee of the New India Foundation, along with fellow trustees Nandan Nilekani, Ramachandra Guha and Srinath Raghavan.

We met Manish at his home-cum-library in the 'old Bengaluru' neighbourhood of Richmond Town on a muggy

Saturday morning. Located in central Bengaluru, Richmond Town is a leafy precinct originally established by the British in 1883 and still housing some of Bengaluru's best convent schools as well as clubs and churches. Manish met us in his large living room where three out of the four walls were covered from floor to ceiling with books. Over many cups of black coffee, green tea and lemonade, we spoke at length about the role of collaboration in our lives.

As his huge library testifies, Manish is an extremely well-read person. In order to substantiate his statements, he quotes extensively and effortlessly from the books he has read. These verbatim quotes also highlight Manish's remarkable memory.

We start with what ails urban India, and he scoffs at the notion that these problems are new. 'Presentism' dates back to the Parthenon, he tells us. The quality of education, for example, has been a topic of debate since the time of Abraham Lincoln, who famously wrote 'defective' when asked about his education on an election form. Manish likes to take a balanced view of things instead of veering to extremes. Often, he quotes the Renaissance physician Paracelsus: 'The dose makes the poison', i.e. any substance taken in extreme concentrations (doses) will have a harmful effect. It is all about balance. In education, for example, Manish says a balance between rote learning and creativity could address issues related to both sides (too much rote learning versus too much creativity). Similarly, on luck versus skill, he believes in a balance and tell us, 'If you believe too much in luck, why bother showing up? If you believe too much in skills, you won't pay attention to context, coalitions, strategy, teamwork, alliances, partnership.'

On collaboration, Manish refers to Doris Kearns Goodwin's book *Team of Rivals: The Political Genius of Abraham Lincoln* and to the idea that people who don't agree with each other could, counter-intuitively, make for a great team. After winning the presidential elections, Lincoln chose his senior team from his rivals for the Republican nomination. In the Indian context, Manish believes that Gandhi's success in gaining independence for India could be attributed to the team of rivals that he assembled, namely Ambedkar and Sardar Patel. He quotes an article[33] in *Hindustan Times* by Ramachandra Guha. The article recounts a brief history of bipartisanship in India and—as mentioned earlier in this chapter—Guha describes in it how independent India's first cabinet consisted not of members from the Indian National Congress but from a range of political parties. However, the most remarkable appointment in the first cabinet was that of Gandhi's bitter opponent, Ambedkar, who was made law minister and, more importantly, the chairman of the drafting committee of the Indian Constitution. Gandhiji made the recommendation of appointing Ambedkar to both Nehru and Patel.

Referring to the concept of the team of rivals, Manish tells us, 'It is a complete recognition of the fact that you don't have to like people to work with them.' Narrating from personal experience, he contrasts his personality with TeamLease's co-founder and managing director, Ashok Reddy, 'We are completely opposite personalities. Ashok is an introvert; I'm an extrovert. He is good at operations; I'm good at selling. He has never met an acquisition he wants to make; I've never met an acquisition I don't want to make. Our board members said that if only Ashok had been around, the company would have been one-hundredth of its size; if only Manish had been around, the company would not have survived. We agree. Therefore, there is a nuclear balance between the two of you. Getting the train out of the station is a different skill set from keeping the trains running on time.' Manish's favourite quote is from the US politician Mario Cuomo, who said in 1985, 'You campaign in poetry. You govern in prose.'

Manish talks of TeamLease with the example of Hoysala architecture, which dates back to the eleventh and fourteenth centuries and can be seen in some of the temples in Belur, Karnataka. The sculptures in these temples often include lions (signifying power), elephants (strength) and horses (speed). So a good king ensures he has all of these in his kingdom because any one animal by itself would just not be enough. The combination of all three goes towards making a great kingdom. Explaining this collaboration, Manish tell us, 'There is a mutual respect and the way to make peace with it is that at different phases, the elephant will get prominence, at different phases the horse will get prominence and so on. That is how it is with Ashok and me. Ashok is this risk-averse middle-class Indian; if I left it to him, we'd do nothing. But if he left it to me, I'd blow it up. So, at some point he has to take the lead and at some point I have to take the lead.'

Can collaboration be taught? Indirectly, says Manish and refers to economist John Kay's book *Obliquity: Why our goals are best achieved indirectly*[34]. 'You can't teach collaboration. You can make people aware of collaboration skills but collaboration is an acquired skill. Soft skills are really learnt through apprenticeship,' he tells us and then refers to one of his favourite lines from what Professor Dumbledore told Harry Potter in *Harry Potter and the Chamber of Secrets*[35]: 'It's our choices, Harry, that show what we truly are, far more than our abilities.'

Finally, we ask Manish for examples of Indian companies that exemplify collaboration and he instantly replies, 'TCS.' When we ask him why, he tells us, 'Because consistently warm beats hot and cold; a twenty-five-year plan is not twenty-five one-year plans.' Manish believes that TCS also always got the right CEO at the right point of the cycle. From Kohli to Ramadorai to Chandra and now Gopinathan—each of them led the organization from strength to strength and, in the process, built teams internally that could collaborate towards a common goal. He ends with a quote from management guru Peter F. Drucker: 'A great orchestra is not composed of great instrumentalists but of adequate ones who produce at their peak.'[36]

Section 4

Applications

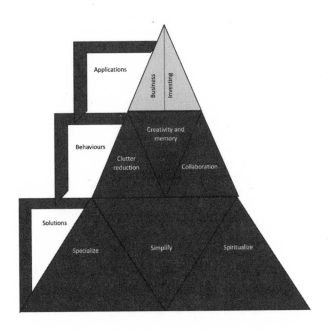

CHAPTER 8

How Simplicity Powers the Best Businesses

'When everything is a priority, nothing is a priority. Attempting to maximize competing variables is a recipe for disaster. Picking one variable and relentlessly focusing on it, which is an effective strategy, diverges from the norm. It's hard to compete with businesses that have correctly identified the right variables to maximize or minimize. When you focus on one variable, you'll increase the odds that you're quick and nimble — and can respond to changes in the terrain.'

—Shane Parrish[1]

In the preceding chapters, we have discussed the specific solutions (specialize, simplify and spiritualize) and behaviours (clutter reduction, creativity and collaboration). In this the final section of our book, we pull everything together and highlight specific applications of our approach which combine the prescribed solutions and behaviours. Given that our professional experience has largely been confined to business and investing, we see two clear applications—simplicity in business and simplicity in investing. This chapter discusses simplicity in business; the next chapter focuses on simplicity in investing.

Simplicity in business is easier said than done. Simple ideas often require complex execution and that in turn can be waylaid by weak teams. The simplest of ideas at the board level can get lost in translation by the time it gets communicated to the workers at the coalface. Similarly, how does a leader of these teams inspire creativity among employees on the one hand and engender unity and cohesiveness on the other? We began this book by describing the stress created in corporate life as individual ambition collides with the misery of navigating India's broken infrastructure. This same compromised infrastructure can also stifle the simplest of ideas. Is simplicity in business even achievable in the Indian context? In this chapter, we look at how giant enterprises have applied the simplicity principle in their businesses.

In their book, *Simplify: How the Best Businesses in the World Succeed*, authors Richard Koch and Greg Lockwood provide several case studies which illustrate that history's most successful business leaders have also been great simplifiers. This list includes Henry Ford, the McDonald brothers and Ray Kroc, Herb Kelleher of Southwest Airlines, Steve Jobs, and many more. And if you thought Steve Jobs was the first business leader to take a complicated technical gadget and simplify its use, this is what Henry Ford said a century ago of his revolutionary Model T car: '[Its] most important feature . . . was its simplicity . . . I thought it was up to me as the designer to make the car so completely simple that no one could fail to understand it.'

Ford made the car affordable to ordinary families in the USA, Jobs created a mobile phone that combined beauty and utility, and Kroc saw the opportunity to scale up McDonald's while retaining its original simplicity. With simplicity at their centre, these icons of corporate America transformed the way large industries operated. Was this easy? Not at all. In *Simplify*, the authors recount Kroc's frustration when the first McDonald's franchise failed to reproduce the same taste in French fries as the original made by the McDonald brothers in their first store in California. The breakthrough, as the book describes, came when a researcher asked Kroc to describe the procedure for making the fries: 'The secret turned out to be that the potatoes were stored in open chicken-wire shaded bins, which allowed plenty of time for the wind to dry out the potatoes and change the sugars to starch.'

The iPhone changed the smartphone as we know it. But turning a palm-sized utility into a beautiful gadget was never easy. There was incredible complexity within the design. In his biography of Steve Jobs, Walter Isaacson quoted Jony Ive describing his own philosophy as follows: 'Why do we assume that simple is good? Because with physical products, we have to feel we can dominate them. As you bring order to complexity, you find a way to make the product defer to you. Simplicity isn't just a visual style. It's not just minimalism or the absence of clutter. It involves digging through the depth of complexity. To be truly simple, you have to go really deep.'[2]

The idea of simplicity and beauty in technology has come a long way since Apple's 2007 introduction of the iPhone. WeChat, the hugely popular messaging app in China, has more than a billion daily users, sending more than forty-five billion messages a day.[3] *Harvard Business Review* (*HBR*) conducted an in-depth study of WeChat to decipher its success. One key component of its success, they found, was that it was conceived as a work of art and not a commercial product. In his interview with *HBR*, this is how Allen Zhang, its founder, described WeChat: 'Before perceiving WeChat as a commercial product,

I'd rather picture it first as an impressive work of art. When I started designing user interactions for Foxmail, I complicated everything. It felt wrong because it no longer looked neat. For WeChat, I now see the necessity of subtraction – making things simpler – and focusing on the product's aesthetic quality.'

Simple ideas, big businesses

Simplicity doesn't always mean that you stick to one simple product. Simplicity can also mean that you go so deep into the product that you begin with, say, trading the product and over the years build everything from the raw material right until the final finished product (referred to in business jargon as 'backward integration').

Successful entrepreneurs take simple ideas and build them into massive businesses. Reliance Industries Limited (RIL) is an important example to highlight this concept. The vast conglomerate whose business today spans petrochemicals, retail and telecom began life in 1957 when RIL founder Dhirubhai Ambani started a yarn business in Mumbai. By 1980, Ambani, who was well-known for his ambition, had already moved up (or 'backward integrated') from a textile factory in Gujarat to a petrochemical factory in Maharashtra. By 1993, RIL was the fourth biggest producer of polyester in the world and the only one with production integrated from naphtha to fabrics. And this was only the beginning since the senior Ambani had plans to enter oil and gas exploration as well. Dhirubhai Ambani's biggest dream, as per Hamish McDonald in his book *Ambani & Sons*[4], was building a full-scale oil refinery. By the time the said aspiration was fulfilled in Jamnagar in June 2000, RIL owned the world's biggest refinery and the Ambani family was on its way to becoming the wealthiest family in India. McDonald puts things into perspective, 'With Jamnagar in production, the

Reliance Group accounted for more than 3 percent of India's gross domestic product and contributed about 10 percent of the central government's indirect taxation revenues.'

Indian corporate history has many examples of entrepreneurs who have started small and simple and then scaled up their businesses over many decades—some, like RIL, by choice and some by compulsion. For example, the TTK Group was a pioneer of the humble pressure cooker and its Prestige brand was the market leader in India. However, in 2003, the group was on the brink of collapse under the strain of excessive debt and weak sales. This is when the chairman, T.T. Jagannathan, took tough decisions, like cutting prices of products and, in parallel, expanding the product line from pressure cookers to cookware such as vessels and appliances (all of which were sold under the well-known Prestige brand). In the book *Disrupt and Conquer*[5], T.T. Jagannathan and Sandhya Mendonca recounted that momentous decision, 'We ventured into cookware - stainless steel and non-stick vessels and appliances. Until now we had only been selling what we made, but we discovered that the intrinsic power of the brand could be used to the maximum.' The strategy worked and TTK Prestige's share price rose 700 times over the next fifteen years, thereby propelling Jagannathan into a very select league—Indian promoters whose net worth is in excess of $1 billion.

Can a product as simple as the zip (or zipper) become a worldwide brand? Yoshida Kogyo Kabushiki-gaisha (Yoshido Manufacturing Corporation), better known as YKK, is the world's largest manufacturer of zippers. This company, which manufactures only one product, generated revenues in excess of $7 billion in 2018.[6] It is highly likely that the clothes you are wearing right now have a zip made by YKK, which has 100 wholly-owned subsidiaries across seventy-three countries. Founded by Tadao Yoshida in 1934, YKK's reputation globally is absolutely top-notch. Yoshida's simple idea was built out over decades into a multi-country business and a brand synonymous with zips. How did this happen?

Tadao worked at a trading company which went bankrupt. The trading company's owner gave him the remains of the business, which included a small subsidiary that made handmade zippers. The rest was sheer determination: 'Tadao, an inquisitive, detail-obsessed man, tried to modernize the manufacturing methods. But machine tool makers weren't interested in his design for a custom-made zipper machine, so he made his own. When knots on large spools of thread kept interrupting his automatic zipper machines, the thread-makers refused to provide him thread without knots. Soon Yoshida had to start making his own thread, too. By the late 1950s the only ingredients YKK needed to buy from outside were plastic chips and its own blend of metal alloys.'[7]

YKK had 95 per cent market share of the Japanese zip market by the 1960s and then opened manufacturing facilities abroad. Eventually, it achieved global domination with its competitors, including many from China, far behind it.

Simple to conceptualize, tough to execute

The examples given above are of world-class brands housed inside companies with able management teams. But the challenge of achieving simplicity involves both uncertainty and complexity. Simplicity in business might be easy to conceptualize but it is very tough to execute. The best ideas get bogged down in execution and lost in detail. A start-up might think of a great product, but getting the right people might be a challenge, leave alone the myriad regulations that can consume all the time of founders. Similarly, for an established market leader, navigating choppy markets, dealing with uncertain growth conditions can take up all the bandwidth of the promoter if he does not have strong and capable teams to help him.

Asian Paints is an excellent example of a homegrown company that has successfully taken on international giants and gone on to dominate the large and lucrative Indian paints market. Not only is paints a lucrative market, it is also complex and difficult. While a consumer may have a preference for Z brand over Y brand in detergents, toothpastes, toothbrushes and other FMCG categories, paints is relatively generic. When we go to a paint store, if we have not already made up our minds, it is difficult to differentiate one product from another. We usually take the advice of the painter painting our homes. From the manufacturer's perspective, he has to carry all types of paints, resulting in a high number of stock-keeping units (SKUs) which are stocked with the dealer. This is incredibly complex in a large and diverse country such as India where colour preferences change from region to region. Given all of this, the margins in the paints industry are typically lower compared to other consumer categories such as automobiles, foods, etc. And yet, Asian Paints has not only sustained its market leadership for decades at a stretch, staving off competition from multinationals such as Kansai Nerolac and AkzoNobel, it has done so with a return on capital employed of 40 per cent.

In Saurabh's book *The Unusual Billionaires*, he has dedicated two chapters to the number one and two paints companies in India—Asian Paints and Berger Paints. Of the two, Asian Paints is far bigger (almost three times bigger).

The roots of Asian Paints' competitive advantages go back to its founder-promoter, Champaklal Choksey, who formed the company back in 1942. From those days, Asian Paints has focused exclusively on the customer and the dealer while cutting out all the other intermediaries who eat up the lion's share of the profit margin in almost any product distribution construct in India.

At its simplest, Choksey's vision for Asian Paints' distribution network was based on cutting out intermediaries, such as wholesalers, cost and freight (C&F) agents and distributors, and going straight to the dealer. This also meant creating a pan-Indian network that delivered paint from its factory directly to the dealer while maintaining sufficient stocks and keeping the dealer happy at all times. Execution thus was complex.

We reproduce an extract from *The Unusual Billionaires* that explains the process: 'Asian Paints has one of the largest number of manufacturing units and depots across the country in its supply chain network. More importantly, the firm leverages on a wider network of manufacturing plants and depots to operate at the highest ratio of revenues per depot or revenues per manufacturing plant, thereby helping improve inventory turnover and working capital turnover for the overall business.

'For instance, over the past decade, Asian Paints has been setting up distribution centres (DCs) next to the manufacturing units. These DCs will serve as large-format hubs for inventory storage of both fast- as well as slow-moving SKUs. Whilst for slow-moving SKUs, the DC network will aim at replacing the RDC network in its entirety, for the fast-moving SKUs, the DC network will aim at reducing the transfer of surplus stock from one depot to another within the distribution network. The company's size and efficiency is visible in the fact that it has the largest number of dealers (35,000 vs 21,000 for Berger). With only around 125 depots in its supply chain, its revenue per depot is approximately Rs 100 crore, more than twice that of the next highest, which is around Rs 40 crore per depot for Kansai Nerolac. Similarly, its revenue per factory is approximately Rs 1,500 crore, twice that of the next highest (just over Rs 700 crore for Kansai Nerolac).'

HDFC Bank is yet another example of how the pursuit of simple goals—such as: (a) building a low-cost current account savings account (CASA) deposit franchise; and (b) prudent lending—led to the creation of India's largest private sector bank by market capitalization.

HDFC Bank defines its strategies, tactics and objectives top-down with the two goals highlighted in the preceding paragraph serving as overarching guideposts. The bank is legendary for how it uses specific systems and procedures to pursue these goals. During his research for *The Unusual Billionaires*, Saurabh spoke to a cross section of HDFC Bank insiders, ex-employees and industry veterans. During these discussions, an industry expert even called HDFC Bank an 'SOP Bank' (SOP stands for standard operating procedure) for its strict adherence to systems and procedures. As customers of the bank, we have seen how employees refuse to budge on simple things (such as the necessary documents required for a banking transaction) when it goes against the bank's stated SOPs.

But achieving these goals has hardly been easy. HDFC Bank has built its reputation and position over the past twenty-five years by assiduously sticking to these goals and its SOPs. The journey wasn't easy. When dematerialization of shares was introduced in India in the mid-to-late 1990s, the opportunity to be captured was huge. For example, while the settlement of shares between buyer and seller may be immediate (from their demat accounts), the transfer of money takes longer. In the mid-to-late 1990s, this was even more tedious since technology then wasn't widely used in the banking sector. But HDFC Bank saw an opportunity in the complex maze of multiple parties.

The following extract from *The Unusual Billionaires* describes how HDFC Bank captured this opportunity:

> HDFC Bank pulled in all the players in the supply chain—buyers, sellers, brokers and exchanges—and got them into an automated settlement system. It offered a solution to both

brokers and exchanges. If brokers had an account with HDFC Bank, exchanges could see in real time whether brokers had money to settle payouts and, if there was a shortfall, there was enough time before the actual settlement to ask the broker to meet this shortfall. This reduced settlement risk for exchanges drove all major exchanges to sign up with HDFC Bank.

The incentive for brokers to sign up with HDFC Bank was that pay-in money was credited immediately to the broker's account, reducing his working capital requirement. This led all the brokers to open their accounts with HDFC Bank for settlements. Since brokers needed bank guarantees for exchanges, the bank also provided credit lines to these brokers. So the bank not only earned a free float on money kept by brokers for their settlement, it also earned fees by providing credit lines to brokers. Starting with the NSE in 1998, the bank became the clearing member of all major exchanges by FY2000. Eight hundred brokers and a majority of custodians were using HDFC Bank's services by FY2000.

In his book *A Bank for the Buck*, veteran banking journalist Tamal Bandyopadhyay wrote about the complexities of banking for stock market transactions and dealing with the ecosystem of brokers and exchanges, in relation to HDFC Bank:

For all this, a bank needs to have the ability to handle very tight processing cycles every single day. It also entails understanding the credit risk of brokers and brokerages as the bank takes exposure on them. This is the hard part, given all the volatility and cycles of the market and of individual broking companies.

'It is the question of marshalling your resources - what we used to call in the early days a Germanic obsession for very tight processes with no tolerance for error and processing risk, and they [HDFC Bank] have built that in the way they operate. It was very clear very early on,' Ravi said.[8]

Page Industries is the India franchise of the premium innerwear brand Jockey. When Page began operations in India in 1993, it had a simple goal—premium quality innerwear at affordable prices. While there was a lot of demand for Jockey products in India, the Genomal family (the promoters of Page) was very clear that it wanted to reach the customer directly instead of navigating through the network of wholesalers and resellers. Sunder Genomal, the managing director of Page, took this proposition to the top hosiery retailers in India's large cities in 1995 and got an overwhelming response. Between 1995 and 1997 he recruited a top-tier team of professionals to help him build the company. But Page also had to contend with the several established brands such as Liberty, Rupa and VIP. Despite his best attempts, however, Genomal did not get off to the start he would have wished for. As Saurabh wrote in *The Unusual Billionaires:*

> Not everything went according to plan for Page in its first years. Given that most innerwear brands were low-end, mass produced and mass-distributed, Page found a distinct lack of quality in the Indian textile manufacturing environment. For example, establishing relationships with high-quality raw material suppliers was a challenge.
>
> Despite initial enthusiasm from Page's distributors, as an overall category, innerwear remained a low-profile product in retail stores. This would ultimately necessitate a high-pitched, pan-India advertising campaign from Page, but the costs were prohibitive. Competitive intensity from incumbents had already increased substantially during 1995–

2000. When the company reached sales of Rs 21 crore in FY2000, Rupa and Maxwell were already at Rs 150 crore each. One level above them, in the mid-premium segment, brands like Liberty, Libertina and Tantex (TTK Tantex) were firmly ensconced. Associated Apparels (Liberty and Libertina) reported sales of Rs 100 crore during the same period.

Page got its break when in 1997 two of its competitors fell prey to labour strikes, thus creating room for Page to ramp up its presence with Jockey. Page never looked back and Jockey's market share went from strength to strength. Page continued to build pan-India distribution much faster and in a far more effective manner than the competition. India's demand for premium quality innerwear at affordable prices with a great brand made the Genomals dollar billionaires and allowed many of their shareholders to become dollar millionaires.

Using the Simplicity Paradigm

Given how useful it is to build an entire business around a simple idea, two questions arise:

- How can organizations use the Simplicity Paradigm to develop simple ideas? *By using specialization and creativity.*
- How can organizations crack the execution challenge for achieving simplicity? *By using collaboration.*

Specialization and creativity

In a highly competitive sector, how does one develop a simple business proposition which can create a pathway to sustainable profitability? One place to start is to ignore industry norms and develop original ideas. In 2010, Saurabh was given charge of a local institutional equities (IE) brokerage in Mumbai. The brokerage industry in Mumbai is a crowded space dominated by established multinational investment banks and domestic bank-run outfits. Both sets of competitors have spent the past twenty years servicing the domestic and foreign fund managers and thus building powerful franchises. In such a market, why would any analyst or salesperson leave his established job and join a brand new domestic house fronted by a person who has never led a frontline brokerage franchise? How does one break into this market?

As described in Chapter 7, Saurabh first focused on building his research team, and carefully chose a mixture of bright chartered accountants and graduates from India's elite institutions of higher learning—the IITs and IIMs. The rationale for this recruitment strategy hinged on the centrality of understanding financial statements in the context of identifying high-quality Indian companies and then combining that skill set with understanding the engineering or science behind the company's products.

Next, Saurabh chose driven but cerebral salespeople—men and women in equal numbers—who were hungry to make their mark (as opposed to well-established senior salespeople who had already built their retirement savings pot). Saurabh also benefited from recruiting some of his ex-colleagues from London who had moved to India with him.

Saurabh's idea was simple: establish cutting-edge equity research as a differentiator. The focus was on publishing path-breaking, differentiated and provocative thematic analysis of the Indian market, which looked at opportunities and threats that would develop over the long-term instead of obsessing over the impact of RBI policies and Union budgets (standard stuff which most brokerages cover extensively).

In a similar vein, company research would be written with a focus on accounting quality and primary data research (i.e. talking to customers, competitors, suppliers, ex-employees of listed companies) instead of regurgitating the dictation that companies give to brokers. These high-quality reports were then marketed by articulate salespeople to open the doors to the largest fund management houses in the world.

The strategy worked. Revenues grew ten-fold in eight years. Fund managers voted Saurabh's team the most improved broker in India for six years in a row and the most 'independent' broker in India three years in a row. And underpinning this success was a simple idea—specialization around outstanding equity research executed relentlessly over the years.

The ideas of simplicity and specialization can be applied across industries. For example, in the unorganized and competitive industry of savoury snacks (or, comfort food for many of us), Haldiram's has built a nearly $1 billion business in India. The roots of the franchise lie in a simple product—*bhujia* (a fried, savoury snack made of besan)—and in a nondescript town in Rajasthan—Bikaner. From that town, the Agarwal family built Haldiram's into a pan-India brand.

As far back as the 1970s, the Agarwals used packaging and branding to differentiate their brand. As Pavitra Kumar writes in her book *Bhujia Barons: The Untold Story of How Haldiram Built a ₹5000-Crore Empire*[9], Manoharlal Agarwal (of the Haldiram's family) focused on differentiating Haldiram's from other generic brands and gave it a high-quality image. He discovered flexo-printing in Delhi, with which multiple inks could be used on plastic without smudging. Although the bhujia was a traditional Marwari snack, flexo-printing was a modern, costly way of packaging the bhujia in bright white-and-red plastic packs. The idea was expectedly resisted by the conservative family that didn't think the extra money was worth it. But Manoharlal persisted with his idea. The results were stellar: 'Luckily, the business did take off. Traders specifically began asking for the Haldiram Bhujiawala product. The brand stood out amongst the crowd, and patrons of the smaller shops began switching over to Haldiram Bhujiawala. Demand increased to such an extent that the Haldiram Bhujiawala store began to have an increasing number of pending orders.'

Going back to the book *Simplify*, Koch and Lockwood recall Henry Ford's vision in the early 1900s to build an affordable car for the masses. That simple idea was the guiding light for the Model T but to bring that idea to light required a lot of creativity and specialization. By focusing on one product, Ford had enough room to specialize. By producing on a large scale, Ford crunched the unit cost of making a car and brought the motor car to the masses. Koch and Lockwood narrate a breakthrough that helped Ford: 'The real breakthrough came with a proprietary innovation, designed by his production managers: the move from batch production to a continuously moving assembly line. This didn't happen until 1913, and it was then that Ford famously insisted that all of his cars would be painted black, because only Japan black paint could dry quickly enough to keep up with the speed of the line.'

Collaboration

Large organizations have teams that seem to work at cross purposes. For example, in the institutional brokerages where we have worked, the research team analyses and recommends stock while the sales team sells these recommendations to clients in order to generate trades and earn commissions. The research analyst bases his recommendations on many hours of painstaking research and meetings with companies and primary sources. The salesperson builds his relationship with the client over many hours of personal contact, timely recommendations, getting access to big chunks of popular stocks and attending to every need of the client (including cricket match tickets, emotional support, data crunching, etc.). The salesperson is the frontline for the brokerage to earn commissions. The research analyst is the foundation on which a brokerage earns credibility, reputation and thought leadership. The research-sales collaboration is the most critical relationship for every successful equity brokerage. This relationship literally starts the business day for the brokerage with the morning meeting, where the research team pitches its key recommendations for the day to the sales team.

And yet, heated morning meetings are normal in the institutional brokerage industry as salespeople and analysts clash routinely. The reasons are predictable: recommendations. While an analyst might be sticking his neck out on, say, a bank stock as 'sell' because the bank has understated non-performing assets, the sales team has heard that the same bank is in fact on the verge of a turnaround because market information indicates a new CEO is about to take charge. Or an FMCG stock is trading at prohibitively high valuations but the analyst still likes it because it is a brand leader and a 'safe' stock with high standards of corporate governance and a visibly steady trajectory for earnings growth. The salesperson knows that every brokerage in Mumbai has a 'buy' on the stock. And with the stock being eye-wateringly expensive, does the world really need another 'buy' recommendation on the stock?

What takes these confrontations to an even higher voltage is when both the analyst and salesperson are highly rated and ranked in industry surveys. How do you resolve an argument between the best analyst and the best salesperson (who will advise the biggest fund managers)? What if the salesperson tells his client to sell a stock to protect his relationship with the client, whereas the analyst stakes his reputation on buying the stock because he has conviction in his research? Such conflicts between research and sales often tear brokerages apart.

Similar conflicts are visible across all large organizations. For example, in banks, the risk function might not like a potential borrowing candidate whereas the sales or lending function believes that the candidate is worthy of a loan. The compliance team might add even more complexity to the relationship.

How, then, can an organization resolve complex relationships and work towards presenting a simple product or service to a client? How can sales teams at brokerages aggressively push their analysts' recommendations to clients without jeopardizing their relationship with the client? How can banks provide loans in a conservative way while maintaining the quality of their book? These objectives aren't impossible but only a small minority of firms are consistently able to achieve these objectives. These firms have strong teams and the ability to collaborate in the face of differences of opinion among team members. Such collaboration in turn requires the team members to be secure, self-confident individuals. Simple rules can then be implemented by teams when everyone is aware of their role in the team and is not riddled with insecurity. *This is where the role of leaders in corralling team members towards a common goal becomes central.*

Saurabh, for example, encouraged analysts to cultivate their own independence of thought and leave conflicts with salespeople to him. Analysts had to be rigorous in their thinking and once they were confident of their recommendations, they would sit with the head of research to convince him. Salesmen, similarly, were trained to think of the analyst as a team member and not as an adversary. Candour was encouraged but rudeness was unacceptable, and nasty morning meetings were stamped out. Salesmen were encouraged to take ownership of the relationship with their clients and work hard in being the first port of call for the client on anything related to a particular stock. Once the identity of both groups was reinforced, research and sales learnt to work with each other and not against each other. Every six months, both research and sales were encouraged to let off steam in each other's company. Once a year, the whole team would decamp to a resort for an extended weekend of full-on partying in scenic locales such as Goa, the backwaters of Kerala or Thailand.

Not every team has to party as frenetically as Saurabh's colleagues did. Leaders can also hold less boisterous events to break the ice. In *A Bank for the Buck*, Bandyopadhyay narrates an example of how Aditya Puri, who has famously held the many teams in the many silos at HDFC Bank together, settled the conflict between the branch banking and retail products teams: 'To break the ice, Aditya called them for an informal outing at Lonavla over a weekend. In the evening, three groups were formed led by Sashi [Sashidhar Jagdishan, currently executive director], Arvind Kapil of the direct sales group and Ravi Narayan of branch banking. The three walked Aditya's dogs – Scooby, a highly energetic Mudhol hound, was given to Sashi; Arvind led Pogo, a mix of a Doberman and an Alsatian; and Ravi, Bushka. There were thirty-odd people and none of them really knew how to walk a dog. So, they had to share tips and help each other manage the three unruly pets. By the time they came back to Aditya's house after the walk, everybody was talking to each other. The party started in right earnest and by nine o'clock Aditya ran out of the stock of booze. It was business as usual in the office next week.'

Why does simplicity in business work?

As all the examples quoted above show, a simple strategy is easy for people to follow. When you deviate from the strategy, the in-built simplicity itself ensures that the deviation is spotted early, course corrected, after which the team gets back on track. If, even by mistake, a loan to a risky borrower is approved within an HDFC Bank, the standard operating procedure in place will ensure that the loan is flagged off before approval. Thus, simplicity in business works because it is effective.

While in recent times General Electric has ceased to be the powerhouse it once was, there are many management lessons from its glory days that still apply to business today. In 1989, *HBR* interviewed the then chairman and CEO of General Electric, the legendary Jack Welch, and asked him what makes an effective organization. His reply was characteristically blunt: 'For a large organization to be effective, it must be simple. For a large organization to be simple, its people must have self-confidence and intellectual self-assurance. Insecure managers create complexity. Frightened, nervous managers use thick, convoluted planning books and busy slides filled with everything they've known since childhood. Real leaders don't need clutter. People must have the self-confidence to be clear, precise, to be sure that every person in their organization—highest to lowest—understands what the business is trying to achieve. But it's not easy. You can't believe how hard it is for people to be simple, how much they fear being simple. They worry that if they're simple, people will think they're simpleminded. In reality, of course, it's just the reverse. Clear, tough-minded people are the most simple.'[10]

Does simplicity in business yield financial results?

The short answer is that it does and that too in ways beyond just profits and return ratios. In *Simplify*, Koch and Lockwood divided firms that simplified into two categories—price simplification and proposition simplification. Price simplification is when a company cuts prices of its new product by half or more such that the new and cheaper product is not the same as the old product but 'fulfils the same basic function'. The new product is a simpler version of the older product and aimed at a new target group of customers who could previously not afford the product. The six case studies used by Koch and Lockwood are Ford, McDonald's, Southwest Airlines, IKEA, Charles Schwab and Honda.

Proposition simplification, on the other hand, '. . . involves creating a product that is useful, appealing and very easy to use, such as the iPad (or any other Apple device of the last decade), the Vespa scooter, the Google search engine or the Uber taxi app.' Thus, proposition simplifying can create markets that didn't exist before; moreover, proposition-simplifying products have the potential to carry a price premium in contrast to price-simplifying products. To investigate the benefits of proposition simplification, the authors studied Amazon, Google, Apple (the iPod years), Advanced RISC Machines (ARM), Tetra Pak and Boston Consulting Group (BCG).

The results of the study of these twelve companies (six price simplifiers and six proposition simplifiers) were summarized as follows: 'The twelve case studies of simplifying companies all display very high increases in market value, high annual rates of increase and significant outperformance when compared with rival companies or stock market indices. The returns from both price-simplifying and proposition-simplifying are very high, with no indication that one type ultimately results in higher financial returns than the other. (The sample sizes are very small, however, so more extensive research might reveal some differences that we have not detected.) The increases in value for all twelve of these simplifiers have persisted for decades, even once the major period of simplifying innovation has ended.'

'Alan Siegel and Robert Gale run the brand strategy and design firm Siegel+Gale, which is part of the Omnicom Group. The firm's tagline is 'Simple is smart', and their website states, 'We believe in the power of simplicity. At Siegel+Gale, we own it, defend it and live by it.'[11]

Siegel+Gale run the Global Brand Simplicity Index, ranking the world's simplest brands. Their 2018–19 report states that the firm '. . . surveyed more than 15,000 people across nine countries to understand which brands and industries provide the simplest experiences.'[12] These ranked companies were Netflix, Aldi, Google, Lidl, Carrefour, McDonald's, Trivago, Spotify, Uniqlo and Subway. The key findings from the report are summarized and quoted as under:

- 55 per cent of people are willing to pay more for simpler experiences.
- 64 per cent of people are more likely to recommend a brand that delivers simple experiences.
- A stock portfolio of the simplest global brands has outperformed the average of the major indexes by 679 per cent since 2009.
- Companies that fail to provide simple experiences leave an estimated share of $98 billion on the table.[13]

Thus, the findings of the study by Koch and Lockwood as well as the returns on the 2018–19 Global Brand Simplicity Index seem to indicate that simplicity does yield impressive financial results too.

* * *

Key takeaways from this chapter

- Simple ideas often require complex execution. The most successful business leaders have also been great simplifiers. For example, Henry Ford, the McDonald brothers and Ray Kroc, Herb Kelleher, Steve Jobs and many more. Successful entrepreneurs take simple ideas and build them into massive businesses.

- So how can one achieve simplicity in business? First, specialization and creativity: start with ignoring industry norms and develop original ideas. Second: build collaboration among diverse teams by aligning conflicting goals to a common organizational objective. Leaders must encourage groups to create and maintain their own identity. And, paradoxically, leaders must be able to help these groups focus on the common goal.

- Simplicity in business works because a simple strategy is easy for people to follow and execute. When there is deviation from a simple strategy, the in-built simplicity itself ensures that the deviation is spotted early, course-corrected, after which the team gets back on track.

- Simplicity in business also yields outsized financial results. An index of the global brand simplicity leaders has outperformed benchmarks by large margins.

How Apurva Purohit Built Radio City around the Tenet of Simplicity

Apurva Purohit is the president of Jagran Prakashan Limited, which owns publications such as *Dainik Jagran* and *Mid-Day* as well as various other media businesses. Apurva is a veteran in the media and entertainment industry and worked with the Zee Group and the Times Television Network before joining the FM radio station Radio City (corporate name Music Broadcast Limited—MBL) in 2005. In 2015, the Jagran Group acquired Radio City, and in 2016, Apurva became president of Jagran Prakashan.

Apurva is a graduate from Stella Maris College in Chennai, where she played hockey for Madras University and then represented Tamil Nadu in state-level hockey tournaments. She holds a PGDM degree from IIM Bangalore and is also the author of two books—*Lady, You're Not a Man!: The Adventures of a Woman at Work*[14] and *Lady, You're the Boss!: The Adventures of a Woman at Work – Part 2*[15].

Apurva has a refreshing take on simplicity in business. In a tough and niche business such as FM radio, Apurva led MBL to profitability in FY13 and the firm has stayed consistently profitable since then, clocking impressive financials along the way. She is a big believer in organizations having a simple, no-nonsense, no-frills vision and communicating it clearly across the firm.

We met Apurva at the colourful MBL office near Bandra Kurla Complex on 12 September 2019, which was the last day of Ganpati Visarjan and also an expectedly rainy Mumbai morning.

Apurva uses a very interesting concept—called F1—to introduce clarity in all business debates which take place under her command. We will explain F1 to you in a bit, but before we do that it is interesting to understand the origins of Apurva's F1 thinking. She told us that the idea went back to her college days when they had to play one sport and she chose hockey, 'My F1 was to be in the team, so I applied for goalkeeper. I knew no one was trying to be the goalkeeper. So I trialled to be the goalkeeper and I got selected and went on to play for the Tamil Nadu state. If I was trying to be centre forward, I would never get in because that was the most fought for position.' Apurva believes that the four ashramas of Hinduism (brahmacharya or student, grihastha or household, vanaprastha or retirement, and sanyasa or renunciation) can teach us what to focus on in each stage of life. 'You can have it all but not at the same time. Clarity comes from reflection,' she told us.

How does one develop thinking with such clarity? Apurva shares from her early life when she was not a very popular student: 'I was this student who comes first, sits very earnestly in class, always reads her books . . . not very popular with people.' This wasn't easy when you are a child and are seeking approval and validation from the entire world. But over time, Apurva learnt that rather than worrying about what people around her were saying she should listen, instead, to her voice within.

Recalling her advertising days setting up Lodestar Media, Apurva told us, 'The good or bad part of the advertising industry then was that agencies were unstructured organizations. I had no mentors, no KRAs [key result areas], no boss.' This lack of a higher authority or a mentor did not affect Apurva. She made it work for her and even today advocates that while we can draw lessons from mentors, we should look within ourselves and not worry about being popular. Apurva is also a big believer in moral compass and fairness. 'I think the earlier you develop a moral compass and know what's fair and what's not, the better it is for you,' she told us.

But life isn't fair and neither is corporate life. How does Apurva then ensure fairness within her organization? She outlined her philosophy to us, saying, 'Fairness is the hallmark of the Radio City culture and it has been difficult to convince managers on this virtue despite my fifteen years of working there. People can tolerate a lot as long as they know you're being fair to them. You need to put your objectives clearly—that it is about the whole process. You need to demonstrate fairness and walk the talk, consistently. For example, I believe in appraisal-based increments that happen once in a year. I would not do mid-term corrections. I can't tell you how much pushback I got for this. But I don't make exceptions. Exceptions are the biggest destroyers of fairness.'

Toughness can cause dissent and alienate people. How does she ensure common ground? Apurva refers to the balanced scorecard (BSC) performance management tool. The BSC tool, as propagated by American accounting academician Robert Samuel Kaplan and management consultant David P. Norton, outlines four areas of measuring performance: financial perspective, customer perspective, internal business perspective, and innovation and learning perspective.[16] Apurva learnt the term 'F1' from the BSC tool, which specifies a primary goal at the top (F = financial). 'If we can do this at a company level, we can do this at a function level,' she told us.

While these concepts in clarity work in small businesses, would they really work in larger, complex, diverse organizations? Apurva believes they can, depending on how exactly your F1 is framed. If the F1 is restricted to increasing margins at the consolidated level, then a company operating in infrastructure can even look at acquiring an IT services firm. But if the F1 is framed as making the core business more efficient, then the firm can look at acquiring companies in the supply chain, distributors, etc. and entering other adjacent/complementary businesses.

How can we apply F1 to our lives, say, for a young person starting his or her career? Apurva tells us that they should start by listing down key motivational factors such as learning, money, power, etc. and choose the non-negotiable ones, without being too bothered with what the world says. 'Prioritize those factors that are non-negotiable and then go for the jobs that deliver those factors,' she tells us. For each of us, Apurva believes, there can be at any point in time only one F1. That F1 is your north star. That is what you need to prioritize above everything else.

'Don't run the race everyone else is running,' she tells us, giving her own example. Apurva laughed about how she wanted to start her career in the unconventional (for IIMB graduates at that time) areas of brand building, communication and creativity: 'I joined advertising straight out of IIM Bangalore. My salary brought down the average of the batch. But then if I'd worried about that, I wouldn't have become the youngest CEO of my batch twenty years ago.' Similarly, for those looking to reinvent themselves in their mid-careers, Apurva believes they should start with the small things that make them happy daily and marry those things with their broader purpose: 'As Annie

Dillard says, "The way we spend our days is, of course, how we spend our lives.'"

Apurva loves reading and when we ask her for her favourite books, she mentions Bertrand Russell's classic *The Conquest of Happiness*[17]. She also mentions *All Things Shining*[18] by Hubert Dreyfus and Sean Dorrance Kelly, which had an immense influence on her.

As we wrapped up, we asked Apurva why she did not carry her mobile to our meeting, as most CEOs are not seen without their mobile phones. 'All of us focus on building a CV but we don't focus enough on building our reputation. But reputation doesn't get built on a piece of paper, reputation is in interactions. As Gulzar wrote: *Ek bar waqt se, lamha gira kahin, wahan dastan mili, lamha kahee nahi* [Loose translation: Once a moment fell out of time, a story was found in that moment even as the moment vanished][19]. So I might never meet you again, but there is a reputation getting formed,' she explains. As we walked towards the Radio City car park we realized that the reputation being formed was a formidable one.

CHAPTER **9**

Building a Simple Framework to Achieve Your Financial Goals

'It's obvious that if a company generates high returns on capital and reinvests at high returns, it will do well. But this wouldn't sell books, so there's a lot of twaddle and fuzzy concepts that have been introduced that don't add much.'

—Charlie Munger[1]

'Complexity tends to be the default option that gets used to persuade investors to buy unnecessary investment products while the vast majority of people just need to understand more conventional options to succeed.'

—Ben Carlson[2]

The quest for lasting wealth

Living a simple but purposeful life requires persistent, focused effort. Running a business using the principles laid out in the preceding chapter of this book is a little trickier. But perhaps even trickier is managing your personal finances in a simple but effective manner. Why? Part of the challenge is that when it comes to your finances—unlike your day-to-day life—you are highly likely to be actively mis-sold to and/or brainwashed into investing in substandard investment products by an assorted army of fund managers, wealth managers and relationship managers from private banks. (It is hard to spot the difference between the various members of this tribe and, in the interests of full disclosure, Saurabh belongs to one of these tribes courtesy his role at Marcellus.)

However, when it comes to saving and investing money, arguably an even bigger problem than greedy intermediaries is you yourself. Most of us are prone to buying assets (stocks, bonds, houses, etc.) when they are expensive and when there is a buzz around these assets. And we are just as likely to sell when asset prices are low and falling lower still. In effect, therefore, most of us 'buy high and sell low'—the opposite of what we should be doing to enhance our wealth.

And just in case our animal instincts were not bad enough, very few of us actually know what our financial goals are. Why are we saving and investing money? What horizon are we saving over? Is our goal of buying a holiday villa in Goa as important as the goal of sending our daughter to study abroad? Is our goal of having a retirement lodge in the Himalayas as essential as our need to have a Rs 10-crore retirement pot?

Saving and investing for yourself is therefore a multilayered problem. The good news is that because it is a well-known problem, a whole industry has been built around solving it; you can easily access dozens of books, videos and coaches/planners who will help you with your financial planning. The bad news is that most of these books, videos and coaches/planners will confuse you as much as they will guide you.

So how can you use the Simplicity Paradigm to make investing simpler, easier and more effective? In this chapter we will draw upon the work done by two investment legends from the USA over the past half century, plus the work done by Saurabh and his associates.[3]

Being market savvy is not very helpful

The common thread that binds the three simplifying ideas for wealth creation presented in this chapter is that market savviness (i.e. being on top of what is happening in the financial markets) has very little to do with how much wealth you generate from your investments. In fact, it can be counterproductive—people who spend their days plugged into financial markets often generate less wealth than sensible investors elsewhere who continue with their day jobs oblivious to the gyrations of financial markets. Why does this happen?

The English poet D.H. Lawrence once noted that if we stare at a map long enough, 'the map appears to us more real than the land'.[4] Extending the metaphor to market data, if one stares at share prices, central bank pronouncements and quarterly results of companies long enough, the financial market appears to be more real (and more relevant) to an investor than the real world. Taken to its extreme, the obsession with prices and high-frequency data becomes a kind of psychological disorder wherein the investor loses all sense of perspective of the real world and builds algorithms to trade based on the smoke signals being generated tick by tick (i.e. nanosecond by nanosecond) by the financial market.

In their different ways, Warren Buffett, Charlie Munger, Rob Kirby and John Bogle understood this form of psychosis earlier than other investors and built varied investment methods to capitalize on this insight (that focusing on financial markets per se does not generate wealth). Buffett and Munger popularized the notion of delving deep into the sustainable competitive advantages of a company and understanding the quality of its accounts. Kirby created the coffee can portfolio method of investing, which one can argue is a powerful simplification of Buffett's and Munger's styles of investing. Bogle's insight was even more profound. We will discuss Kirby's and Bogle's insights in more detail further on in this chapter.

Kahneman's famous 'System 1 vs System 2' framework (from his book *Thinking, Fast and Slow*) can also be used to understand why being on top of stock market data does little to generate wealth or happiness. Brian Portnoy in his enjoyable book *The Geometry of Wealth: How to Shape a Life of Money and Meaning*[5] explains why System 1—which he calls our fast brain, i.e. the part of the brain most exposed to financial market data—leads to poor decision-making:

> The fast brain loves consistency. It is biased to confirm beliefs and see patterns even when they don't exist. It shies away from ambiguity and doubt. It accepts given categories and isn't fond of thinking in terms of probability, preferring specific predictions. It anchors on what you already think you know and ignores evidence that is hard to find. In Kahneman's terms, 'what you see is all there is'.

Notice the similarity between this last sentence excerpted from Portnoy's book and the D.H. Lawrence quote—financial markets create an illusory world which can drown those who immerse themselves in market data. This in turn leads to investment mirages, such as the one which led investors to buy shares in Indian non-bank lenders through 2015–18. Most of these shares turned out to be worth very little by 2019.

Saurabh does not have a single financial market app or social media app on his phone (which itself is a battered five-year-old thing). When he needs to check prices (which he sometimes does, given that he and his colleagues at Marcellus manage considerable sums of money for thousands of investors in India and abroad), he goes to the stock exchange's website using his phone. This process takes twenty to thirty seconds. That time lag switches off his fast brain/System 1. Most of Saurabh's colleagues at Marcellus— with the exception of Marcellus' traders—access stock price data using similar techniques.

Readers of this book who are not experts on financial markets therefore shouldn't worry about their lack of expertise. The path to a sustainable investment corpus actually begins with assessing and understanding your life goals.

Simplifying Idea 1: Ashvin B. Chhabra's goal-based investing

> 'Wealth, truly defined, is only achievable in the context of a life in which purpose and practice are thoughtfully calibrated. In isolation, neither deep thoughts nor long checklists is up to the task. To succeed, clear minds and dirty hands must work together.'
>
> —Brian Portnoy[6]

We all have goals; some of them are personal and some are for our broader family. Almost all of these goals carry a financial cost and our ability to meet those costs becomes the bedrock of our peace of mind and happiness. Financial planners in the USA have created a goal-based system of financial planning over the past twenty years. There are several variants of this system but the core message remains that you have to broadly segment your goals into three categories:

1. **Security**: These goals are extremely important to us and provide protection from anxiety.
2. **Stability**: These goals are not as important as the security-related goals; however, they ensure that we maintain a certain desired standard of living.
3. **Ambitions**: These goals may not be necessities but they help us achieve upward wealth mobility and give us a certain status in our social circle.

In this section we use the simple goal-based investing framework laid down by Ashvin B. Chhabra's superb book, *The Aspirational Investor: Investing in the Pursuit of Wealth and Happiness.*[7] We use examples from the lives of Akanksha Sharma and Suraj Trivedi, two fictitious (and yet familiar) characters introduced in the prologue of this book, to illustrate how this goal-based framework can be used to create investment plans that address Akanksha and Suraj's specific aspirations and goals, using their current salaries and financial positions as starting points. This approach to creating an investing plan is elaborated upon in much more detail in the final two chapters of *Coffee Can Investing: The Low-Risk Road to Stupendous Wealth.*

Exhibit 6: Akanksha's goals divided into three categories[8]

To add to Akanksha's disillusionment in regard to her career was the feeling of underachievement in her personal finances. A salary of Rs 1 crore per annum and heading a large product at a prestigious company with very bright prospects would be a dream come true for many of her peers and seniors as well. Akanksha also had a high savings rate, a habit that her father had trained her in since she was young. Unfortunately, Akanksha had made serious mistakes while handling her personal finances.

Firstly, carried away by the bull-market frenzy of 2008, she invested in poor-quality stocks (recommended to her by a discount brokerage) and ended up losing almost all her money in them in the stock market crash that followed. Secondly, whatever money she had left then, she invested in a real-estate project in the far-flung suburbs of Mumbai. The builder (then touted as 'safe' by her friends and family) had recently gone bankrupt and there was no news on when, if at all, the project would be completed. Having burnt her hands in stocks and real estate, Akanksha thought she had learnt her lessons and so to 'protect' her money in 'safe' asset investments, she had, for the past few years, turned to bank fixed deposits with a vengeance. Akanksha's quandary resembles what we call the 'dumbbell' approach to investing—namely, moving from one heavy side (too aggressive) of a dumbbell to the opposite side (too conservative).

As luck would have it, Akanksha's neighbour Smriti was a financial adviser with a stellar reputation for honesty and trust among high-net-worth individuals. Over many cups of coffee, hand-holding and hand-wringing, Smriti heard out Akanksha's journey and prepared a simple diagram capturing Akanksha's goals (see Exhibit 6), and a projected statement of fund requirements (see Exhibit 7).

Category	Goals	Current Cost in 2019 (₹ lakh)	Inflation	Year of Goal	Target Corpus (₹ lakh)
Security	Retirement corpus	39	8%	2034	2069
Stability	Daughter's higher education abroad	100	8%	2034	317
Ambition	Holiday home in Ranikhet	75	8%	2034	238
Total					2624

Exhibit 7: Projected statement of funds
required by Akanksha[9]

Smriti then took Akanksha's current savings (around Rs 66 lakh spread across savings and fixed deposit accounts) and prepared an investment plan with an allocation of 80 per cent towards equity and 20 per cent towards debt. The equity component was further split into index funds, Marcellus Investment Managers' Consistent Compounders Portfolio from their portfolio management services division (referred to here as 'Marcellus Consistent Compounders PMS'), and high-quality mid and small-cap mutual fund schemes. Smriti refused to allocate any money to real estate and gold.

Finally, Smriti assumed a) Akanksha's annual remuneration would grow at 12 per cent per annum and b) Akanksha would let Smriti's proposed investment plan run through fifteen years from 2019 to 2034. Based on these assumptions and the gross returns given in the table below, Smriti forecasted Akanksha's finances in 2034 at the end of the plan. By then, Akanksha would have achieved all her financial goals and could look forward to a well-funded retirement in which she could pursue her hobbies (travel, art and voluntary work). Interestingly enough, this plan is solely for Akanksha and doesn't include her husband Akash's personal finances.

	Percentage of Allocation	Gross Returns Pre-Tax (CAGR)
Equities	**80%**	
Stability (index funds)	10%	10%
Wealth compounding (Marcellus Consistent Compounders PMS)	45%	13%
Mid- and small-cap funds	25%	15%
Fixed income	**20%**	7%
Real estate	**0%**	Not applicable
Gold	**0%**	Not applicable
Total	**100%**	

Exhibit 8: Asset allocation and return assumptions for Akanksha's initial investible corpus[10]

(*Note: All calculations are based on assumptions and estimates. These recommendations have been made for representational purposes for this book and should not be considered as financial advice.*)

Income		Monthly (₹ lakh)	Yearly (₹ lakh)
2034 salary plus bonus (post-tax)		30	356
Expenses	**Percentage of Income**	**Monthly (₹lakh)**	**Yearly (₹ lakh)**
Daughter's education	9%	3	31
Household expenses	9%	3	31
Leisure	20%	6	72
Medical expenses	6%	2	21
Total	**43%**	**13**	**155**
Value of Akanksha's investment in equities (Rs)	**A**		**2,686**
Value of Akanksha's investment in fixed income (Rs)	**B**		**414**
Total Net worth in equities + fixed income (Rs)	**C = A + B**		**3,099**

Exhibit 9: Akanksha's Financial Position in 2034[11]

The second character from our opening story—young Suraj Trivedi—has several ambitions with very little time to achieve them. In less than fifteen years, he wants a dedicated corpus of Rs 1 crore for his own start-up. In these fifteen years, Suraj expects to have built his core skills, honed his talent, proved his mettle and, most importantly, developed a large enough network of people to launch his own start-up. He also knows that he doesn't have to wait to hit forty; he could also easily quit in the next three to five years and call on the mighty IIT-IIM network to help him get venture capital funding. That is what most of his friends were doing. But Suraj wants to get deep industry experience and have the freedom to test a few of his own ideas within his existing job without risking his own capital and maintaining the safety and security of a monthly salary. And Suraj's monthly salary is very important for him since it supports his fifty-year-old mother. Suraj is a single child and the only earning member of his family after his father died an untimely death when Suraj was just fifteen years old.

Even though Suraj's Rs 25-lakh salary is secure at Vedanga Capital, he is doing a bad job at managing his expenses and savings. Every other month he has been scrambling to his friends, asking them for money to pay his rent. The reason for this fund crunch? Day trading. Suraj is mindlessly punting his salary in futures and options. Suraj thinks he has developed a foolproof intraday trading system. And the system even worked for the first few months. But as soon as there were major, unexpected events (demonetization, Fed rate hikes/cuts, etc.) the markets caught him on the wrong foot, wiped out all his profits and ate into his capital. Suraj follows all the masters of trading on social media and is lured by the screenshots of trading positions that these 'celebrity' traders share publicly. Since Suraj spends most of his trading day (9 a.m. to 3.30 p.m.) tracking markets, he ends up spending late nights at work, adding to his overall stress. His bosses know of this but as long as Suraj delivers on his work, they aren't overly concerned.

On one such stressed out evening, Suraj bumped into Urvashi, his senior at IIM, at an IIM reunion at a microbrewery in Lower Parel. Urvashi had worked at one of India's largest wealth management firms and had recently started her own fee-based investment advisory service. Over a few drinks, Urvashi heard out Suraj's dilemma and told him that she would get back to him with a few thoughts a week from then.

Suraj forgot about the meeting when he hit his work desk on Monday but on Thursday evening, he got an email that would change his life. In a small attachment, Urvashi outlined Suraj's goals and what it would take financially to achieve these goals. He met Urvashi over the weekend and Urvashi explained her plan: 'Suraj, I think you should set your goals on a three-tier structure: a) the base is your security, which is a basic and comfortable lifestyle for yourself and your mother. This means enough money to cover rent, electricity, grocery, domestic help salaries and other minimum sustenance expenses. b) On top of that base we build stability. You need a good work-life balance considering how hard you work. Focus on your health, get enough time off. So shift your home closer to work, catch up with friends on weekends, and learn to enjoy life in Mumbai. All this will mean an increase in expenses but that would be worth it for the improved quality of life. Finally, c) we need to build that Rs 1-crore corpus for your start-up.' For starters, Suraj needed to immediately stop his day trading and then he needed to follow Urvashi's plan.

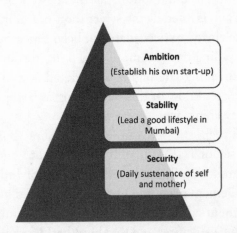

Exhibit 10: Suraj's goals divided into three tiers[12]

Category	Goals	Current Cost in 2019 (₹ lakh)	Inflation	Year of Goal	Future Cost (₹ lakh)
Security	Daily sustenance of self and mother	11	8%	2034	36
Stability	Leisure lifestyle in Mumbai	5	10%	2034	20
Ambition	Establish a start-up	100	8%	2034	317

Exhibit 11: Projected statement of funds required by Suraj[13]

Urvashi designed an investment charter for Suraj wherein she clearly explained that considering Suraj's risk-return profile, allocating 100 per cent of his savings towards equities would be ideal. The equity component was further split into index funds, Marcellus Consistent Compounders PMS, and a mix of mid-cap and small-cap mutual fund schemes. Assuming that Suraj's income would grow by 12 per cent per annum and he would not deviate from the financial plan, by the end of fifteen years or 2034, Suraj would have accumulated a corpus (from his net cash flows after removing the expenses for stability and security) that would be more than what he had targeted for his start-up, and hence he could look forward to running his own start-up and leading a well-rounded life.

	Percentage of Allocation	Gross Returns Pre-Tax (CAGR)
Equities	**100%**	
Stability (index funds)	10%	10%
Wealth compounding (Marcellus Consistent Compounders PMS)	55%	13%
Mid- and small-cap funds	35%	15%
Fixed income	**0%**	Not applicable
Real estate	**0%**	Not applicable
Gold	**0%**	Not applicable
Total	**100%**	

Exhibit 12: Asset allocation for Suraj's initial investible corpus[14]

(*Note: All calculations are based on assumptions and estimates. These recommendations have been made for representational purposes for this book and should not be considered as financial advice.*)

Income		Monthly (₹ lakh)	Yearly (₹ lakh)
2034 salary plus bonus (post-tax)		7	89
Expenses	**Percentage of Income**	**Monthly (₹ lakh)**	**Yearly (₹ lakh)**
Rent/household expenses	26%	2	23
Mother's expenses	9%	1	8
Leisure (including any monthly instalments)	23%	2	20
Medical expenses (self + mother)	6%	0.4	5
Total	**63%**	**5**	**56**
Value of Suraj's investment in equities			**334**

Exhibit 13: Suraj's Financial Position in 2034[15]

While a goal-oriented financial plan gives you a broad sense of how much of your wealth you should invest in equities, it does not tell you how to go about choosing stocks or funds which will give you the ideal exposure to equities. To understand how to do so we turn to investing legends and their simple but powerful investment constructs.

Simplifying Idea 2: John Bogle and index funds

'Many investors are under the mistaken impression that mutual funds are a secure and relatively matter-of-fact way to gain the benefits of diversification at low cost. In reality . . . mutual funds have a large incentive to benefit from the economics of their business, rather than look after their investors' long-term wealth. Thus we see some mutual funds not only charge outsized fees, but also practice portfolio management strategies which leave investors behind market index averages . . .'

—Arthur Levitt, the longest serving chairman of the US Securities and Exchange Commission (SEC)[16]

'If a statue is ever erected to honour the person who has done the most for American investors, the hands down choice should be Jack Bogle. For decades, Jack has urged investors to invest in ultra-low-cost index funds. In his crusade, he amassed only a tiny percentage of the wealth that has typically flowed to managers who have promised their investors large rewards while delivering them nothing . . . of added value. In his early years, Jack was frequently mocked by the investment-management industry. Today, however, he has the satisfaction of knowing that he helped millions of investors realize far better returns on their savings than they otherwise would have earned.'

—Warren Buffett[17] on John Bogle

Bogle's journey from being a Princeton University student to becoming an investment legend

Born in 1929 in Montclair, New Jersey, to an American family hit hard by the Great Depression, John Clifton Bogle is arguably the most radically influential figure to emerge from the world of investing in the past 100 years. Having studied economics and investing at Princeton University and having written a 130-page thesis on the US mutual fund industry—titled *The Economic Role of the Investment Company*—while at Princeton, Bogle was by his mid-twenties one of the smartest thinkers in the US investment management industry.

His industry knowledge and work ethic ensured a rapid ascent at Wellington Fund and in 1970, aged forty-one, he was named as the chairman of this pioneering mutual fund house. Four years later, an unwise merger approved by Bogle led to his downfall and he was 'fired with enthusiasm', amidst much acrimony, by the board of Wellington. In one of the most celebrated comebacks in American business, Bogle not only bounced back to found Vanguard in 1975 but also pioneered a new style of investing, which has become over the last twenty years the default method for investing in developed markets such as the USA.

When Bogle launched Vanguard, the great and the good in America launched an attack on him. Edward Johnson, the Chairman of Fidelity, led the sceptics, assuring the world that Fidelity had no intention of following Vanguard's lead. 'I can't believe that the great mass of investors are going to be satisfied with just receiving average returns. The name of the game is to be the best,' said Johnson.[18] Fidelity now runs nearly $500 billion worth of indexed assets.

Never one to care too much about what the establishment was saying, Bogle drew inspiration from the path-breaking research published by Nobel laureate Paul Samuelson. Samuelson is the foremost academic economist of the preceding century not least because of his seminal textbook, *Economics: An Introductory Analysis*, which was first published in 1948 and has served as a primer on the subject for millions of youngsters across the world. Among Samuelson's several path-breaking insights, the one which has had the greatest impact on financial markets is the efficient-market theory, which says that asset prices fully reflect all available information. By implication, therefore, it is impossible to 'beat the market' consistently on a risk-adjusted basis since market prices should only react to new information.

Bogle took the efficient-market theory to heart and was among the first executives in the mutual fund industry to fully understand its profound implication, namely, it makes little or no sense to pay juicy fees to a fund manager to manage your money given that the fund manager has little or no chance of consistently beating the market. Thus was born Bogle's breakthrough idea—in 1976, Vanguard launched the world's first index mutual fund. Instead of beating the index and charging high fees, the index fund would mimic the index performance over the long run—thus achieving higher returns with lower costs than the costs associated with actively managed funds.

Take the following example: suppose two people—Sarbani and Saurabh—graduate from university on the same day and get jobs with identical salaries. Assume further that throughout their forty-year-long careers, they save identical amounts and invest with fund managers who generate identical returns of 12 per cent per annum (before fees). The only difference is that Sarbani uses an index fund which charges 0.1 per cent per annum, and Saurabh uses an active fund manager, which charges 2.5 per cent per annum. As a result, over her entire career, Sarbani generates 2.4 per cent per annum more than Saurabh and thus retires with a corpus that is *2.3 times* as large as Saurabh's! This is because fees and expenses borne by customers of mutual funds have an exponential impact—the 2.4 per cent that Sarbani saves relative to Saurabh compounds over time to make her twice as rich as Saurabh.

In fact, Bogle's central insight—that actively managed mutual funds are not worth the fees they charge—has a deeper implication. Bogle figured out that even if the efficient-market theory does *not* hold—and therefore even if markets are 'wildly inefficient'—by definition, around half of the fund managers would underperform the index *before* fees and expenses are taken into account. Therefore, once you subtract the fees and expenses from fund performance, you get:

Net returns to the investor = (Gross returns from the fund) – (Fees and expenses of running the fund)

On this basis, more than half the fund managers will underperform the market. In separate studies, Bogle, Morningstar and Rob Arnott (of Research Affiliates) have found that over the past three decades, around 75–90 per cent of US mutual funds underperform the index[19]. In India, if we take the last three years' track record (up to the end of 2018), the ratio for underperforming large-cap mutual funds is around 90 per cent, i.e. barely 10 per cent of large-cap mutual funds in India are able to justify their fees.[20]

Even more remarkably, as we highlight in the next section, it is impossible to predict which large-cap mutual funds will outperform going forward—outperformance by such funds seems to be a random affair. Furthermore, in India as in the USA, most mutual funds which outperform are small (in terms of the assets under management). In particular, in India we have noticed that once a large-cap fund exceeds Rs 10,000 crore ($1.4 billion) in assets, outperformance ebbs away.

In 1975, Bogle took this simple insight with regard to the importance of costs and proceeded to build a firm which crushed the cost of money management in several ways, including:

- **Portfolio turnover-related costs:** In order to minimize the costs associated with brokerage, price impact and taxes, Bogle believed that portfolio turnover should be at most 3–5 per cent. In most large stock markets, most funds have portfolio turnover in excess of 30 per cent. Over a ten-year period in India, such a fund will end up giving away a quarter of the investor's wealth to stockbrokers (via commissions) and to the taxman (via transaction taxes and capital gains taxes).

- **Advertising costs**: In his book *The Clash of the Cultures: Investment vs. Speculation*, Bogle wrote: 'There is no evidence whatsoever that advertising benefits fund investors by bringing in an amount of new assets adequate to create economies of scale that offset the amount spent.' As a result, for the first thirty years of its existence, Vanguard barely advertised. Over the past decade it has stepped up its spending but even now: (a) it spends much less on advertising than its mainstream competitors; (b) almost all of its spend is on digital media (no mainstream newspaper or TV spend); and (c) every dollar spent on advertising is tracked carefully.[21]

- **Distribution costs**: The world over, fund managers use distributors/brokers to sell their products to the ultimate investor. In return, the fund manager pays commissions to these intermediaries. In India, these commissions can be as high as 70 per cent of the fees paid by the ultimate investor to the fund manager. When Vanguard was two years old, Bogle severed links with all the intermediaries who sold Vanguard's funds and moved the entire sales and marketing function in-house. Bogle thus gave the world its first fund with no distribution costs associated with it. In 2013, SEBI declared that all Indian mutual funds had to have a 'direct' option, i.e. an option wherein the investor can invest directly without having to go through a distributor.

As a result of Bogle's vision, the expense ratio for Vanguard's funds is 11 basis points (bps) compared to the 64 bps for an average mutual fund in the USA. (The expense ratio is a mutual fund's annual operating expenses, expressed as a percentage of the fund's average net assets.) That 53 bps differential is huge. It almost ensures that Vanguard's funds will outperform the vast majority of actively managed funds on a consistent basis. As a result, Vanguard's clients would make much more money than the clients of most active managers. Such is the centrality of costs in the world of investing that Morningstar and Bogle have shown in separate number-crunching exercises that the most reliable predictor of a fund's future performance is its expense ratio.

In India, the cost differential between active versus passive investing is much bigger than it is in the USA. Large-cap ETFs in India are now available with an expense ratio of 5 bps. In contrast, the expense ratio of large-cap mutual funds in India is in excess of 100 bps. Assuming an expense ratio advantage of just 100 bps in favour of ETFs implies that Indian investors would save Rs 800 crore ($120 million) per annum if they invested in ETFs rather than large-cap mutual funds. Given that less than 4 per cent of the Indian mutual fund industry's assets under management (AUM) is in passively managed assets, you can draw your conclusions regarding the direction in which the share of index funds and ETFs will go in India.[22]

But there is much more to Bogle's legacy than just low-cost index mutual funds. He realized that there is a two-tier principal-agent problem in the fund management industry: the first between the fund manager and his client (this is the problem which the index fund addresses) and the second between the fund manager and the owners/shareholders of the fund management house (the standard principal-agent problem in any business).

To address the latter issue, Bogle came up with an utterly novel construct: Vanguard would be owned by its clients! This solution actually addresses both the principal-agent problems: if the clients control the fund manager, not only does that compel the fund manager to keep his costs—including compensation costs—low, it also forces him to responsibly build a long-term franchise which is in the best interests of the shareholders who also happen to be the clients. The fund manager is therefore answerable to only one master—the client—and not two (as is the case in most privately owned companies).

Thirdly, Bogle figured out that beyond greedy fund managers, the investor is surrounded by other agents—promoters/CEOs, auditors, investment bankers, sell-side analysts, lawyers—who collude with the promoter to gouge the investor. He called this the 'double agency society' problem. To quote him:

> The nature of this largely tacit conspiracy is not complex, and its web is wide. It includes the managers of our giant corporations – their CEOs and CFOs, directors, auditors, and lawyers – and Wall Street – investment bankers, sell-side analysts, buy-side research departments, and the managers of giant investment institutions. Their shared goal: to increase the price of a firm's stock . . . to raise the value of its currency for acquisitions, to enhance the profits executives realise when they exercise their stock options . . .
>
> How to accomplish this objective? Project high long-term earnings growth, offer regular guidance to the financial community as to your short-term progress and, whether by fair means or foul, *never* fall short of the expectations you've established. Ultimately, these ambitious goals are doomed to fail for corporations as a group.[23]

While Bogle worked in the USA, much of what he says is equally applicable to India. By implication, the Indian investor is not only battling against the high fees charged by Indian fund managers but also against a system loaded in favour of promoters.

In Chapter 3 of *Coffee Can Investing*, Saurabh and his colleagues have shown how high Indian mutual funds' fees are relative to their very modest ability to outperform the Indian stock market.

In Chapter 10 of *The Unusual Billionaires*, Saurabh showed that there is very strong empirical evidence that in India the poorer a company's accounting quality, the weaker its shareholders' returns. The chapter also highlights how the majority of listed companies in India have subpar accounting quality (when measured using a battery of forensic accounting ratios).

At Marcellus Investment Managers, Saurabh and his colleagues have broken free of this construct by: (a) using in-house forensic accounting models rather than believing the audited financial statements published by companies; (b) conducting in-depth research in-house rather than using the research published by investment banks; and (c) crushing the fixed costs that have to be borne by investors to negligible levels.

Implications for investors

Nearly two-thirds of the Rs 7,20,000 crore (around $100 billion) equity assets managed by Indian mutual funds are invested in large-cap and mid-cap stocks (defined by the Indian regulator as the top 250 companies by market cap).[24]

As mentioned earlier, credible studies of Indian mutual funds now show that 80–90 per cent of large-cap mutual funds fail to beat the relevant benchmarks. Such sustained underperformance actually masks even deeper challenges for these funds. In Saurabh's previous co-authored book, *Coffee Can Investing*, it has been shown that:

- Of the thirty to forty leading large-cap mutual fund schemes in India that managed to generate top quartile performance in a given three-year period, around 45 per cent deliver subpar returns (i.e. returns in the bottom two quartiles) in the subsequent three-year period[25].
- This reversion to mean implies that over the past decade, there have been *only three* leading mutual funds in India which have managed to consistently stay in the top quartile.

The remaining ninety-seven have either been outside the top quartile for the entire decade, or have sporadically entered the top quartile—suggesting that luck, as much as skill, is responsible for their performance.

- The two preceding bullets are flattered by 'survivorship bias' because the mutual fund industry's trade body, AMFI, reports all fund performance data after deleting the results of the funds which have been shut down. Since over 30 per cent of Indian large-cap mutual fund schemes have been wound up between 2009 and 2019, excluding these dead schemes obviously flatters the industry's performance (on the reasonable presumption that the funds which have been shut down were the worst performing funds).[26]

In light of the above, it is not surprising that Indian equity investors are migrating away from large-cap funds towards the alternative asset management industry. Even though the alternatives industry in India is not exactly populated by saints, assets under management for it have rocketed from negligible levels a decade ago to Rs 2,50,000 crore as of February 2020 (or $35 billion; Rs 1,10,000 crore for AIF + Rs 1,40,000 crore for PMS). As one would expect, wealthier and better informed Indian investors are at the forefront of this shift from mutual funds to alternative assets but if the American experience is anything to go by, less affluent investors are unlikely to be far behind.

Simplifying Idea 3: Robert Kirby and Coffee Can Investing

'In investing, as in auto racing, you don't have to win every lap to win the race, but you absolutely do have to finish the race. While a driver must be

> prepared to take some risks, if he takes too many
> risks, he'll wind up against the fence. There are
> sensible risks—and there are risks that make no
> sense at all.'

—Robert G. Kirby of Capital Group[27]

Headquartered in Los Angeles, Capital Group is one of the world's largest asset management firms with assets under management in excess of $1.4 trillion. In the late 1960s, Capital Group set up an entity called Capital Guardian Trust Company, whose aim was to provide traditional investment counselling services to wealthy individuals. Robert Kirby joined Capital in 1965 as the main investment manager at Capital Guardian Trust, where his job involved advising high-net-worth clients on their investments and managing their portfolios. Nearly twenty years later he wrote a remarkable article which introduced to the world the concept of the 'coffee can portfolio'.

In the article[28] written in 1984, Kirby narrated an incident involving his client's husband. The gentleman had purchased stocks recommended by Kirby in denominations of $5,000 each but, unlike Kirby, did not sell anything from the portfolio. This process (of buying when Kirby bought but not selling thereafter) led to enormous wealth creation for the client over a period of about ten years. The wealth creation was mainly on account of one position transforming to a jumbo holding worth over $800,000 which came from 'a zillion shares of Xerox'. Impressed by this approach of 'buy and forget' followed by this gentleman, Kirby coined the term 'coffee can portfolio', in which the 'coffee can' harkens back to the Wild West, when Americans, before the widespread advent of banks, saved their valuables in a coffee can and kept it under a mattress.

Although Kirby made the discovery of the coffee can portfolio sound serendipitous, the central insight behind this construct—that in order to truly get rich, an investor has to let a sensibly constructed portfolio stay untouched for a long period of time—is as powerful as it is profound. After all, the instinctive thing for a hard-working, intelligent investor is to try to optimize his portfolio periodically, usually once a year. It is very, very hard for investors to leave a portfolio untouched for ten years. A retail investor will be tempted to intervene whenever he sees stocks in the portfolio sag in price. A professional investor will feel that he has a fiduciary responsibility to intervene if parts of the portfolio are underperforming. But Kirby's counter-intuitive insight is that an investor will make way more money if he leaves the portfolio untouched.

It is possible to recreate Kirby's coffee can investing approach for the Indian stock market, and this exercise has been described in detail in Saurabh's previous book, *Coffee Can Investing* (co-authored with Rakshit Ranjan and Pranab Uniyal). What follows is a summary of the approach described in that book.

Robert Kirby's construct applied to India

We use straightforward investment filters to identify 10–25 high-quality stocks and we then leave the portfolio untouched for a decade. Both in backtesting and in live portfolios we find that this simple approach delivers consistently impressive results. In particular, the portfolio not only outperforms the benchmark consistently, it also delivers healthy absolute returns and, more specifically, it performs extremely well when the broader market is experiencing stress.

Before we detail the returns delivered by this investment approach, let us explain the simple investment filters that can be used to build a portfolio which is aligned to Kirby's philosophy of buying great companies and leaving them alone in your portfolio for long periods of time. To begin with, of the approximately 6,000 listed companies in India, we limit our search to companies with a minimum market capitalization of Rs 100 crore, as the reliability of the data on companies smaller than this is somewhat suspect. There are around 1,500 listed companies in India with a market cap above Rs 100 crore. Within this universe we look for companies that over the preceding decade have grown sales each year by at least 10 per cent alongside generating return on capital employed (pre-tax) of at least 15 per cent.

Why return on capital employed (ROCE)? A company deploys capital in assets which in turn generates cash flows and profits. The total capital deployed by the company consists of equity and debt. ROCE is a metric that measures the efficiency of capital deployment for a company, calculated as a ratio of 'earnings before interest and tax' (EBIT) in the numerator and capital employed (sum of debt liabilities and shareholder's equity) in the denominator. The higher the ROCE, the better the company's efficiency of capital deployment.

Why use a ROCE filter of 15 per cent? We use 15 per cent as a minimum because we believe that is the bare minimum return required to beat the cost of capital. Adding the risk-free rate (8 per cent in India) to the equity risk premium[29] of 6.5–7 per cent gives a cost of capital broadly in that range. The equity risk premium, in turn, is calculated as 4 per cent (the long-term US equity risk premium) plus 2.5 per cent to account for

India's credit rating (BBB–, as per S&P). A country's credit rating affects the risk premium as a higher rating (e.g. AAA, AA) indicates greater economic stability in the country which lowers the risk premium for investing in that country, and a lower credit rating indicates comparatively lower economic stability which, in turn, raises the risk premium for investing in that country.

Why use a revenue growth filter of 10 per cent every year? India's nominal GDP growth rate has averaged 13 per cent over the past ten years. Nominal GDP growth is different from real GDP growth in that unlike the latter, nominal GDP growth is *not* adjusted for inflation. In simple terms, it is gross domestic product (GDP) evaluated at current market prices (GDP being the monetary value of all the finished goods and services produced within a country's borders in a specific time period). A credible firm operating in India should, therefore, be able to deliver sales growth of at least that much every year. However, very few listed companies, only six out of the nearly 1,500 firms screened by Marcellus Investment Managers, have managed to achieve this! Therefore, Saurabh has reduced this filter rate modestly to 10 per cent, i.e. he looks for companies that have delivered revenue growth of 10 per cent every year for ten consecutive years.[30]

For financial services stocks, we modify the filters of return on equity (ROE) and sales growth as follows:

ROE of 15 per cent: We prefer return on equity[31] over return on assets (ROA)[32] because this is a fairer measure of the ability of banks and non-bank lenders to generate higher income efficiently on a given equity capital base over time.[33]

Loan growth of 15 per cent: Given that nominal GDP growth in India has averaged 13 per cent over the past ten years, a loan growth of at least 15 per cent is an indication of a bank's ability to lend over business cycles.

Now, let us look at the results. Detailed backtesting of this investment approach based on data going back to 1991 shows that *such a portfolio beats benchmarks across most time periods*. The portfolio also performs admirably well during stressful periods (like the Lehman crisis in 2008) when the overall stock market nosedived. If invested for over a decade with no churn, this portfolio generates returns that are substantially higher than the benchmark (median compounded annualized outperformance over the last nineteen years of 7 per cent points).

iterations[34]

Kick-off Year	No. of Stocks #	Portfolio Start Date	Value	Portfolio End Date	Value	Portfolio TSR CAGR	Sensex TSR CAGR	Outperformance relative to Sensex
2000	5	01-07-2000	500	30-06-2010	3,831	22.6%	16.0%	6.6%
2001	6	01-07-2001	600	30-06-2011	9,802	32.2%	20.5%	11.7%
2002	8	01-07-2002	800	30-06-2012	7,631	25.3%	20.2%	5.1%
2003	9	01-07-2003	900	30-06-2013	10,117	27.4%	20.2%	7.2%
2004	10	01-07-2004	1,000	30-06-2014	16,880	32.7%	19.7%	12.9%
2005	9	01-07-2005	900	30-06-2015	6,659	22.2%	16.1%	6.0%
2006	10	01-07-2006	1,000	30-06-2016	6,376	20.4%	11.4%	9.0%
2007	15	01-07-2007	1,500	30-06-2017	9,030	19.7%	9.3%	10.3%
2008	11	01-07-2008	1,100	30-06-2018	7,442	21.1%	12.2%	8.9%
2009	11	01-07-2009	1,100	30-06-2019	5,950	18.4%	12.0%	6.4%
2010	7	01-07-2010	700	30-06-2019	2,137	13.2%	11.0%	2.2%
2011	14	01-07-2011	1,400	30-06-2019	2,911	9.6%	11.3%	-1.7%
2012	22	01-07-2012	2,200	30-06-2019	8,645	21.6%	14.0%	7.6%
2013	18	01-07-2013	1,800	30-06-2019	6,643	24.3%	13.9%	10.4%
2014	17	01-07-2014	1,700	30-06-2019	4,351	20.7%	10.5%	10.1%
2015	20	01-07-2015	2,000	30-06-2019	3,314	13.5%	10.3%	3.1%
2016	17	01-07-2016	1,700	30-06-2019	2,332	11.1%	14.6%	-3.5%
2017	12	01-07-2017	1,200	30-06-2019	1,480	11.0%	14.2%	-3.2%
2018	9	01-07-2018	900	30-06-2019	964	7.1%	12.5%	-5.4%

For any stock, and indeed for any portfolio, one can disaggregate the source of investment returns into two sources: (a) the growth in profits; and (b) the growth in the price/earnings (P/E) multiple. Even more interesting than the ability of Kirby's approach to consistently outperform the Sensex is the source of this outperformance—namely healthy profit growth (measured by earnings per share [EPS] CAGR in Exhibit 15) rather than P/E rerating of the stocks in the portfolios. As the final three columns of the table show, in the vast majority of the iterations, the dominant driver of returns is profit growth (measured by EPS growth).

Date	Value	Date	Value	EPS CAGR*	P/E CAGR*	TSR** CAGR
2000	500	2010	3,831	19%	3%	22.6%
2001	600	2011	9,802	17%	13%	32.2%
2002	800	2012	7,631	17%	7%	25.3%
2003	900	2013	10,117	19%	7%	27.4%
2004	1,000	2014	16,880	19%	12%	32.7%
2005	900	2015	6,659	15%	6%	22.2%
2006	1,000	2016	6,376	19%	1%	20.4%
2007	1,500	2017	9,030	16%	3%	19.7%
2008	1,100	2018	7,442	12%	8%	21.1%
2009	1,100	2019	5,950	13%	5%	18.4%
2010	700	2019	2,137	5%	8%	13.2%
2011	1,400	2019	2,911	1%	9%	9.6%
2012	2,200	2019	8,645	4%	17%	21.6%
2013	1,800	2019	6,643	8%	15%	24.3%
2014	1,700	2019	4,351	13%	6%	20.7%
2015	2,000	2019	3,314	12%	1%	13.5%
2016	1,700	2019	2,332	9%	2%	11.1%
2017	1,200	2019	1,480	15%	-4%	11.0%
2018	900	2019	964	13%	-5%	7.1%

Exhibit 15: Disaggregating the returns from Kirby's investment approach into profit growth (measured by EPS CAGR) and P/E growth[35]

In the next exhibit we have analysed the performance of these nineteen historical iterations of our application of Kirby's approach with each portfolio lasting for up to ten years of holding period, i.e. nearly 150 years of cumulative portfolio investments. The median portfolio return[36] (compounded and annualized) has remained robust at around 24–25 per cent historically. Moreover, this investment approach also delivers an extremely low level of volatility in these annualized returns for all holding periods—a necessary condition for investors to have a large exposure to equities in their net worth.

In more technical terms, analysing the numbers behind Exhibit 15 shows that over the past nineteen years, the returns generated from this approach are positive for all holding periods of three years or more, and have been in excess of 9 per cent per annum for all holding periods of five years or more. In simple terms, it means that Kirby's approach offers more than a 95 per cent probability of generating a positive return as long as investors hold the portfolio for at least three years. If held for at least five years, there is more than 95 per cent probability of generating a return greater than 9 per cent.

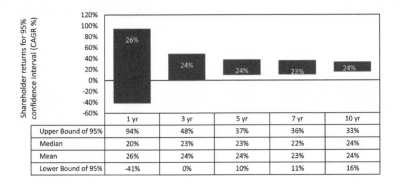

	1 yr	3 yr	5 yr	7 yr	10 yr
Upper Bound of 95%	94%	48%	37%	36%	33%
Median	20%	23%	23%	22%	24%
Mean	26%	24%	24%	23%	24%
Lower Bound of 95%	-41%	0%	10%	11%	16%

Exhibit 16: Returns from Kirby's investment approach have been robust across various holding periods (X-axis), with limited volatility in these returns, as depicted by the height of vertical bars which measure two standard deviations (95 per cent confidence interval) of returns[37]

Just to emphasize the importance of 24–25 per cent CAGR returns, a run-rate of 26 per cent return per annum results in the portfolio growing in size to ten times in ten years, 100 times in twenty years and 1,000 times in thirty years.

Why does Kirby's investment approach perform so well?

> 'The ancient Romans were used to being defeated.
> Like the rulers of history's great empires, they
> could lose battle after battle but still win the war.
> An empire that cannot sustain a blow and remain
> standing is not really an empire.'
>
> —Yuval Noah Harari[38]

Many historians take the view that the 'greatness' of a kingdom or an empire should be measured by its longevity. How long did the empire sustain? How durable was the empire? By this measure, the first great empire was arguably the Persian Empire. Founded around 550 BCE, it lasted for around 200 years until Alexander the Great brought it to an end in 330 BCE by defeating King Darius III. However, by the same measure, the Roman Empire is by some distance the greatest empire that the world has ever seen. While the first Roman Republic, headquartered in Rome, lasted from 100 BCE to 400 CE, the imperial successor to the Republic lasted for a staggering 1,400 years before falling to the Ottoman Turks in 1453. So ubiquitous is the influence of this empire that the language in which we are writing this book, the legal system which forms the basis of the contract between the publisher and the authors of this book, the mathematical concept of compounding which underpins much of this book, all of them come more or less directly from the Roman Empire!

When it comes to investing in stock markets, as Saurabh explains in the opening chapter of *The Unusual Billionaires*, greatness is defined as the ability of a company to grow while sustaining its moats over long periods of time[39]. This then enables such great companies to sustain superior financial performance over several decades.

Our application of Kirby's philosophy of investing is built upon using these twin filters to identify great companies that have the DNA to sustain their competitive advantages over ten to twenty years (or longer). This is because 'greatness' is not temporary and it is surely not a short-term phenomenon. Greatness does not change from one quarterly result to another. In fact, great companies can endure difficult economic conditions. Their growth is not beholden to domestic or global growth—they thrive in economic down cycles as well. Great companies do not get disrupted by evolution in their customers' preferences or competitors or the operational aspects of their business. Their management teams have strategies that deliver results better than their competition can. These great companies effectively separate themselves from their competition using these strategies. Over time, they learn from their mistakes and increase the distance between themselves and their competition. Often, such companies appear conservative. However, they do not confuse conservatism with complacency—these companies simply bide their time to make the right moves. These traits are common among great companies and are rarely found outside great companies.

Secondly, a critical feature of our application of Kirby's investment approach is that not only does it use the twin filters (ROCE above 15 per cent and revenue growth of 10 per cent) to identify great companies, it then holds these companies for ten years. In fact, during that decade, this investing approach does not make any changes to the portfolio. That might strike several readers to be strange to the point of irresponsible.

We believe that there are very compelling reasons to not touch investment portfolios for long periods of time. In fact, churn in a portfolio goes against the basic philosophy of long-term investing, which is a cornerstone of Robert Kirby's original 'coffee can' construct. Here are *four* compelling factors which go against churn in a portfolio composed of great companies:

Reason 1—Higher probability of profits over longer periods of time: As is well understood, equities as an asset class is prone to extreme movements in the short term. For example, while the Sensex has returned more than 15 per cent CAGR returns over the last twenty-five years, there have been intermittent periods of unusually high drawdowns. In 2008, for instance, an investor entering the market near the peak in January would have lost over 60 per cent of value in less than twelve months of investing. Thus, while over longer time horizons, the odds of profiting from equity investments are very high, the same cannot be said of shorter time frames. In his book, *More Than You Know: Finding Financial Wisdom in Unconventional Places*[40], the celebrated American strategist Michael J. Mauboussin illustrates this concept using simple math in the context of US equities. We use that illustration and apply it in the context of Indian equities here.

The Sensex's returns over the past thirty years have been 15 per cent on a compounded annualized basis, while the standard deviation of returns has been 29 per cent. Now using these values of returns and standard deviation and assuming a normal distribution of returns (admittedly a simplifying assumption), the probability of generating positive returns over a one-day time horizon works out to 51.2 per cent. As the time horizon increases, the probability of generating positive returns goes up. The probability of generating positive returns goes up to 70 per cent if the time horizon increases to one year; the probability tends towards 100 per cent if the time horizon is increased to ten years.

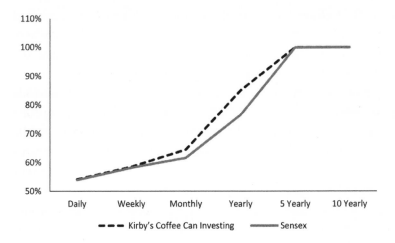

Exhibit 17: Probability of gains from equity investing in India (Sensex) increases disproportionately with increase in holding horizons[41]

Reason 2—The power of compounding: Holding a portfolio of stock for periods as long as ten years or more allows the power of compounding to play out its magic. Over the longer term, the portfolio comes to be dominated by the winning stocks while the losing stocks keep declining to eventually become inconsequential. Thus, the positive contribution of the winners disproportionately outweighs the negative contribution of the losers to eventually help the portfolio compound handsomely. We will illustrate the point here using simple mathematics. Let us consider a hypothetical portfolio that consists only of two stocks. One of these stocks, Stock A, grows at 26 per cent per annum while the other, say Stock B, declines at the same rate, i.e. at 26 per cent per annum. Overall, not only do we assume a fifty-fifty strike rate, we also assume symmetry around the magnitude of positive and negative returns generated by the winner and the loser respectively.

In Exhibit 18, we track the progress of this portfolio over a ten-year holding horizon. As time progresses, Stock B declines to irrelevance while the portfolio value starts converging to the value of holding in Stock A. Even with the assumed 50 per cent strike rate with symmetry around the magnitude of winning and losing returns, the portfolio compounds at a healthy 17.6 per cent per annum over this ten-year period, a pretty healthy rate of return. This example demonstrates how powerful compounding can be for investor portfolios if only sufficient time is allowed for it to work its magic.

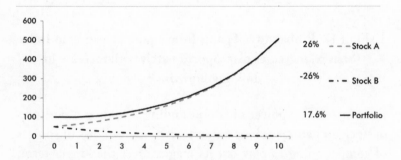

Exhibit 18: A hypothetical portfolio with 50 per cent strike rate and symmetry around positive and negative returns[42]

Reason 3—Neutralizing the negatives of 'noise': Investing and holding for the long term is the most effective way of killing the 'noise' that interferes with investment decisions. Often, deep-rooted psychological issues outweigh this commonsensical advice. It is easy to say that we should ignore the noise in the market but quite another thing to master the psychological effects of that noise. What investors need is a process that allows them to reduce the noise, which then makes it easier to make rational decisions. As an example, we highlight how, over the long term, Asian Paints' stock price has withstood short-term disappointments to eventually compound at an impressive 26 per cent CAGR since January 2010 to September 2019.

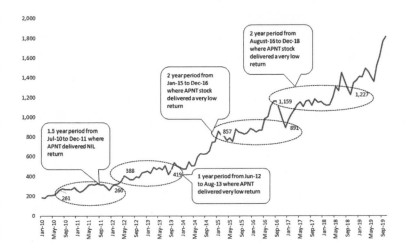

Exhibit 19: Asian Paints' stock price compounded at an impressive 26 per cent per annum between 2010 to 2019, in spite of the several time periods when the stock delivered negligible returns[43]

However, Exhibit 19 also highlights that over the past ten years, there have been several extended time periods when Asian Paints' share price did not generate impressive returns (circled in the graph). In spite of remaining flat over these periods, Asian Paints has performed so well in the remaining period that the ten-year compounded annualized investment return from the stock is 26 per cent. At its simplest, this is why the concept of investing for longer time horizons works—once you have identified a great franchise and you have the ability to hold on to it for a long period of time, there is no point trying to be too precise about timing your entry or your exit. As soon as you try to time that entry/exit, you run the risk of 'noise' rather than fundamentals driving your investment decisions.

Reason 4—Transaction costs: By holding a portfolio of stocks for over ten years, a fund manager resists the temptation to buy/sell in the short term. This approach reduces transaction costs which add to the overall portfolio performance over the long term. We illustrate this with an example. Assume that you invest Rs 10 crore in a hypothetical portfolio on 30 June 2006. Assume further that you churn this portfolio by 50 per cent per annum (implying that a typical position is held for two years) and this portfolio compounds at the rate of Sensex Index. Assuming a total price impact cost and brokerage cost of 100 bps for every trade done over a ten-year period, this portfolio would generate CAGR returns of 13.3 per cent. Left untouched, however, the same portfolio would have generated CAGR returns of 14.5 per cent. This implies that around 9 per cent of the final corpus (around Rs 3.5 crore in value terms) is lost to churn over the ten-year period. Thus, a Rs 10-crore portfolio that would have grown to Rs 38.2 crore over the ten-year period (30 June 2006 to 30 June 2016) in effect grows to Rs 34.7 crore due to high churn. The shortfall in the return is obviously the returns that the broking community earns for helping the investor churn his portfolio.

Emulate Rob Kirby and create your own portfolio

Having discussed the virtues of Kirby's investment approach, if in December 2019 one were to screen the entire spectrum of listed companies with market cap greater than Rs 100 crore using our twin filters of revenue growth (or loan book growth for banks) and profitability every year over FY09–19, we get the list of nine stocks mentioned in Exhibit 20.

Company Name	Amt. Invested (₹)	Mcap (₹ Mn)*	Mcap ($ Mn)*
Abbott India Ltd	100	2,67,590	3,743
Amara Raja Batteries Ltd	100	1,31,449	1,838
Cera Sanitaryware Ltd	100	33,179	464
Dr Lal PathLabs Ltd	100	1,32,601	1,855
HDFC Bank Ltd	100	69,79,260	97,612
LIC Housing Finance Ltd	100	2,19,983	3,077
Page Industries Ltd	100	2,39,656	3,352
Astral Poly Technik Ltd**	100	1,74,911	2,446
Thyrocare Technologies Ltd	100	29,723	416

Exhibit 20: Applying Kirby's investment approach in 2019[44]

As discussed in the preceding pages, a portfolio constructed today using this approach needs to be invested equally in all the stocks mentioned in this list. This portfolio should be left untouched for the next ten years regardless of how well or badly it does in a short-term period within this ten-year holding period. Will such a portfolio make money for you? There are no guaranteed returns with equity investments but if we go by the historical track record of this form of investing, Exhibits 20 and 21 show that not only does Kirby's investment approach outperform the Sensex in the vast majority of time periods, it (a) rarely gives you negative returns, and (b) in most time periods it generates significant positive returns.

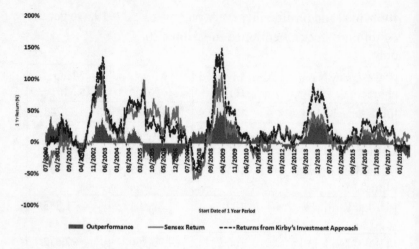

Exhibit 21: Total shareholder return from Kirby's investment approach versus the Sensex on a one-year rolling basis[45]

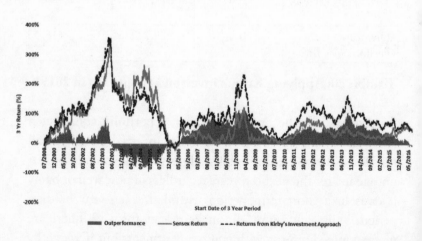

Exhibit 22: Total shareholder return from Kirby's investment approach versus the Sensex on a three-year rolling basis[46]

In fact, as Exhibit 22 shows, over the past twenty years if you had followed this approach for a period of at least three years, only on one occasion you would have got negative returns (namely in the three-year period starting 2006, i.e. the period characterized by the global financial crisis when the Sensex more than halved in value in the space of nine months).

Leaving aside the absolute level of returns, you can actually see in Exhibits 20 and 21 the markedly lower volatility of returns generated from this investment approach as compared to the returns from the Sensex. Those who would like to understand this phenomenon in more detail are encouraged to turn to Appendix I for more details.

* * *

Key takeaways from this chapter

- For the vast majority of equity investors in India, investment becomes a complicated affair, not only because they are surrounded by substandard advisers, but also because they imbibe (or are fed) incorrect investment theories—the most common one being, 'To make higher returns from the stock markets, one must take higher risks.'
- We all have goals—some of them are personal and some are for our broader family. Almost all of these goals carry a financial cost. A goal-based financial plan segments our goals into three buckets—security, stability, ambitions—and tells us how much of our portfolio needs to be invested in equities, bonds and cash.
- Instead of trying to beat the index and charging high fees, an index fund mimics the index performance over the long

run—thus achieving higher returns with lower costs than the costs associated with actively managed funds.

- Rob Kirby's coffee can portfolio (CCP) is a powerful construct. In the Indian context, one can build the CCP using a simple method: look for companies having above Rs 100 crore market capitalization, that over the preceding decade have grown sales each year by at least 10 per cent alongside generating a return on capital employed (pre-tax) of at least 15 per cent each year. Detailed backtesting of the CCP approach in India shows that *such a portfolio beats benchmarks consistently*. If invested for over a decade with no churn, this portfolio generates returns that are substantially higher than the benchmark.

Mark Mobius's Legendary Journey in Emerging Markets Investing

Mark Mobius is the founder of Mobius Capital Partners and an emerging-markets legend. Dr Mobius has a BA in fine arts and MS in mass communications from Boston University, and a PhD in economics from MIT. Dr Mobius has spent more than forty years working in and travelling throughout emerging and frontier markets. During this time he has been in charge of actively managed funds totalling more than $50 billion in assets. Prior to launching Mobius Capital Partners in May 2018, Dr Mobius was with Franklin Templeton Investments for more than thirty years, most recently as executive chairman of the Templeton Emerging Markets Group. During his tenure, the group expanded assets under management from $100 million to more than $50 billion and launched a number of emerging market and frontier funds focusing on Asia, Latin America, Africa and Eastern Europe. Dr Mobius has also been a key figure in developing international policy for emerging markets and has received numerous industry awards. He has religiously followed a simple framework for investing in stocks: finding high-quality companies that are undervalued and sticking with them for the long term. Thus, for our book, he embodies the concept of simplicity in investing.

In their careers on the sell-side, both the authors have serviced Franklin Templeton as a client. Hence, this rare occasion to talk to Dr Mobius for our book was a 'fanboy' moment for both of us (we do not easily get a chance to speak to an investing legend on topics other than which stock to buy or sell). We got on to the Zoom video conferencing service for a call with Dr Mobius on 11 October 2019.

We began our conversation with how Dr Mobius entered the asset management industry. Before he became an investor, Dr Mobius had a diverse résumé—from working at a talent agency to teaching communications and marketing Snoopy toys in Asia. Prior to joining Templeton, Dr Mobius worked at Vickers Da Costa, an international securities firm. As part of his role as a sell-side analyst, Dr Mobius had met the legendary value investor Sir John Templeton (then running the firm Templeton, Galbraith & Hansberger) many times in Nassau, Bahamas. In 1987, Sir John asked Dr Mobius to run one of the world's first emerging markets funds, handing him the task of investing $100 million in what were then only six markets that qualified for investment. In 1992, Templeton, Galbraith & Hansberger merged with Franklin Resources to form what is now known as Franklin Templeton.

What did Dr Mobius learn from Sir Templeton back in the late 1980s when investing in emerging markets was still in its early days? He told us: 'Three things—a contrarian approach, a long-term view and fundamental analysis.' But things were challenging because back in the 1980s and 1990s, the first challenge was depth—since in terms of liquidity, emerging markets weren't as deep as developed markets. The second challenge was finding reliable audited financial statements and then translating them to international accounting standards. A lot of time was thus spent in understanding the real story behind the published financial statements. Thus, to understand the companies better and to meet their managements required Dr Mobius and his team to travel extensively. This was a huge learning process. 'At that time, we put a lot of emphasis on the numbers and probably less on the people behind the company. But as time went on, we began to realize that it was more important to understand the people behind the company. That was something we learned the hard way,' he told us. This approach—of understanding the people and their motivation behind running the company—would eventually become a cornerstone of Dr Mobius's investing approach.

How has Dr Mobius's investment philosophy evolved over these decades? 'The main transition has been from strictly fundamental analysis to two directions: first, major orientation on the people behind the company and second, an intense look at the future,' he told us. In a 2018 interview to *Barron's*, Dr Mobius admitted to being too rigid in the early days: 'We would focus too much on metrics like price/earnings and price/book ratios, and didn't pay enough attention to the total picture. We didn't have the imagination of what could happen over five or ten years and missed a lot of technology stocks during the boom.'[47]

In his current firm, Dr Mobius is focusing on 'ESG' (environment, social, governance) criteria while investing. 'Our emphasis is on governance. We talk to managements who, a) look at environmental and social risks, and b) are willing to have independent views from outside the organization, for example, an independent board of directors and listening to shareholders,' he told us.

Dr Mobius's travels are well-known in the investment world and his passion for travel is indefatigable. Thus, travel has played a major role in shaping Dr Mobius's investment philosophy in general and world view in particular. 'Travel opens up your mind. You have to open your mind because you are being confronted with different people, different images, different environments, and you are not going to survive very long if you are close-minded. You have to be willing to learn,' he explained. Dr Mobius recalled traveling to Japan (before it became an economic giant) as a scholarship student, telling us: 'I was staying with a family in Kyoto and their way of life and their outlook was so different that it was quite a big lesson for me.'

As we wrap up the interview, we ask Dr Mobius for his advice to a twenty-five-year-old starting his career. 'Learn the fundamental skills like reading and writing. Go to museums because art gives you a hint about how the future can look. Develop your creativity—so learn to play an instrument, learn to draw, learn creative writing. Machines and robotics will take away a lot of the normal work that we do and we will be relegated more and more to the creative aspects like creating new concepts,' he told us. His advice for a mid-career professional is blunt, 'Ask yourself: do you like what you are doing? If you don't, then get out, quit. You have to enjoy what you are doing, otherwise you won't be able to do a good job and it will affect not only you but the people around you. Secondly, think about your life and ask yourself if you regret not having done something. And if the answer is yes, then start doing it, go back and do what you failed to do up to now.'

CHAPTER 10

Boiling It All Down to the Simplicity Checklist

In this chapter we summarize the key findings of our book into a simple checklist that can be used by readers. We then conclude the book with a case study which exemplifies many of the items highlighted in the checklist and in the preceding chapters.

No.	Task	Response
	Specialize	
1	Have you found an area/field/specialization which sparks your imagination and motivates you?	Yes / No
2	If the answer to the first question is yes, then have you prepared a timeline of how your career will proceed?	Yes / No
3	If the answer to the first question is no, then have you found your inclinations and prioritized them?	Yes / No
4	Have you found a great mentor for the current phase of your career?	Yes / No

No.	Task	Response
Specialize		
5	Are you expanding your knowledge into related fields by reading extensively?	Yes / No
Simplify		
6	Have you made a list of good habits (e.g. healthy nutrition, physical exercise, reading, etc.), which you will inject into your routine? Have you injected these habits into your routine?	Yes / No
7	Do you work in an intense, focused way and—if possible—in solitude and away from any distractions?	Yes / No
8	Do you actively seek high-quality feedback for your work from your peers, bosses, friends, relatives and mentors?	Yes / No
9	Do you actively seek and accept criticism?	Yes / No
10	Have you defined your daily routine in terms of time, and once defined, do you follow that routine without deviation?	Yes / No
Spiritualize		
11	Do you dedicate specific time(s) every day to meditation, and do you adhere to meditation as a daily practice?	Yes / No
12	Do you use a defined meditation technique and improve on it over time?	Yes / No
13	Do you endeavour to live a frugal life, including cutting down on unnecessary purchases?	Yes / No
14	Do you stay positive and constructive as a habit, instead of giving in to negativity and cynicism?	Yes / No
15	Do you use meditation to improve your ability to focus?	Yes / No

No.	Task	Response
Specialize		
Declutter		
16	Do you maintain a clean, neat and tidy workspace and home, and do you get rid of unnecessary clutter?	Yes / No
17	Do you prioritize your goals using checklists?	Yes / No
18	Do you consciously reduce smartphone usage and remove all unnecessary notifications and disturbances?	Yes / No
19	Have you removed all social media apps? If you still desperately need them, do you use their website versions instead?	Yes / No
Creativity		
20	Have you created an extensive reading list, and have you dedicated specific hours within your day towards reading?	Yes / No
21	Have you made a travel schedule to explore new places?	Yes / No
22	Do you actively find groups of people with similar interests and interact with them to develop new thoughts and new ideas?	Yes / No
23	Do you improve your memory with techniques such as memory palace and actively use your memory in your specialization?	Yes / No
Collaboration		
24	If feasible, do you work with colleagues from diverse backgrounds at your workplace?	Yes / No
25	Do you actively seek perspectives and viewpoints that are different from yours and try to understand and appreciate them?	Yes / No
27	Do you align your personal development with the goals of your team and organization?	Yes / No

No.	Task	Response
Specialize		
Simplicity in Business		
28	Do you define your organization's goals and vision in simple terms and keep revisiting these goals over time?	Yes / No
29	Do you identify how you can simplify your business's offering—in terms of price and/or in terms of proposition?	Yes / No
30	Do you lay down standard operating procedures and note deviations to improve on them in the future?	Yes / No
31	Do you specialize deep within your product and develop original thinking around how to improve and expand on it?	Yes / No
32	Do you ensure that your team members come from diverse backgrounds and bring a variety of experiences, skills and personalities to the table?	Yes / No
33	Do you ensure teams are led by leaders who encourage groups to maintain their own identity while mediating disagreements and conflicts between these groups?	Yes / No
Simplicity in Investing		
34	Do you make a list of your goals for which you are investing your hard-earned money?	Yes / No
35	Do you have a financial adviser for developing a financial plan in alignment with your goals?	Yes / No
36	Do you stick to simple investments such as index funds, government bonds and Rob Kirby's coffee can portfolio approach?	Yes / No
37	Do you track your investments and goals, and do you adjust and realign them as part of the plan?	Yes / No

Our readers would, we hope, come from diverse backgrounds and therefore, a single to-do list that applies to all of them is not practical. For example, a twenty-five-year-old who is just starting his career would hardly have any control over who his colleagues and team members are, leave alone ensuring that they come from diverse backgrounds. Similarly, a consultant or a freelancer would not have organizational goals to align his personal goals to. Therefore, the above list is an indicative one and should be used as the starting point of your journey towards simplicity. The list above summarizes the concepts in the preceding chapters and should be used more as a guide and less as a rigid instruction manual. Having said that, we believe that if you have ticked 'No' more times than you have ticked 'Yes', then you need to rethink your approach to peak performance. If, on the other hand, you have ticked 'Yes' more times than you have ticked 'No', we reckon that you are on your way to peak performance. In such a happy scenario, we hope that you will pass on this book to a friend or a relative who might benefit from reading it.

R.D. Burman and A.R. Rahman: A Case Study of Two Creative Giants

'Time works in a strange way. However, successful you may be, if your success is only a matter of chance or circumstances, not based on real talent, it will not stand the test of time. But if you are really great, you become greater with time. And time makes a bigger and bigger idol of you. And that is what is happening to R.D. Burman. Because time is kind to great people. And R.D. Burman was great.'

—Javed Akhtar[1]

'First you have the prelude and then the music comes, then you have an interlude, followed by a cross-line . . . From the start, songs were written this way. Rahman broke the pattern . . . the horizon . . . at what stage the song will return to the refrain, one never knows . . . Like classical and semi-classical musicians, he elaborates the tune. These elaborations build links and keep unfolding.'

—Gulzar[2]

Brief bios of the two legends

Rahul Dev Burman—or Pancham, as the veteran Indian actor Ashok Kumar had named him when he was a mere toddler—was born in Kolkata in 1939 to a branch of the Tripura royal family. He did not distinguish himself in school but his father, the legendary music director S.D. Burman, deserves the gratitude of generations of Indian music lovers for beginning his son's training in Hindustani classical music by the time Pancham was ten years old. The teenaged Pancham was precocious—among other songs, he composed 'Sar Jo Tera Chakraye' for Guru Dutt's iconic move *Pyaasa* (1957).

When he was sixteen, his father relocated him to Mumbai, where Pancham became an assistant to his famous father. Personal success however continued to elude him, even though his friend, the comedian Mehmood, hired Pancham as the music director for *Chhote Nawab* (1961). Pancham's first critically acclaimed hit came with *Padosan* (1968), a movie whose true worth has become more obvious to music lovers with the passage of time. Then, in the years following *Padosan*, Pancham composed the music for four smash hits whose music towered over everything that was composed in Bollywood in the sixties, seventies and eighties.

Teesri Manzil (1966) was Pancham's entry into the premier league with the full-on brass band and hundred-piece orchestra of 'O Haseena Zulfon Waali', transforming the Bollywood song-and-dance number, once and for all, into a big-budget spectacular. In Dev Anand's *Haré Rama Haré Krishna* (1971), Pancham memorably brought rock music, English lyrics and vocalists trained in Western music to Bollywood, with 'Dum Maro Dum' being the most memorable outcome of this fusion between the East and West. In *Kati Patang* (1971), Pancham's music resulted in Filmfare awards for superstar Rajesh Khanna, director Shakti Samanta and singer Kishore Kumar. For the next Rajesh Khanna blockbuster—*Amar Prem* (1972)—Pancham composed four songs[3] that pay glorious tribute to India's rich heritage of Hindustani classical music and are regarded by the cognoscenti as the greatest songs composed for the Hindi screen.

More hits followed in the 1970s and the early 1980s, until younger composers imitating the legend undercut him and left him financially stranded in the late 1980s. R.D. Burman died of a heart attack in 1994 soon after finishing work on *1942: A Love Story* (1994). He was honoured with a Filmfare award posthumously for his work in his last film, which itself went on to become a smash hit and put singer Kumar Sanu's career into the orbit.

Allahrakka Rahman was born in Chennai in 1967. His father, the music composer R.K. Shekhar, died when Rahman was nine years old. By then, Rahman had already become an assistant to his father in the studio. Following his father's death, Rahman supported his family by renting out his father's music equipment. By the time he dropped out of school in his mid-teens, he had already mastered the keyboard, piano, synthesizer, harmonium and guitar. The young Rahman was particularly interested in the synthesizer, because it was the 'ideal combination of music and technology'.[4]

Through his teenage years Rahman made a name for himself in Chennai, first as a synthesizer player in movie soundtracks and then as a sought-after composer of advertising jingles. His big break came when Mani Ratnam approached him to compose music for *Roja* (1992). The movie was one of the first multilingual hits across India, with the freshness of Rahman's music being a big driver of the movie's success. *Time* magazine included *Roja* in the ten best movie soundtracks of all time.[5]

Even as Rahman's popularity rocketed in the Tamil movie market, further success in Bollywood came through his consistently fresh and resonant music for *Bombay* (1995)—another multilingual hit from Mani Ratnam—followed by *Rangeela* (1995) and then *Dil Se..* (1998). These critically acclaimed and commercially successful movies brought a completely new genre of music to Indian cinema.

In the new millennium, while Rahman continued making memorable movie music in India—notable successes being *Rang De Basanti* (2006), *Guru* (2007) and *Jodhaa Akbar* (2008)—he also expanded his reach and his skill set with ventures that no Indian musician had ever undertaken before.

In 2002, Rahman composed music for Andrew Lloyd Webber's West End and Broadway musical *Bombay Dreams*. Rahman's music for Danny Boyle's *Slumdog Millionaire* (2008) won two Academy Awards, a first for an Asian[6], which sparked wild celebrations across Chennai. In 2012, Rahman composed a Punjabi song for the opening ceremony of the London Olympics. In 2017, he made his debut as a director and writer for the upcoming virtual reality film *Le Musk*. Rahman remains India's most expensive and most sought-after music composer, someone whose name is enough to set the cash registers ringing.

Striking parallels between the two lives

Burman and Rahman completely redefined movie music in their respective eras, and although the two men grew up and lived in different cities, the parallels between their careers and working habits is striking. We draw upon two biographies of these music legends—Anirudha Bhattacharjee and Balaji Vittal's award-winning *R.D. Burman: The Man, The Music* and Krishna Trilok's *Notes of a Dream: The Authorized Biography of A.R. Rahman*[7]—to outline their strikingly similar paths to stardom:

• **Deep immersion in music by their mid-teens:** Alongside formal training in music (Pancham from Ustad Ali Akbar Khan in Kolkata, and Rahman from Musee Musicals, Nithyanandam Master and Dakshinamoorthy in Chennai), both men were working as professional musicians in the film industry by their mid-teens. While Burman was an assistant to his famous father S.D. Burman (a role which became ever more important as Burman senior aged through the 1960s), he was also regarded as the best harmonica player in Mumbai. Most memorably, he played the harmonica in the song 'Hai Apna Dil To Awara' in the movie *Solva Saal* (1958). His father's untimely demise meant that by the time he was ten years old, Rahman was the family's main breadwinner. He alternated between his classes at school and his early career as a session recording artist for Tamil movies. If we assume that these composers did a forty-hour week between the ages of fifteen and twenty, by the time these men entered their twenties, we can safely say that they would have clocked Malcolm Gladwell's 10,000 hours required for the mastery of their chosen profession.

Interestingly, but not accidentally, both men were highly focused musicians. Pancham repeatedly turned down acting roles in the 1960s and made his intention to become a notable composer in his own right clear to everyone in Mumbai. Rahman quit school in his mid-teens to focus exclusively on music.

- **Blazing desire to challenge conventions and norms:** Pancham consciously and deliberately broke away from the traditional form of Bollywood music. He mixed jazz, rock, bossa nova, calypso, samba and Middle Eastern melodies with Hindustani classical to create sounds which had never before been heard in Indian cinema. He brought instruments like the electric guitar, trumpet, trombone, conga, xylophone, bongo and vibraphone into mainstream movie music.

  Partly due to the musical education his father had imparted to him, Rahman brought to Indian movie music a mastery of electronic and synthesizer sounds that simply did not exist in the country in the 1990s. With the aid of these instruments, he proceeded to fuse Hindustani classical, reggae, Western pop and rock.

- **Restless, curious musicians constantly looking for new sounds:** Before he moved to Mumbai at the age of sixteen, Pancham had already acquired in-depth knowledge of Hindustani classical, jazz and bossa nova. He then fused these different types of music to Indianize the bossa nova by stripping it of the complicated chords while incorporating the rhythm. As his fame grew, Pancham become even more innovative: 'One morning, a household help was rubbing a piece of newspaper against the floor with her foot to remove stains. The act of rubbing at a particular pace resulted in a different kind of sound, which aroused Pancham's interest. He summoned the household help to continue generating the sound, which he recreated in the studio by running a piece of aluminium foil on a khol . . .'[8]

  Rahman's authorized biography contains even more remarkable stories regarding the composer's hunger to discover new sounds. When the legendary qawwali singer Nusrat Fateh Ali Khan came to Mumbai, Rahman 'went to Nusrat's room at some unearthly hour, knocked on the door and politely introduced himself . . . AR said to him, "I want to learn qawwali from you." And Nusrat just wakes up his musicians and calls them up to his room and they just played all night. Nusrat told Rahman a few things and AR took notes while they were playing.' In fact, in Rahman's case his curiosity extends beyond music. 'He finds the technicians, the visual effects guys and cinematographers and just keeps talking to them.'

- **Perfectionists and deep workers:** Both men are known to have worked twelve hours a day to produce their best work. Rahman's success means that the studios at his homes in Chennai and Mumbai have world-class recording equipment, and this allows him to work from 5 p.m. to 5 a.m. in the privacy of his residence. No phone calls and no interruptions from visitors are entertained during these twelve hours. Sometimes Rahman takes an entire twelve-hour session just to get one note right. Apparently, this was how the sublime opening notes of 'Jaage Hain' for the film *Guru* were composed.

While living a more bohemian life than Rahman, Pancham worked a slightly more conventional twelve-hour day from 9 a.m. to 9 p.m. in recording studios. He would be surrounded during these twelve hours by an army of musicians, most of whom worked with him for several decades. However, his musical ear was so finely honed that as soon as rehearsal began, even with a 100-piece orchestra, Pancham could hear that, say, the sixth violin in the third row was out of tune.

- **Collaborators supreme:** In a competitive high-stakes, commercially charged environment, the ability to win the trust of a diverse group of stakeholders is as important as one's innate talent. Both music composers befriended and collaborated with a wide variety of people, an essential skill if one is to succeed in the cut-throat movie markets of Mumbai and Chennai. Pancham's deep friendship with singers (Kishore Kumar, Lata Mangeshkar, Asha Bhosle), with lyricists (Gulzar, Gulshan Bawra, Javed Akhtar), with film stars (Shammi Kapoor, Mehmood, Rajesh Khanna, Amitabh Bachchan) and with directors (Shakti Samanta, Nasir Hussain, Ramesh Sippy, Hrishikesh Mukherjee) placed him firmly at the centre of the Bollywood movie market of the 1970s. Similarly, Rahman's long-standing friendships with a diverse group of cutting-edge directors, such as Mani Ratnam, Imtiaz Ali, Danny Boyle, Rakeysh

Omprakash Mehra, Shekhar Kapur and Ashutosh Gowariker, allow him the latitude to give full vent to his creativity.

Not only did Burman and Rahman change the way movie music is made in India, there are striking similarities between their careers. Both men were professional musicians by their mid-teens. Both turned away from conventional styles of movie music. Both were masters of their craft, which was primarily composing music for movies. And yet their range of knowledge extended far beyond their chosen profession. As highlighted in Chapter 2, this combination of in-depth specialization in one area alongside a vast body of knowledge is a powerful driver of creativity and original thought.

Epilogue

It was 5 p.m., and Akanksha and Akash were done with their counselling session. Akanksha was in the fifth week of counselling and the effects were evident to her and, more importantly, to her family. Akash had accompanied her in many of the sessions and one of the breakthroughs they had achieved was a date night. 'Commit yourselves to being with each other at least one night a week; no compromises. Go back to the old days and live the good times again,' Akanksha's counsellor told her. No matter how busy their schedules were, both Akash and Akanksha would take Wednesday nights off to go to Café Noorani in Tardeo, their favourite haunt when they were dating. The counsellor was still working on their myriad issues, but date night was a personal win for Akash and Akanksha.

Akanksha's day had changed radically after the counselling sessions. After getting out of bed, her first activity now wasn't an hour on the laptop but an hour spread across the gym and the swimming pool. Their home in the luxury tower had superb sports facilities which came at a hefty cost and were typically left unused by the power couple. Akanksha now ensured that she hit the gym and the pool at least six days a week, including one fun workout on Sunday in the pool with the family. She hired trainers for both the routines—for functional training at the gym and for learning to swim at the pool. Some things never changed, of course; Akanksha was still an early riser, but now she used the time to literally open the gym at 6 a.m.

The results began showing on Akanksha in the first few weeks. She didn't feel tired, the dark circles under her eyes were gone and—thanks to deliberate practice—she was getting better at both the gym and the swimming pool. She enjoyed both routines, especially swimming because it gave her a stretch of solitude; she could carry her phone on the treadmill but not in the pool. Even on the treadmill, Akanksha listened to music on her iPhone and stopped watching financial news channels. She began meditating at home, using a popular app on her phone. She started with the beginner packs and was soon on guided meditations. Before long, meditation became a routine for her, like gymming and swimming.

And then there was CerysIn. 'Ajay, here is my mobile phone; keep it with you for the next two hours and let me know only in case of urgent calls. Route everything else via Ria,' Akansha told Ajay Mittal, her executive assistant who handled all incoming calls and emails. Ria Malhotra, who reported directly to Akanksha, was young, ambitious, and just five years into CerysIn. Ria reminded Akanksha of herself— she had a large capacity to take on work and find her way around challenges without asking for too much help; and she loved to travel and learn the tricks of the trade on the ground instead of sitting in an air-conditioned office. 'Ria, you are taking over strategy for dealers and distributors. Divide your work in your team and give me all the numbers on Deknext. I want to know where they are hurting us and how. I also need you to prepare a travel schedule for the next quarter,' Akanksha told Ria. One of the reasons Akanksha had more time for her personal life was because Ria's travel schedule had freed up Akanksha's time.

Inside her cabin, Akanksha did twenty-five-minute spurts of focused work without any interruptions for emails or phone calls. She took five-minute breaks only to get up and walk around her cabin, so as not to stay seated for too long. No calls, no emails. And she was surprised at how much she could focus on work without these interruptions. Her first phone call was to her batchmate and good friend Amrita, who was also the senior vice president at FDGH Bank. 'Amrita, I need a channel financing arrangement with you. Let us figure out a way wherein FDGH will provide lines of credit to CerysIn dealers at zero cost,' Akanksha told Amrita. 'Sure, buddy, this can be done. It shouldn't cost much since CerysIn are old customers for us and your balance sheet is rock solid. I can push this internally. Let me get back to you by end of day,' Amrita replied.

When Akanksha opened Ria's analysis on Deknext, she realized that it was more than six months since she had spoken personally to CerysIn dealers and distributors. Over the next few days, Akanksha worked the phones and called the large dealers and distributors, reminding them of their long-term relations with CerysIn. 'Kalpenbhai, I remember your daughter's tenth birthday, how you were struggling to find the exact doll your daughter wanted and we flew it in from one of our branches,' she told Kalpen Shah, a dealer for CerysIn products in the suburb of Borivali. As she spoke to the dealers, she reminded them of how CerysIn had been with them during their ups and downs and how, as CerysIn grew, the dealers grew as well. As she put the emotional connect in place, she knew it was time to use some money to give the last push.

'Mukul, I need an increase in the commission for the dealers and distributors. They are with us but they also need a reason to push back Deknext. This increase will narrow the gap,' Akanksha told Mukul. 'But Akanksha, we don't have the budget and you know times are tough. It'll be tough for me to get this approved,' Mukul replied. 'We're losing market share to Deknext and we need to fight back. Get this done for me and I know I can regain lost share,' Akanksha told Mukul. Eventually, Mukul came through and got the increase in commission. After the raise, while CerysIn commissions were still lower than Deknext, Akanksha's conversations and meetings with the dealers and distributors served as a major morale booster. Akanksha used an aggressive advertising campaign, supported by Ria's suggestion of including digital channels as well. The following week Amrita called Akanksha to inform her that FDGH would enhance the credit lines available to CerysIn dealers. Slowly and surely CerysIn recovered the market share that it had lost to Deknext.

'Well done Akanksha, this was one of the toughest battles we have fought and I'm glad you won!' Mukul congratulated her. But the best was yet to come. 'You have really proved yourself here, Akanksha, and the time has come. I'm recommending you as my successor to the board,' Mukul told her.

Not too far away from Akanksha's office, as the sun was setting in Bandra, Suraj Trivedi was finishing his five-kilometre jog on Carter Road. 'Hey Suraj, the usual? SlimJhim?' Rohit, the juice truck guy, asked Suraj. 'Yes, Rohit, the same,' Suraj replied. Rohit quickly crushed together a concoction of apples, spinach, bitter gourd, lemon, and much more to make a SlimJhim. It was Suraj's favourite drink after his run. Flushed with the drink, he walked to his new home, which was less than 500 metres from Carter Road. It was still a long walk, and Suraj used to smoked on long walks but not any more. Suraj had quit smoking as part of the overhaul of his health. Bandra was expensive and the extra rent ate into Suraj's salary, but that sea-facing view was to die for. And Suraj's commute from office to home was now down to just half an hour. Tired of the long commutes, Suraj had bit the bullet and shifted out of Kandivali.

It took him a while to accept the higher rent, but the extra time he got for himself made him feel much better.

'*Kya baat hai*, boss, you've lost a lot of weight!' Gaurav told Suraj. A strict diet and workout routine had helped Suraj shed ten kilograms in the past eight weeks. The evening run alternated with a morning gym routine. It helped that the gym was in the same building as Suraj's office and he had got a good deal thanks to a promotional scheme. Suraj would leave his Bandra home at 7.30 a.m. and hit the gym at 8.15 a.m. Forty-five minutes of varied workout routines followed by ten minutes of meditation had done wonders to his body. More importantly, he felt refreshed when he began work every day. He had deleted all his social media apps on his smartphone and mandated that his friends would have to call him and talk to him. 'I've had enough of the constant pings on WhatsApp and notifications of new photos on Facebook and Instagram. If you want to talk, call me from now on,' Suraj had told his friends. It took time but his friends did go old-school.

Free from the clutter of social media and with more time on his hands, Suraj went after his favourite activity at IIT—coding and programming. He had decided to keep his start-up plans on hold. Instead, he focused on developing ways to streamline the preparation of a pitch deck. This became his pet project on which he would spend focused time every day. Suraj even worked through many weekends and holidays to develop this idea. First, he automated the procedure of downloading and analysing a firm's financials into a specially designed spreadsheet template. Next, he ran algorithms that simulated the firm's financial performance under various market scenarios, such as a change in regulation, the entry of a new competitor, price wars, etc. And finally, he integrated all of his programming within his spreadsheets, documents and presentations. As a result, all he had to do was put the name of a company and his programme would pull data across multiple sources and throw up a simple five-slide presentation deck. He refined his programme even further, making a mobile app with real-time live updates for breaking news related to the company or the sector.

'This is fantastic, Suraj; super-useful stuff. Heck, this is way cheaper than the imported financial data terminals that we buy! And it looks like you are adding more and more features to this. I think it is time for you to move on to pitching for deals on your own to smaller clients. No need for us to hand-hold you any more. Time to make you a senior associate!' Gaurav told him a few weeks after everyone at Vedanga Capital had used his algorithm and programme. 'Mom, you won't believe it; I've got a promotion!' Suraj told his mother when he reached home that night after his jog. 'That is great to know, *beta*; I hope you are doing yoga like I told you?' his Mom replied. 'Yes, yes, Ma, don't worry. Yoga and meditation—I'm doing all of that every day. Now stop worrying about me,' Suraj calmed his mother.

Suraj began his yoga sessions on Saturday evenings after discovering a yoga class near his house. This wasn't heavy-duty stuff but basic yoga, which aimed at getting his breathing and blood circulation in order. He hadn't taken pranayama seriously until he was trained at the yoga class. A few sessions in and he could feel the difference. He could handle his anxiety much better now by centring all his attention on his breathing. 'Suraj, I have no idea how you handle those pitches, but I wish I was as calm as you,' Anil Dua, the new recruit and Suraj's junior, told him. Mentally, Suraj felt a lot tougher than before. It helped that he was finally rid of all the envy and anxiety regarding his friends doing much better than him. 'I've come to terms with my choice, yaar, and I've made peace with myself. I chose this job because I wanted to be close to my mother, and because I want to be a big fish in a small pond. It is all coming together now,' Suraj told Karan. 'Yeah, dude, whatever rocks your boat. I just heard about that new kick-ass algo you developed at Vedanga. They've recognized and rewarded your efforts, so hey, it is all good,' Karan told him.

Suraj began travelling around the country, making deal pitches to Vedanga's smaller clients. With his new programme, he was able to create pitch decks much quicker than before. Wherever there were gaps to be filled in and client queries to be handled, Suraj would give that work to Anil, who would resolve them at the office. 'Anil, you need to develop a way to tackle queries quickly. I need you to start accompanying me on deal pitches so that you learn this much faster than I did,' Suraj told Anil. Suraj knew the drudgery of being chained to the desk doing mind-numbingly dull tasks only too well. But he had learnt to focus on work and find ways to upgrade his skills. Decluttering and detaching from distractions had only helped his mind to focus better. And finally, exercising and meditating had helped strengthen his mind even more. He could feel that this was the beginning of a new chapter in his career.

* * *

We hope that the end of this book becomes a starting point for you, the reader. Writing this book has been a labour of love for us. Cynics will say that it is easy to write books with high-flown ideas and ideals but it is harder to implement the same in our daily lives. We disagree. We firmly believe that, despite all the doom and gloom that social media injects into our lives, there is a good life waiting for us. From simple goals (such as losing weight and becoming fitter) to fulfilling our professional ambitions (such as launching a start-up or becoming the CEO), our lives are filled with challenges. These challenges can be surmounted successfully before they become a source of heartburn and frustration. As evidenced by our personal experiences recounted in this book, as well as by the wise words from the masters quoted here, we believe that a simple life with minimal distractions and deep focus is one way of achieving these goals.

Building a Portfolio That Lasts Forever

We have included in this appendix a series of exhibits which aims to give you a more visual understanding of why Rob Kirby's investment approach (adapted for Indian conditions) consistently delivers market-beating returns. We begin with a histogram of the Sensex which shows that in twenty-one out of the last thirty-one years (i.e. in 68 per cent of the years), the Sensex has delivered positive returns. In these twenty-one years of positive returns, in the majority of the years, the Sensex has given returns below 30 per cent per annum.

Sensex

	NEGATIVE RETURNS			POSITIVE RETURNS			
< -30%	-20% to -30%	-10% to -20%	0% to -10%	0% to +10%	+10% to +20%	+20% to +30%	> +30%
FY93	FY01	FY95	FY97	FY96	FY98	FY08	FY91
FY09		FY03	FY99	FY13	FY05	FY15	FY92
		FY12	FY02	FY90	FY07		FY94
			FY16		FY11		FY00
					FY14		FY04
					FY17		FY06
					FY18		FY10
					FY19		FY89

The stock-specific histograms that follow are those of typical companies identified employing the investment approach enumerated in the final section of Chapter 9 ('Simplifying Idea 3: Robert Kirby and Coffee Can Investing'). We have shown that for these companies:

- Positive returns occur with significantly greater consistency than with the Sensex. Most companies which pass our filters delivered positive returns in twenty-six out of thirty-one years, i.e. in 84 per cent of the years as opposed to 68 per cent for the Sensex.
- In the years in which returns are positive, these companies' returns are typically above 30 per cent per annum.
- The years in which these companies give negative returns (such as FY99, FY01 and FY09) are typically followed by years in which these companies give returns above 30 per cent per annum.

Finally, in the last exhibit shown in this appendix, we have crunched the data from all the iterations of Kirby's investment approach to illustrate what is happening over long periods of time. Firstly, for any portfolio, the returns improve with time (we call this the 'patience premium'). Secondly, if you invest in a high-quality portfolio such as the ones which we have built in Chapter 9 of this book, you improve your returns further (we call this the 'quality premium').

Asian Paints

	NEGATIVE RETURNS			POSITIVE RETURNS			
< -30%	-20% to -30%	-10% to -20%	0% to -10%	0% to +10%	+10% to +20%	+20% to +30%	> +30%
FY09		FY97	FY01	FY90	FY91	FY05	FY89
		FY99		FY93	FY95	FY11	FY92
				FY03	FY96	FY12	FY94
				FY16	FY98	FY14	FY00
				FY18	FY07	FY17	FY02
							FY04
							FY06
							FY08
							FY10
							FY13
							FY15
							FY19

Berger Paints

	NEGATIVE RETURNS			POSITIVE RETURNS			
< -30%	-20% to -30%	-10% to -20%	0% to -10%	0% to +10%	+10% to +20%	+20% to +30%	> +30%
FY93		FY01	FY91	FY97	FY14	FY12	FY92
FY96		FY02	FY03	FY18	FY16	FY19	FY94
FY07			FY08				FY95
			FY09				FY98
							FY99
							FY00
							FY04
							FY05
							FY06
							FY10
							FY11
							FY13
							FY15
							FY17

Relaxo

	NEGATIVE RETURNS			POSITIVE RETURNS			
< -30%	-20% to -30%	-10% to -20%	0% to -10%	0% to +10%	+10% to +20%	+20% to +30%	> +30%
FY97			FY98	FY03	FY19	FY05	FY00
FY02			FY99	FY12		FY06	FY04
FY09			FY01	FY16		FY08	FY10
			FY07			FY11	FY13
							FY14
							FY15
							FY17
							FY18

HDFC Bank

	NEGATIVE RETURNS			POSITIVE RETURNS			
< -30%	-20% to -30%	-10% to -20%	0% to -10%	0% to +10%	+10% to +20%	+20% to +30%	> +30%
FY09		FY01	FY99	FY02	FY12	FY07	FY97
			FY03	FY16		FY11	FY98
						FY13	FY00
						FY14	FY04
						FY19	FY05
							FY06
							FY08
							FY10
							FY15
							FY17
							FY18

Pidilite

	NEGATIVE RETURNS			POSITIVE RETURNS			
< -30%	-20% to -30%	-10% to -20%	0% to -10%	0% to +10%	+10% to +20%	+20% to +30%	> +30%
FY01	FY96	FY02	FY16	FY97	FY98	FY03	FY95
FY09				FY07	FY08		FY99
					FY12		FY00
					FY14		FY04
					FY17		FY05
							FY06
							FY10
							FY11
							FY13
							FY15
							FY18
							FY19

Marico

	NEGATIVE RETURNS			POSITIVE RETURNS			
< -30%	-20% to -30%	-10% to -20%	0% to -10%	0% to +10%	+10% to +20%	+20% to +30%	> +30%
FY00		FY09	FY01	FY98	FY02	FY11	FY99
			FY14	FY08	FY03	FY12	FY04
				FY19	FY07	FY13	FY05
					FY18	FY16	FY06
						FY17	FY10
							FY15

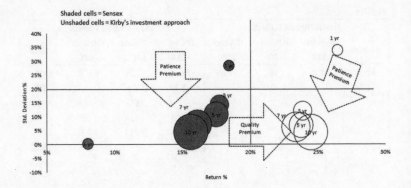

The risk-reward trade-off in Kirby's investment approach relative to the Sensex and government bonds[*]

---

[*] Source: Marcellus Investment Managers, Ace Equity. The return from Kirby's investment approach is the average of all portfolio iterations highlighted in Chapter 9 of this book.

List of Articles Written by the Authors for *The Ken*

Date	Title	URL
1 September 2018	'Tsundoku: The burden of the unread book'	https://the-ken.com/story/tsundoku-mental-clutter/
6 October 2018	'Of pride and prejudice: Inside the human mind'	https://the-ken.com/story/human-mind-limits-multitasking/
3 November 2018	'Keep it simple, silly'	https://the-ken.com/story/keep-it-simple-silly/
1 December 2018	'Step into the memory palace'	https://the-ken.com/story/step-into-the-memory-palace/
5 January 2019	'The spirituality of simplicity'	https://the-ken.com/story/the-spirituality-of-simplicity/
2 February 2019	'The power of thinking differently'	https://the-ken.com/story/the-power-of-thinking-differently/
2 March 2019	'The final step— and the first'	https://the-ken.com/story/the-final-step-and-the-first/

Acknowledgements

The ideas behind this book began to germinate in early July 2018 when Durgesh Shah of FLAME University invited Saurabh to address the seasoned investors who attend FLAME's three-day investment camp during the monsoon each year. At the university's scenic campus on the outskirts of Pune, we presented for the first time the ideas which we have developed further in this book. We thank Durgeshbhai and FLAME University for giving us the opportunity to present the concepts contained in this book, when they were in their nascency, to an experienced group of investors.

These concepts were developed further when Rohin Dharmakumar and Seema Singh at *The Ken*, and Ashish K. Mishra (then at *The Ken*) invited us to write a series of articles. We met Rohin and Ashish at Café Zoe in Mumbai in July 2018 to discuss the ideas Saurabh had presented at FLAME University and we fondly recall their energy and enthusiasm for publishing material on what we thought were unexplored areas. *The Ken* is an Indian news website, and from the autumn of 2018 to the opening months of 2019 we wrote seven articles for them around some of the concepts which are contained in this book. Some of the material published here originally appeared in *The Ken*, and we thank *The Ken* for granting us a licence to reuse this material.

Lohit Jagwani was the editor at Penguin Random House who had commissioned Saurabh to write his two previous bestsellers, *The Unusual Billionaires* (2016) and *Coffee Can Investing: The Low-Risk Road to Stupendous Wealth* (co-authored with Rakshit Ranjan and Pranab Uniyal, 2018). He was equally constructive when we approached him with the idea for this book. Sadly for us, Lohit migrated to Canada before we could complete the book. Lohit's inputs played a big role in helping us shape its structure. We miss working with him and we wish him the very best with life in the New World.

The young and energetic Manish Kumar has stepped into Lohit's oversized shoes at Penguin Random House. Manish has provided us with invaluable assistance not only in putting together this book but also in dealing with our myriad requests around the look and feel of the book. We owe Manish several lunches in the swish eateries surrounding his office in Gurgaon.

In addition to Manish's inputs, the book has benefited from the meticulous and fastidious copyediting of Vineet Gill and Roshan Kumar Mogali. This is the fifth book that Saurabh has had the good fortune to author and Vineet and Roshan are the best copy editors Saurabh has worked with to date.

Mukti Seth was a stellar research lead as we tossed around data and abstract concepts in an attempt to give colour and definition to the trickier sections of this book. Apart from offering insights, she also played a key role in writing up the interviews. We thank Mukti for her interest, enthusiasm and persistence—all while managing her professional responsibilities as a senior investment product specialist in a premier wealth management firm in Mumbai.

Saurabh's colleagues at Marcellus Investment Managers were subjected—sometimes involuntarily so—to discussions around the concepts detailed in this book. These concepts were also fleshed out in the blog posts that Saurabh writes for Marcellus's website. Clients and friends of Marcellus responded to these blogs with insightful comments. Those inputs helped us sharpen our thinking further. We are grateful to the staff, clients and friends of Marcellus Investment Managers for the manner in which they have supported the development of this book.

We are particularly grateful to Deven Kulkarni of Marcellus Investment Managers for the charts and analysis presented in the penultimate chapter of the book, 'Building a Simple Framework to Achieve Your Financial Goals'. These charts have allowed us to illustrate the power of the simple, but highly effective, investment approach created by the late Rob Kirby, whose work continues to guide and inspire us.

Saurabh would like to thank Ashok Wadhwa and Rahul Gupta for their guidance during his years in Ambit Capital. These gentlemen taught Saurabh the merits of staying calm, working collaboratively and constantly learning new skills regardless of whatever else was happening around him.

Saurabh's family—Sarbani, Jeet and Malini—watched him frown and scowl as he tried to inject structure and meaning into this book. The fact that they tolerated him doing this during the weekends, even as he was helping build Marcellus Investment Managers during his weekdays, means that they should be deemed worthy of receiving a civilian honour or two from the highest authorities in the land. Many thanks to Sarbani, Jeet and Malini for their patience, their understanding and for their love.

Much of the heavy lifting for this book was done by Saurabh. Anupam is grateful to Saurabh for generously sharing the writing credit for the book and sharing his thoughts and ideas over several litres of coffee at his house, at his office and at the assorted coffee shops they frequented across many cities and airports for this book. At a broader level, working and writing with Saurabh since 2014 has been, and continues to be, an incredible learning experience for Anupam.

Anupam thanks his family—his mother, Shubhra Saran; his wife, Vanita; and his son, Varun—for their patience with him while he wrote this book. Anupam grabbed as much time as he could from his freelance writing assignments and podcast recordings to help write this tome. His family calmly adjusted their lives as he skipped school annual days, parent-teacher meetings and family gatherings every once in a while to meet a writing deadline or to rush to meet with an expert who had agreed to give his or her valuable time for the book.

The authors thank Rakshit Ranjan and Pranab Uniyal for their permissions to use concepts from the bestselling book they co-authored with Saurabh, *Coffee Can Investing: The Low-Risk Road to Stupendous Wealth*. The authors also thank Anirudha Dutta for his invaluable guidance as a sounding board for the theme of this book and for his help in fleshing out the ideas contained here.

Our interviewees gave us their valuable time. Often this meant meeting us during the weekends. We are very grateful to the following people (in alphabetical order) for sharing with us their time and knowledge: Raamdeo Agrawal, Prof. Sanjay Bakshi, Dr Sharmila Banwat, Sanjeev Bikhchandani, Gurcharan Das, Harsh Mariwala, Mark Mobius, T.V. Mohandas Pai, Apurva Purohit, Manish Sabharwal and Jason Voss. The many hours spent with this unique group of individuals have given us some of our fondest memories of the two fulfilling years we spent writing this book.

By the time we put the final touches to *The Victory Project*, India, along with many other countries, had entered the prolonged lockdown triggered by COVID-19. As, like millions of other people, we worked from home to finish this book, we were even more thankful for the opportunities we have enjoyed over the last few years to learn from some of the brightest minds in the world.

Mumbai   Saurabh Mukherjea (saurabh@marcellus.in)
April 2020   Anupam Gupta (anupam9gupta@gmail.com)

Notes

Section 1: Introduction

Prologue

1. Lyrics from a song that features in *C.I.D.*, directed by Raj Khosla (1956). Loose translation: 'My heart, it is tough to live here, so be careful and watch your back; this is Bombay, my love.'
2. Soutik Biswas, 'What divorce and separation tell us about modern India', *BBC*, 29 September 2016, https://www.bbc.com/news/world-asia-india-37481054
3. Times News Network, '40% marriages in Mumbai, Delhi end in divorce', *Times of India*, 26 March 2018, https://timesofindia.indiatimes.com/city/nagpur/40-marriages-in-mum-delhi-end-in-divorce/articleshow/63453211.cms
4. 'The world's biggest disease is what will people say if you go against societal norms.'
5. Times News Network, 'India is the 6th most depressed country: WHO report', *Times of India*, 12 October 2018, https://timesofindia.indiatimes.com/life-style/health-fitness/de-stress/india-is-the-6th-most-depressed-country-who-report/articleshow/66179026.cms
6. From a discussion the authors had with T.V. Mohandas Pai in Bengaluru on 11 May 2019.
7. Ibid.

Chapter 1: A Peek into the Human Mind

1. Parts of this chapter first appeared in *The Ken* as part of a series of articles written by the authors (see Appendix 2 for a list of these).

The text contained in these parts has been edited before being included in this chapter.

2. William Makepeace Thackeray, *Vanity Fair* (London: Alma Classics, 2019).

3. Baruch Spinoza, Ethics (Cambridge: Hackett, 1982).

4. Nick Chater, *The Mind is Flat: The Illusion of Mental Depth and the Improvised Mind* (London: Penguin Books, 2019).

5. Amos Tversky and Daniel Kahneman, 'Judgment under Uncertainty: Heuristics and Biases', *Science* 185, no. 4157 (1974), http://www.its.caltech.edu/~camerer/Ec101/JudgementUncertainty.pdf

6. Comment by Daniel Kahneman: https://replicationindex.com/2017/02/02/reconstruction-of-a-train-wreck-how-priming-research-went-of-the-rails/comment-page-1/#comment-1454

7. Source: Redrawn from available material for the Johari window on the Communication Theory website, https://www.communicationtheory.org/the-johari-window-model/

8. Michael Shermer, 'Rumsfeld's Wisdom', *Scientific American*, 1 September 2005, https://www.scientificamerican.com/article/rumsfelds-wisdom/

9. Steven Sloman and Philip Fernbach, *The Knowledge Illusion: Why We Never Think Alone* (London: Macmillan, 2017); Chater, *The Mind is Flat*.

10. See Tod Perry, 'Astrophysicist Shoots Down Climate Change Denier', *Good*, 30 October 2017, https://www.good.is/articles/deny-global-warming-you-get-burned/

11. David Eagleman, *The Brain: The Story of You* (Edinburgh: Canongate Books, 2015).

12. Fiona MacRae, 'It's not just men who can't multi-task: New research says women are just as bad at juggling tasks', *Daily Mail*, 7 March 2013, http://www.dailymail.co.uk/sciencetech/article-2289664/Smug-women-beware--new-research-suggests-just-bad-multi-tasking-men-are.html

13. Sneha Alexander, 'Black Money, Terror & Fake Notes: Did Note Ban Achieve Its Goals?', *Quint*, 9 November 2017, https://www.thequint.com/news/india/did-demonetisation-achieve-its-goals

14. George Soros with Byron Wien and Krisztina Koenen, *Soros on Soros: Staying Ahead of the Curve* (New York: John Wiley & Sons, 1995).

15. J. Oliver Conroy, 'An apocalyptic cult, 900 dead: remembering the Jonestown massacre, 40 years on', *Guardian*, 17 November 2018, https://www.theguardian.com/world/2018/nov/17/an-apocalyptic-cult-900-dead-remembering-the-jonestown-massacre-40-years-on

16. 'When Tamagotchis briefly conquered the world', *BBC*, 23 November 2016, https://www.bbc.com/news/av/technology-38066730/when-tamagotchis-briefly-conquered-the-world

17. W.E. Hill, 'My wife and my mother-in-law. They are both in this picture – find them', 1915, https://www.loc.gov/pictures/item/2010652001/

18. Tom Michael, 'What is The Knowledge taxi test and why is the exam taken by London's black cab drivers so tough?', *The Sun*, 17 October 2017, https://www.thesun.co.uk/news/3307245/the-knowledge-taxi-test-london-black-cab-drivers-exam/

Chapter 2: Discovering the World of Specialization

1. Parts of this chapter first appeared in *The Ken* as part of a series of articles written by the authors (see Appendix 2 for a list of these). The text contained in these parts has been edited before being included in this chapter.

2. Johann Wolfgang von Goethe, *Goethe: The Collected Works—Volume 9: Wilhelm Meister's Apprenticeship*, ed. and trans. Eric A. Blackall (Princeton: Princeton University Press, 1995).

3. As quoted in Bruce Thomas, *Bruce Lee: Fighting Spirit* (London: Sidgwick & Jackson, 2008).

4. Adam Smith, *The Wealth of Nations* (Indianapolis: Hackett, 1993).

5. Malcolm Gladwell, *Outliers: The Story of Success* (New York: Little, Brown & Co, 2008).

6. Matthew Syed, *Bounce: The Myth of Talent and the Power of Practice* (London: Fourth Estate—HarperCollins, 2011).

7. Saurabh Mukherjea, *Gurus of Chaos: Modern India's Money Masters* (New Delhi: Bloomsbury, 2015).

8. Anders Ericsson, *Peak: Secrets from the New Science of Expertise* (London: The Bodley Head, 2016).

9. David Epstein, *Range: Why Generalists Triumph in a Specialized World* (London: Macmillan, 2019).

10. Matthew Polly, *Bruce Lee: A Life* (London: Simon & Schuster, 2018).

11. Igor Chirashnya, 'Bruce Lee – The World's Most Famous Fencer?', *Academy of Fencing Masters Blog*, 3 December 2015, https://academyoffencingmasters.com/blog/bruce-lee-the-worlds-most-famous-fencer/

12. Jiddu Krishnamurti (1895–1986) was a well-known and highly regarded Indian philosopher whose teachings are available on the website www.jkrishnamurti.org

13. Bruce Lee, *Chinese Gung Fu: The Philosophical Art of Self-Defense* (Burbank: Ohara Publications, 2008).

14. Bruce Lee, *Tao of Jeet Kune Do* (Santa Clarita: Ohara Publications, 1973).

15. Included in *Bruce Lee: A Warrior's Journey* (2000), a documentary from Warner Home Video. YouTube link: https://youtu.be/5D48N21WOtc?t=1667

16. https://quoteinvestigator.com/2016/06/22/why/

17. Elle Luna, 'The Crossroads of Should and Must', Medium, 8 April 2014, https://medium.com/@elleluna/the-crossroads-of-should-and-must-90c75eb7c5b0/

18. Robert Greene, *Mastery* (London: Profile Books, 2012).

19. See Science ABC's YouTube channel: https://www.youtube.com/watch?v=yuD34tEpRFw/

20. Peter Bevelin, *Seeking Wisdom: From Darwin to Munger* (Malmö: PCA Publications, 2007); Trenholme J. Griffin, *Charlie Munger: The Complete Investor* (New York: Columbia Business School Publishing, 2015); Charles T. Munger, *Poor Charlie's Almanack: The Wit and Wisdom of Charles T. Munger*, ed. Peter D. Kaufman (Virginia: Donning Company Publishers, 2008).

21. Brian Leiberman, 'The Second Half of the Chessboard — Understanding Exponential Leaps Forward in Tech', *Medium*, 23 January 2018, https://medium.com/@brian.leiberman1/the-second-half-of-the-chessboard-understanding-exponential-leaps-forward-1ee0832a10c3

22. Munger, *Poor Charlie's Almanack*.

23. Herbert A. Simon, 'What is an "Explanation" of Behavior?', *Psychological Science 3*, No. 3 (1992): 150–61.

24. https://www.youtube.com/watch?v=3WkpQ4PpId4

25. Griffin, *Charlie Munger*.

26. Shane Parrish, 'Charlie Munger on Getting Rich, Wisdom, Focus, Fake Knowledge and More', *Farnam Street*, https://fs.blog/2017/02/charlie-munger-wisdom/

27. Griffin, *Charlie Munger*.

28. Shane Parrish, 'Peter Bevelin on Seeking Wisdom, Mental Models, Learning, and a Lot More', *Farnam Street*, https://fs.blog/2016/10/peter-bevelin-seeking-wisdom-mental-models/

29. Janet Lowe, *Damn Right!: Behind The Scenes With Berkshire Hathaway Billionaire Charlie Munger* (New York: Wiley, 2000).

30. Griffin, *Charlie Munger*.

31. Ibid.

32. Griffin, *Charlie Munger*.

Chapter 3: How to Simplify Your Life

1. Parts of this chapter first appeared in *The Ken* as part of a series of articles written by the authors (see Appendix 2 for a list of these). The text contained in these parts has been edited before being included in this chapter.

2. Often attributed to Einstein but there's no conclusive evidence that he actually said it. The statement, in its various versions, is widely quoted by many people; for example, by entrepreneur Naval Ravikant in a tweet dated 12 March2017: https://twitter.com/naval/status/840799984014376960?lang=en

3. Walter Isaacson, *Steve Jobs: The Exclusive Biography* (New York: Simon & Schuster, 2011).

4. Cliff Edwards, 'Commentary: Sorry, Steve: Here's Why Apple Stores Won't Work', *Bloomberg Businessweek*, 21 May 2001, https://www.bloomberg.com/news/articles/2001-05-20/commentary-sorry-steve-heres-why-apple-stores-wont-work

5. George Stephanopoulos, 'Walter Isaacson on Steve Jobs: Not "Exceptionally" Smart, But a "Genius"', *ABC News*, 24 October 2011, https://abcnews.go.com/blogs/politics/2011/10/walter-isaacson-on-steve-jobs-not-exceptionally-smart-but-a-genius

6. Mark Gurman and Shawn Donnan, 'Apple's tariff tradeoff: Raise iPhone prices or suffer a big hit to profits', *Financial Post*, 15 May 2019, https://business.financialpost.com/technology/apples-tariff-tradeoff-raise-iphone-prices-or-suffer-a-big-hit-to-profits

7. https://quoteinvestigator.com/2011/05/13/einstein-simple/

8. https://www.lexico.com/definition/simplicity/

9. https://www.simplicityindex.com

10. https://www.amfiindia.com/mutual-fund (data available till January 2020, last accessed 6 March 2020)

11. This $35 billion, or Rs 2,40,000 crore, is split between Rs 1,40,000 crore in AIFs and Rs 100,00,000 crore in PMS (this refers only to discretionary PMS in order to give a like-for-like comparison). The AIF data, as of 31 December 2019, is from SEBI's website, https://www.sebi.gov.in/statistics/1392982252002.html; the PMS data, as of April 2019, is from a SEBI Working Group paper on PMS providers (published in August 2019): https://www.sebi.gov.in/sebi_data/commondocs/aug-2019/Report%20of%20Working%20Group%20on%20PMS_p.pdf

12. Nicholas Foulkes, 'Jony Ive on the Apple Watch and Big Tech's responsibilities', *Financial Times*, 19 October 2018, https://www.ft.com/content/20aad4d4-d2ba-11e8-a9f2-7574db66bcd5/

13. Paul Farhi, 'Jeffrey Bezos, Washington Post's next owner, aims for a new 'golden era' at the newspaper', *Washington Post*, 3 September 2013, https://www.washingtonpost.com/lifestyle/style/jeffrey-bezos-washington-posts-next-owner-aims-for-a-new-golden-era-at-the-newspaper/2013/09/02/30c00b60-13f6-11e3-b182-1b3bb2eb474c_story.html?

14. Richard Koch and Greg Lockwood, *Simplify: How the Best Businesses in the World Succeed* (London: Piatkus, 2016).

15. Mason Currey, *Daily Rituals: How Artists Work* (New York: Alfred A. Knopf, 2013).

16. Manu S. Pillai, *Rebel Sultans: The Deccan from Khilji to Shivaji* (New Delhi: Juggernaut, 2018).

17. Charles Duhigg, *The Power of Habit: Why We Do What We Do in Life and Business* (New York: Random House, 2012).

18. Gretchen Rubin, *Better Than Before: What I Learned About Making and Breaking Habits—to Sleep More, Quit Sugar, Procrastinate*

Less, and Generally Build a Happier Life (London: Two Roads, 2015).

19. Saurabh Mukherjea, *The Unusual Billionaires* (Gurugram: Penguin Random House, 2016).

20. Mason Currey, *Daily Rituals.*

21. Shane Parrish, 'Charlie Munger: 20 Book Recommendations That will Make you Smarter', *Farnam Street*, https://fs.blog/2014/06/charlie-munger-recommended-books/

22. Shane Parrish, 'Hemingway's Routine', *Farnham Street*, https://fs.blog/2013/05/hemingways-routine/

23. Saul McLeod, 'Solomon Asch - Conformity Experiment', *SimplyPyschology*, 28 December 2018, https://www.simplypsychology.org/asch-conformity.html

24. James Williams, *Stand Out of Our Light: Freedom and Resistance in the Attention Economy* (Cambridge: Cambridge University Press, 2018).

25. Cal Newport, *Deep Work: Rules for Focused Success in a Distracted World* (New York: Grand Central Publishing, 2016).

26. Emotional intelligence is the ability to understand, differentiate and identify our emotions and the emotions of others.

27. Daniel Goleman, *Focus: The Hidden Driver of Excellence* (London: Bloomsbury, 2014).

28. Adam Grant, 'The surprising habits of original thinkers', https://www.ted.com/talks/adam_grant_the_surprising_habits_of_original_thinkers?language=en

29. Peter Drucker, *The Effective Executive* (London: Heinemann, 1967).

30. Saurabh Mukherjea, Rakshit Ranjan and Pranab Uniyal, *Coffee Can Investing: The Low-Risk Road to Stupendous Wealth* (Gurugram: Penguin Random House, 2018).

31. Daniel Kahneman, *Thinking, Fast and Slow* (USA, Farrar, Straus and Giroux, 2011).

32. See https://www.youtube.com/watch?v=VtQutUM1NsM/

33. https://www.youtube.com/watch?v=lt9OcLynjwE/

34. Eric Johnson, 'Warren Buffett and the "avoid at all cost list"', *Excellent Journey*, 13 April 2015, https://excellentjourney.net/2015/04/13/warren-buffett-and-the-avoid-at-all-cost-list/

35. Robert T. Kiyosaki, *Rich Dad Poor Dad: What the Rich Teach Their Kids About Money That the Poor and Middle Class Do Not!* (London: Time Warner Paperbacks, 1998).

Chapter 4: Connecting with Your Inner Self

1. Parts of this chapter first appeared in *The Ken* as part of a series of articles written by the authors (see Appendix 2 for a list of these). The text contained in these parts has been edited before being included in this chapter.
2. *Fight Club*, directed by David Fincher (1999).
3. Yoda (*Star Wars*), Gandalf (*The Lord of the Rings*), Master Shifu (*Kung Fu Panda*) are taken from popular movies and books. Gibran an author, and Tolle a spiritual teacher.
4. Khushwant Singh, *The End of India* (New Delhi: Penguin, 2003).
5. Leonard Mlodinow, *Subliminal: The New Unconscious and What it Teaches Us* (London: Allen Lane, 2012).
6. Chuck Palahniuk, *Fight Club* (New York: W.W. Norton & Company, 2005).
7. Liz Mineo, 'Good genes are nice, but joy is better', *Harvard Gazette*, 11 April 2017, https://news.harvard.edu/gazette/story/2017/04/over-nearly-80-years-harvard-study-has-been-showing-how-to-live-a-healthy-and-happy-life/
8. Ray Dalio, *Principles* (New York: Simon & Schuster, 2017).
9. Marcus Aurelius, *Meditations* (Auckland: Floating Press, 1800).
10. Phil Dobson, *The Brain Book: How to Think and Work Smarter* (London: LID, 2016).
11. Jason Apollo Voss, *The Intuitive Investor: A Radical Guide for Manifesting Wealth* (New York: Select Books, 2010).
12. John Selby, *Seven Masters, One Path: Meditation Secrets from the World's Greatest Teachers* (London: Rider, 2003).
13. Dalio, *Principles;* Voss, *The Intuitive Investor;* Selby, *Seven Masters, One Path.*
14. Sue McGreevey, 'Eight weeks to a better brain', *The Harvard Gazette*, 21 January 2011, https://news.harvard.edu/gazette/story/2011/01/eight-weeks-to-a-better-brain/
15. *Wall Street* (1987).

16. Mihaly Csikszentmihalyi, *Flow: The Psychology of Optimal Experience* (New York: HarperPerennial, 2008).

17. Results include the effects of dividends and stock splits on total return. The results were calculated based on data published by Yahoo! Finance and covering the period from 22 September 2000 to 18 August 2005—the length of Voss's tenure as co-portfolio manager of DAIF. The DAIF ticker symbol is DCSYX.

18. Emerging Technology from the arXiv, 'A quantum experiment suggests there's no such thing as objective reality', *MIT Technology Review*, 12 March 2019, https://www.technologyreview.com/s/613092/a-quantum-experiment-suggests-theres-no-such-thing-as-objective-reality/

Chapter 5: Reduce, Reduce, Reduce: Getting Rid of Clutter

1. Mary Shelley, *Frankenstein; or, The Modern Prometheus* (London: Lackington, Hughes, Harding, Mavor, & Jones, 1818).

2. Lauren Feiner, '"Facebook is the new cigarettes," says Salesforce CEO', *CNBC*, 14 November 2018, https://www.cnbc.com/2018/11/14/salesforce-ceo-marc-benioff-facebook-is-the-new-cigarettes.html

3. Cal Newport, *Digital Minimalism: On Living Better with Less Technology* (London: Portfolio, Penguin, 2019).

4. Matthew D. Lieberman, *Social: Why Our Brains Are Wired to Connect* (New York: Crown Publishers, 2013).

5. Brian A. Primack, et al., 'Social Media Use and Perceived Social Isolation Among Young Adults in the U.S.', *American Journal of Preventive Medicine*, Vol. 53, Issue 1 (2017).

6. Lydia Denworth, 'Worry Over Social Media Use and Well-Being May Be Misplaced', *Psychology Today*, 30 May 2019, https://www.psychologytoday.com/us/blog/brain-waves/201905/worry-over-social-media-use-and-well-being-may-be-misplaced

7. Lydia Denworth, 'Social Media Has Not Destroyed a Generation', *Scientific American*, November 2019, https://www.scientificamerican.com/article/social-media-has-not-destroyed-a-generation/

8. Greg McKeown, *Essentialism: The Disciplined Pursuit of Less* (London: Virgin Books, 2014).

9. Brian Christian and Tom Griffiths, *Algorithms to Live By: The Computer Science of Human Decisions* (London: William Collins, 2016).

10. Ray Zinn, *Tough Things First: Leadership Lessons from Silicon Valley's Longest Serving CEO* (New York: McGraw-Hill, 2015).

11. Atul Gawande, *The Checklist Manifesto* (London: Profile Books, 2010).

12. See WHO Surgical Safety Checklist, https://www.who.int/patientsafety/topics/safe-surgery/checklist/en/

13. Source: Nikhil Sonad, 'You probably won't remember this, but the "forgetting curve" theory explains why learning is hard', *Quartz*, 1 March 2018, https://qz.com/1213768/the-forgetting-curve-explains-why-humans-struggle-to-memorize/

14. Watch Cal Newport lay out the basics of digital detox: https://www.youtube.com/watch?v=3E7hkPZ-HTk/

15. Stephen R. Covey, *The 7 Habits of Highly Effective People* (New York: Free Press, 1989).

16. Jim Collins and Jerry I. Porras, *Built to Last: Successful Habits of Visionary Companies* (New York: HarperCollins, 1994).

17. Daniel Goleman, *Focus: the hidden driver of excellence* (New York: Harper, 2014).

18. Navi Radjou, Jaideep Prabhu & Simone Ahuja, *Jugaad Innovation: A Frugal and Flexible Approach to Innovation for the 21st Century* (Noida : Random House, 2012).

19. Source: Harsh Mariwala. The wording, underlining and emphasis have been replicated from Harsh's diary.

20. Loose translation: 'Have you had your head massaged yet?'

Chapter 6: Develop Your Creativity and Memory

1. Parts of this chapter first appeared in *The Ken* as part of a series of articles written by the authors (see Appendix 2 for a list of these). The text contained in these parts has been edited before being included in this chapter.

2. Bernard Shaw, *Man and Superman: A Comedy and a Philosophy* (London, Westminster: Archibald Constable & Co., 1903).

3. For a fuller discourse on this subject, please refer to Mukherjea, Ranjan and Uniyal, *Coffee Can Investing*.

4. Doris B. Wallace and Howard E. Gruber, *Creative People at Work* (New York: Oxford University Press, 1989).

5. Paul Arthur Schilpp, *Albert Einstein: Autobiographical Notes* (New York: Evanston, 1949).

6. For an illustrated account of what Einstein is talking about, see John D. Norton, 'Chasing a Beam of Light: Einstein's Most Famous Thought Experiment', University of Pittsburgh, December 2004, https://www.pitt.edu/~jdnorton/Goodies/Chasing_the_light/

7. Wallace and Gruber, *Creative People at Work*.

8. Stang, Nicholas F., 'Kant's Transcendental Idealism', *The Stanford Encyclopedia of Philosophy* (Winter 2018 Edition), Edward N. Zalta (ed.), https://plato.stanford.edu/archives/win2018/entries/kant-transcendental-idealism

9. Adam Grant, *Originals: How Non-Conformists Move the World* (London: Penguin Random House, 2016).

10. Ludwig van Beethoven, *Beethoven: Letters, Journals and Conversations*, ed. Michael Hamburger (New York: Pantheon, 1952).

11. Kahneman, *Thinking, Fast and Slow*.

12. Benedict Carey, 'Remembering, as an Extreme Sport', *New York Times*, 19 May 2014, https://well.blogs.nytimes.com/2014/05/19/remembering-as-an-extreme-sport/

13. Anthony Metivier, 'How to Remember Things: 21 Techniques for Memory Improvement', *Magnetic Memory Method*, 22 February 2019, https://www.magneticmemorymethod.com/how-to-remember-things/

14. Rachel Becker, *An ancient memorization strategy might cause lasting changes to the brain*, https://www.theverge.com/2017/3/16/14950798/memory-palace-method-of-loci-brain-fmri-activity-neuroscience

15. Robert I. Sutton, *Weird Ideas that Work: How to Build a Creative Company* (New York: Free Press, 2002).

16. Wallace and Gruber, *Creative People at Work*.

17. Ibid.

18. W.A. Pannapacker, 'How to Procrastinate Like Leonardo da Vinci', *Chronicle of Higher Education*, 20 February 2009, https://www.chronicle.com/article/How-to-Procrastinate-Like/26491

19. The last two lines of this verse, as quoted in *Creative People at Work*, are slightly different from those that appear in the original

poem by Wordsworth: 'Beside the lake, beneath the trees,/ Fluttering and dancing in the breeze . . .'

20. Ed Catmull, *Creativity, Inc.: Overcoming the Unseen Forces that Stand in the Way of True Inspiration* (New York: Transworld Publishers, 2014).

21. Steve Coll, *On the Grand Trunk Road: A Journey into South Asia*, (New York: Penguin, 2009).

22. David A. Vise and Steve Coll, *Eagle on the Street: Based on the Pulitzer Prize-Winning Account of the Sec's Battle With Wall Street* (New York: Collier Books, 1992).

23. Steve Coll, *Ghost Wars: The Secret History of the CIA, Afghanistan, and Bin Laden, from the Soviet Invasion to September 10, 2001* (London: Penguin, 2005).

24. Steve Coll, *The Bin Ladens: The Story of a Family and its Fortune* (London: Penguin, 2009).

25. Ramachandra Guha, *India After Gandhi: The History of the World's Largest Democracy* (India: Picador, 2007).

26. Ramachandra Guha, *Gandhi Before India* (London: Allen Lane, 2013).

27. Ramachandra Guha, *Gandhi: The Years that Changed the World: 1914-1948* (London: Allen Lane, 2018).

28. Ramachandra Guha, *A Corner of a Foreign Field: The Indian History of a British Sport* (London: Picador, 2002).

29. Sunil Khilnani, Incarnations: *India in 50 Lives* (London: Allen Lane, 2016).

30. Manu S. Pillai, *The Ivory Throne: Chronicles of the House of Travancore* (Noida: HarperCollins Publishers, 2015).

31. Manu S. Pillai, *Rebel Sultans: The Deccan from Khilji to Shivaji* (New Delhi: Juggernaut, 2018).

32. Manu S. Pillai, *The Courtesan, the Mahatma and the Italian Brahmin: Tales from Indian History* (Context, 2019)

33. Ramachandra Guha, *Gandhi: The Years that Changed the World, 1914-48* (London: Allen Lane, 2018).

34. Aristotle, *Rhetorica* (New York: Penguin, 1991).

35. Nidhi Verma, interview of Manu S. Pillai, *Platform*, https://www. platform-mag.com/literature/manu-s-pillai.html

36. 'Info Edge IPO lists at hefty 94.93% premium', *Financial Express*, 21 November 2006, https://www.financialexpress.com/archive/info-edge-ipo-lists-at-hefty-9493-premium/184612/

37. https://www.bseindia.com/stock-share-price/info-edge-(india)-ltd/naukri/532777/

Chapter 7: Teaming Up with the Best

1. Doris Kearns Goodwin, *Team of Rivals: The Political Genius of Abraham Lincoln* (New York: Simon & Schuster, 2005).

2. Yuval Noah Harari, *Sapiens: A Brief History of Humankind* (London: Vintage Books, 2014).

3. Rich Karlgaard, *The Soft Edge: Where Great Companies Find Lasting Success* (San Francisco: Jossey Bass, 2014).

4. Tamal Bandyopadhyay, *HDFC Bank 2.0: From Dawn to Digital* (Mumbai: Jaico Publishing House, 2019).

5. Bandyopadhyay, *A Bank for the Buck* (Mumbai: Jaico Publishing House, 2013).

6. A creamery is an establishment where butter, cheese, cream and milk are prepared and sold.

7. Source: Annual reports for Nestlé and HUL, and GCMMF's website for the GCMMF-related data.

8. Verghese Kurien, as told to Gouri Salvi, *I Too Had a Dream* (New Delhi: Lotus Collection, 2005).

9. Harish Damodaran, *India's New Capitalists: Caste, Business, and Industry in a Modern Nation* (Basingstoke: Palgrave Macmillan, 2008).

10. Kurien, *I Too Had a Dream*.

11. Vivian Hunt, Lareina Yee, Sara Prince and Sundiatu Dixon-Fyle, *Delivering through diversity* (New York: McKinsey & Company, 2018), https://www.mckinsey.com/business-functions/organization/our-insights/delivering-through-diversity

12. Walter Isaacson, 'How Steve Jobs' Love of Simplicity Fueled A Design Revolution', *Smithsonian Magazine*, September 2012, https://www.smithsonianmag.com/arts-culture/how-steve-jobs-love-of-simplicity-fueled-a-design-revolution-23868877/

13. Helen Lee Bouygues, '3 Simple Habits to Improve Your Critical Thinking', *Harvard Business Review*, 6 May 2019, https://hbr.org/2019/05/3-simple-habits-to-improve-your-critical-thinking

14. Jonah Lehrer, 'Steve Jobs: "Technology Alone Is Not Enough"', *The New Yorker*, 7 October 2011, https://www.newyorker.com/news/news-desk/steve-jobs-technology-alone-is-not-enough

15. Steven Levy, 'One More Thing Inside Apple's Insanely Great (or Just Insane) New Mothership', *Wired*, 16 May 2017, https://www.wired.com/2017/05/apple-park-new-silicon-valley-campus/

16. Shashank Shah, *Win-Win Corporations: The Indian Way of Shaping Successful Strategies* (Gurugram: Penguin Random House, 2016).

17. Charles Duhigg, 'What Google Learned From Its Quest to Build the Perfect Team', *The New York Times Magazine*, 25 February 2016, https://www.nytimes.com/2016/02/28/magazine/what-google-learned-from-its-quest-to-build-the-perfect-team.html.

18. Judith A. Ross, 'Make Your Good Team Great', *Harvard Business Review*, 28 February 2008, https://hbr.org/2008/02/make-your-good-team-great-1.

19. Thomas A. Timberg, *The Marwaris: From Jagat Seth to the Birlas* (New Delhi: Allen Lane, 2014).

20. Gita Piramal, *Business Maharajas* (Gurugram: Penguin Random House, 2000).

21. Kumar Mangalam Birla, 'Butter chicken at Birla', McKinsey.com, December 2013, https://www.mckinsey.com/featured-insights/asia-pacific/butter-chicken-at-birla

22. Serenitie Wang and Daniel Shane, 'Jack Ma endorses China's controversial 12 hours a day, 6 days a week work culture', *CNN*, 16 April 2019, https://edition.cnn.com/2019/04/15/business/jack-ma-996-china/index.html

23. Jason Fried and David Heinemeier Hansson, *It Doesn't Have to Be Crazy at Work* (New York: Harper Business, 2018).

24. Katherine Bindley, 'The Phone Call Isn't Dead, It's Evolving', *Wall Street Journal*, 19 October 2019, https://www.wsj.com/articles/the-phone-call-isnt-dead-its-evolving-11571457605

25. Cal Newport, 'Was E-mail a Mistake?', *The New Yorker*, 6 August 2019, https://www.newyorker.com/tech/annals-of-technology/was-e-mail-a-mistake

26. Ramachandra Guha, 'A Brief History of Bipartisanship', *Hindustan Times*, 23 March 2010, http://ramachandraguha.in/archives/a-brief-history-of-bipartisanship.html

27. All market capitalization data is as per the Bombay Stock Exchange and INR/USD rates existing on those dates.

28. Robert Hunt, *Case Study: State Bank of India, World's Largest Centralized Core Processing Implementation* (Needham, USA: TowerGroup, 2009), https://www.tcs.com/content/dam/tcs-bancs/pdf/bancsprotected/TCSBaNCS_SBI_TowerGroup.pdf

29. 'TCS edges past US-based DXC to become world's 3rd largest IT firm by revenue', *Business Today*, 24 May 2019, https://www.businesstoday.in/sectors/it/tcs-third-largest-it-firm-by-revenue-in-the-world/story/349954.html

30. Jason Del Rey, 'The making of Amazon Prime, the internet's most successful and devastating membership program', *Vox*, 3 May 2019, https://www.vox.com/recode/2019/5/3/18511544/amazon-prime-oral-history-jeff-bezos-one-day-shipping

31. Brad Stone, *The Everything Store: Jeff Bezos and the Age of Amazon* (New York: Little, Brown and Company, 2013).

32. Jodi Kantor and David Streitfeld, 'Inside Amazon: Wrestling Big Ideas in a Bruising Workplace', *The New York Times*, 15 August 2015, https://www.nytimes.com/2015/08/16/technology/inside-amazon-wrestling-big-ideas-in-a-bruising-workplace.html

33. Guha, 'A Brief History of Bipartisanship'.

34. John Kay, *Obliquity: Why Our Goals Are Best Achieved Indirectly* (New York: Penguin Press, 2011).

35. J.K. Rowling, *Harry Potter and the Chamber of Secrets* (London: Bloomsbury 1998).

36. Peter F. Drucker, 'They're Not Employees, They're People', *Harvard Business Review*, February 2002, https://hbr.org/2002/02/theyre-not-employees-theyre-people

Chapter 8: How Simplicity Powers the Best Businesses

1. Shane Parrish, 'Charlie Munger on Getting Rich, Wisdom, Focus, Fake Knowledge and More', *Farnam Street*, https://fs.blog/2017/02/charlie-munger-wisdom/

2. Isaacson, *Steve Jobs*.
3. Julian Birkinshaw Dickie Liang-Hong Ke and Enrique de Diego, 'The Kind of Creative Thinking That Fueled WeChat's Success', *Harvard Business Review*, 29 October 2019, https://hbr.org/2019/10/the-kind-of-creative-thinking-that-fueled-wechats-success
4. Hamish McDonald, *Ambani & Sons* (Sydney: UNSW Press, 2010).
5. T.T. Jagannathan and Sandhya Mendonca, *Disrupt and Conquer* (Gurugram: Penguin Random House, 2013).
6. 'Main Financial Data (Consolidated)', YKK.com, https://www.ykk.com/english/corporate/financial/highlights/c_graph.html
7. Benjamin Fulford, 'Zipping Up the World', *Forbes*, 24 November 2003, https://www.forbes.com/global/2003/1124/089.html
8. Ravi refers to Ravi Narain, a former managing director of the National Stock Exchange (NSE).
9. Pavitra Kumar, *Bhujia Barons: The Untold Story of How Haldiram Built a ₹5000-Crore Empire* (Gurugram: Penguin Random House, 2016).
10. Noel Tichy and Ram Charan, 'Speed, Simplicity, Self-Confidence: An Interview with Jack Welch', *Harvard Business Review*, September–October 1989, https://hbr.org/1989/09/speed-simplicity-self-confidence-an-interview-with-jack-welch
11. https://www.siegelgale.com/about/
12. Siegal+Gale, 'The World's Simplest Brands, 2018–2019', available on https://simplicityindex.com
13. Molly Muldoon, 'Netflix revealed as World's Simplest Brand, according to annual study from Siegel+Gale', Siegel+Gale, November 2018, https://www.siegelgale.com/netflix-revealed-worlds-simplest-brand-according-annual-study-siegelgale/
14. Apurva Purohit, *Lady, You're Not a Man!: The Adventures of a Woman at Work* (Mumbai: Rupa Publications India, 2014).
15. Apurva Purohit, *Lady, You're the Boss!: The Adventures of a Woman at Work – Part 2* (Mumbai: Westland, 2019).
16. Robert S. Kaplan and David P. Norton, 'The Balanced Scorecard—Measures that Drive Performance', *Harvard Business Review*, January–February 1992, https://hbr.org/1992/01/the-balanced-scorecard-measures-that-drive-performance-2

17. Bertrand Russell, *The Conquest of Happiness* (New York: Liveright, 1930).

18. Hubert Dreyfus and Sean Dorrance Kelly, *All Things Shining: Reading the Western Classics to Find Meaning in a Secular Age* (New York: Free Press, 2011).

19. Lyrics from a song that features in *Gol Maal*, directed by Hrishikesh Mukherjee (1979).

Chapter 9: Building a Simple Framework to Achieve Your Financial Goals

1. Griffin, *Charlie Munger.*

2. Ben Carlson, *A Wealth of Common Sense: Why Simplicity Trumps Complexity in Any Investment Plan* (Hoboken, USA: John Wiley & Sons, 2015).

3. A significant part of this chapter draws upon the material presented in Saurabh's two previous books—*The Unusual Billionaires* and *Coffee Can Investing: The Low-Risk Road to Stupendous Wealth.*

4. D.H. Lawrence, *Phoenix: The Posthumous Papers of D.H. Lawrence* (London: W. Heinemann, 1936).

5. Brian Portnoy, *The Geometry of Wealth: How to Shape a Life of Money and Meaning* (Petersfield, UK: Harriman House, 2018).

6. Ibid.

7. Ashvin B. Chhabra, *The Aspirational Investor: Investing in the Pursuit of Wealth and Happiness* (Noida: HarperCollins, 2015)

8. Source: Marcellus Investment Managers. Our construct here has been influenced by Chhabra's book, *The Aspirational Investor.*

9. Source: Mukti Seth. All calculations are based on assumptions and estimates. These recommendations have been made for representational purposes for this book and should not be considered as financial advice.

10. Ibid.

11. Ibid.

12. Source: Marcellus Investment Managers. Our construct here has been influenced by Chhabra's book, *The Aspirational Investor.*

13. Source: Mukti Seth. All calculations are based on assumptions and estimates. These recommendations have been made for

representational purposes for this book and should not be considered as financial advice.

14. Ibid.

15. Ibid.

16. From the foreword to John C. Bogle's *The Clash of the Cultures: Investment vs. Speculation* (Hoboken, USA: John Wiley & Sons, 2012).

17. *Berkshire Hathaway Annual Report 24*, www.berkshirehathaway. com, p. 24.

18. Source: Gary M. Brinson Distinguished Lecture delivered by Bogle at Washington State University on 13 April 2014.

19. Knut A. Rostad (ed.), *The Man in the Arena: Vanguard Founder John C. Bogle and His Lifelong Battle to Serve Investors First* (Hoboken, New Jersey: Wiley, 2013). Rob Arnott's studies are cited on p. 23; John Bogle's studies are cited on p. 165; and Morningstar's research on this subject is cited on p. 154.

20. Akash Jain and Arpit Gupta, *SPIVA® India Scorecard* (New York: S&P Global, 2018), https://us.spindices.com/documents/spiva/ spiva-india-year-end-2018.pdf

21. Natalie Zmuda, 'Vanguard Proves It Pays to Advertise', *AdAge*, 26 November 2012, https://adage.com/article/special-report-marketer-alist-2012/vanguard-proves-pays-advertise/238421

22. Disha Sanghvi, Lisa Pallavi Barbora, 'Passive investing rises as large-cap funds underperform', *Livemint*, 27 November 2018, https:// www.livemint.com/Money/5uy7XNtE6cEXxoa5UfCiPL/Passive-investing-rises-as-largecap-funds-underperform.html

23. Bogle, *The Clash of the Cultures*.

24. 'Funds Mobilised and Total Assets - According To Investment Objectives', Securities and Exchange Board of India, https://www. sebi.gov.in/statistics/mutual-fund/mf-investment-objectives.html

25. Saurabh Mukherjea, Rakshit Ranjan, Pranab Uniyal, *Coffee Can Investing: The Low Risk Road to Stupendous Wealth*, (Mumbai: Penguin Portfolio, 2018).

26. Akash Jain, Arpit Gupta, 'SPIVA India Scorecard Mid-year 2019', www.asiaindex.co.in › documents › spiva › spiva-india-mid-year-2019

27. Quoted in Charles D. Ellis, *Capital: The Story of Long-Term Investment Excellence* (Hoboken: John Wiley & Sons, 2004).

28. Robert G. Kirby, 'The Coffee Can Portfolio', *Journal of Portfolio Management* 11, No. 1 (1984), pp. 76–80.

29. The equity risk premium denotes the additional return that the investor expects over and above the risk-free rate of return, for investing in equity.

30. It is important to note that we are *not* looking for companies which have grown sales over a ten-year period at a compounded annualized rate of at least 10 per cent. Instead we *are* looking for companies which have grown sales every single year for ten consecutive years by at least 10 per cent.

31. ROE is the amount of profits earned (after paying corporate taxes) as a percentage of shareholders' equity.

32. ROA gives a sense of how efficient a management team is at using its assets to generate earnings. It is calculated by dividing a company's annual profits (after paying corporate taxes) by its total assets.

33. The assets of a bank are its equity plus the amount of money the bank has borrowed. Therefore, by looking at ROE, rather than ROA, we are not only able to measure a bank's ability to lend money profitably but also measure its ability to gauge exactly how much money the bank should borrow.

34. Source: Marcellus Investment Managers, Ace Equity. All stock prices in this table are as of 30 June 2019. 'Portfolio Start' denotes an equal allocation of Rs 100 for the stocks qualifying to be in the portfolio for that year. The portfolio kicks off on 30 June of every year. The CAGR returns for all the portfolios since 2010 have been calculated until 30 June 2019. Both portfolio returns and Sensex returns in this table have been computed using TSR, i.e. total shareholder return, which includes dividends for both portfolio as well as for Sensex. The 2019 iteration started on 1 July 2019 and hence its returns could not be computed. The sales growth filter has been relaxed to 9.5 per cent in FY18 to include Astral Poly, because it was part of the 2017 iteration and missed the filter by a very narrow margin.

35. Source: Marcellus Investment Managers, Ace Equity. All stock prices in this table are as of 30 June 2019. EPS CAGR and P/E CAGR have been calculated for the April–March period due to inconsistency of trailing twelve-month EPS data for various stocks, whereas TSR CAGR is for the July–June period. TSR, i.e. total

shareholder return, is the stock price change plus cash returned to shareholders in the form of dividends and buy-backs.

36. Median denotes the midpoint of returns, such that there is an equal probability of falling above or below it.

37. Source: Marcellus Investment Managers, Ace Equity. Note: Period under consideration is July 2000 to June 2019. The investment horizons are calculated on a weekly rolling basis. For instance, the standard deviation of one-year return is the standard deviation of returns generated by considering 6,855 one-year periods (for all the CCP iterations) including 01/07/2000 to 01/07/2001, 08/07/2000 to 08/07/2001 and so on.

38. Harari, *Sapiens*.

39. Saurabh Mukherjea, *The Unusual Billionaires*, (Mumbai: Penguin, 2016).

40. Michael J. Mauboussin, *More Than You Know: Finding Financial Wisdom in Unconventional Places* (New York: Columbia University Press, 2006).

41. This study is for the thirty-two-year period from March 1987 to November 2019. Source: Marcellus Investment Managers, Ace Equity. Kirby's Coffee Can Investing curve is based on the simple average of the 'probability of gains' of all the nineteen portfolio iterations highlighted in the tables presented earlier in this chapter.

42. The returns have been simulated over a ten-year period with the investments made on the first day of the first year. Source: Marcellus Investment Managers.

43. Source: Marcellus Investment Managers, Ace Equity.

44. Source: Marcellus Investment Managers, Ace Equity. *This data is as of 26 November 2019. ** The sales growth filter has been relaxed to 9.5 per cent in FY18 to include Astral Poly.

45. Source: Marcellus Investment Managers, Ace Equity. The returns from Kirby's investment approach are taken as the average of all live portfolio iterations during the period.

46. Ibid. Total shareholder return is the stock price change plus cash returned to shareholders in the form of dividends and buy-backs.

47. Reshma Kapadia, 'Exit Interview: Mark Mobius on 30 Years of Emerging Markets', *Barron's*, 9 February 2018, https://www.

barrons.com/articles/exit-interview-mark-mobius-on-30-years-of-emerging-markets-1518183233

Chapter 10: Boiling It All Down to the Simplicity Checklist

1. In the foreword to Anirudha Bhattacharjee and Balaji Vittal, *R.D. Burman: The Man, The Music* (Noida: HarperCollins, 2011).
2. Nandini Ramnath, '"Mozart from Madras": New documentary celebrates AR Rahman', *Scroll.in*, 5 January 2015, https://scroll.in/article/698525/mozart-from-madras-new-documentary-celebrates-ar-rahman
3. 'Chingari Koi Bhadke', 'Kuch Toh Log Kahenge', 'Raina Beeti Jaye' and 'Yeh Kya Hua . . .'
4. Anirudha Bhattacharjee and Balaji Vittal, *R.D. Burman: The Man, The Music* (Noida: HarperCollins, 2011).
5. Richard Corliss, 'All-TIME 100 Movies', *TIME*, 19 January 2010, http://entertainment.time.com/2005/02/12/all-time-100-movies/slide/roja/
6. Krishna Trilok, *Notes of a Dream: The Authorized Biography of A.R. Rahman* (Gurugram: Penguin Viking, 2018).
7. Ibid.
8. Anirudha Bhattacharjee and Balaji Vittal, *R.D. Burman: The Man, The Music* (Noida: HarperCollins, 2011).